Writing
Interpreters and Compilers
for the
Raspberry Pi Using Python
Second Edition

```
Source program
                        a = 2 + 3 + 5

Postfix
                        a 2 3 + 5 + =

Python Bytecode

    co_names  =  ['a']
    co_consts =  [2, 3, 5]
    co_code   =  [100, 0, 100, 1, 23, 100, 2, 23, 90, 0]
```

```
Abstract Syntax Tree           Assembler code

      <program>                       .global main
          |                           .text
         '='                 main:    push {lr}
        /   \
      'a'   '+'                @ a = 2 + 3 + 5
           /   \                       mov r4, #10
         '+'   '5'
        /   \                          mov r0, #0
      '2'   '3'                        pop {pc}
```

Anthony J. Dos Reis

Writing Interpreters and Compilers for the Raspberry Pi Using Python Second Edition
Copyright © 2020 by Anthony J. Dos Reis, all rights reserved.

ISBN: 9798635920329

To the fullest extent of the law, neither the author nor the copyright holders nor the publisher assume any liability for any injury and/or damage to persons or property as a matter of products liability, negligence or otherwise, or from any use or operation of any methods, products, instructions, or ideas contained in the material herein.

To all my students

Table of Contents

Preface, *ix*

1   Basic concepts, 1

> Creating Your Work Directory, 1
> Installing Python 3, 2
> Starting Your Work, 2
> Which Text Editor to Use, 3
> Running Python 3, 3
> Difference between Interpretation and Compilation, 3
> What Happens When an Interpreter Interprets, 6
> Advantages of Interpreters over Compilers, 9
> Problems, 10

2   Defining Languages with Regular Expressions, 12

> Introduction, 12
> Basic Language Concepts, 12
> Operations on Strings and Languages, 13
> Regular Expressions, 14
> Problems, 15

3   Defining Languages with Context-free Grammars, 16

> Introduction, 16
> Context-free Grammars Defined, 16
> Examples of Context-free Grammars, 18
> Grammars for Arithmetic Expressions, 19
> Problems, 24

4   Recursive-Descent Parsing, 25

> Introduction, 25
> Implementing a Recursive-Descent Top-down Parser, 25
> When Not to Use Recursion, 31
> Using Grammars with the *, +, |, and [ ] Operators, 32
> Problems, 33

5   Predict Sets, 35

> Introduction, 35
> Analyzing Grammars for Predictive Recursive-Descent Parsing, 35
> Productions with a Choice, 41
> Problems, 43

6 Constructing a Tokenizer for a Python Subset, 45

>   Introduction, 45
>   Tokenizer-Parser Interface, 45
>   Structure of the `t1.py` Tokenizer, 48
>   Problems, 55

7 Constructing a Parser for a Python Subset, 57

>   Introduction, 57
>   Grammar for Our Python Subset, 57
>   Problems, 63

8 Constructing a Pure Interpreter, 64

>   Introduction, 64
>   Structures Needed for a Pure Interpreter, 64
>   Modifications to our Parsing Functions, 65
>   Problems, 68

9 Bytecode, 70

>   Introduction, 70
>   What is Python Bytecode, 70
>   Structures Produced by the Parser in a Hybrid Interpreter, 71
>   Code Generation for a Small Program, 71
>   Bytecode Interpretation of a Small Program, 72
>   Displaying Bytecode, 74
>   Opcodes for Our First Hybrid Interpreter, 76
>   Problems, 77

10 Constructing a Hybrid Interpreter, 78

>   Introduction, 78
>   Global Constants and Variables in Our Hybrid Interpreter, 78
>   Embedding the Code Generator in the Parser, 79
>   Modifying the `printstmt()` Function, 82
>   Modifying the `assignmentstmt()` Function, 82
>   Implementing a Bytecode Interpreter, 83
>   Problems, 87

11 Raspberry Pi Assembly Language, 88

>   Introduction, 88
>   Architecture of the Raspberry Pi (a Simplified View), 88
>   How Machine Instructions are Executed, 90
>   Some Simple Assembly Language Programs, 94
>   User and Supervisor Modes, 97

How an Address Fits into a Machine Instruction, 99
Using the `.text` and `.data` Directives, 100
Linking Separately Assembled Modules, 102
Problems, 104

12 Calling C Functions from Assembler Code, 106

Introduction, 106
Converting to and from Binary, 106
Structure of a C Program in Executable Form, 107
Calling `printf()` from an Assembly Language Program, 109
Calling `scanf()` from an Assembly Language Program, 112
Problems, 113

13 Constructing a Compiler, 115

Introduction, 115
Using Both `.text` and `.data` Segments, 115
Minimizing Compiler Complexity, 115
Structure of the Compiler, 117
`assigmentstmt()` and `printstmt()`, 124
Commenting the Assembler Code, 125
Problems, 127

14 Constructing a Tokenizer Level 2, 129

Introduction, 129
Required Modifications, 130
Adding Support for Two-character Tokens, 131
Adding Support for Floating-Point Constants, 131
Adding Support for Comments, 132
Adding Support for String Data, 132
Adding Support for Python Indentation, 132
Problems, 134

15 Constructing a Parser Level 2, 136

Introduction, 136
Our New Grammar, 136
Shortcomings of our Grammar, 140
Problems, 141

16 Constructing a Pure Interpreter Level 2, 142

Introduction, 142
Determining the Branch-to Address in a Backward Branch, 142
Implementing a Forward Branch, 143
Executing a Relational Expression, 145
Problems, 146

17   Constructing a Hybrid Interpreter Level 2, 148

    Introduction, 148
    Some More Bytecode Instructions, 148
    Compiling Backward Branches to Bytecode, 150
    Compiling Forward Branches to Bytecode, 150
    `whilestmt()`, 151
    `ifstmt()`, 151
    `printstmt()`, 152
    `factor()`, 153
    `interpreter()`, 153
    Problems, 154

18   Constructing a Compiler Level 2, 156

    Introduction, 156
    Temporary Variable Re-use, 156
    Constant Folding, 157
    Putting Constants in the `.text` Segment, 159
    Register Allocation, 159
    Unoptimized Version, 163
    Optimized Version, 166
    Problems, 167

19   Constructing a Pure Interpreter Level 3, 171

    Introduction, 171
    New Symbol Tables, 171
    How a Function Definition is Handled, 174
    Saving Return Addresses, 175
    Saving the Local Symbol Table, 175
    Saving Global Declarations, 176
    Structure of the `funtioncall()` Function, 177
    Structure of the `functiondef()` Function, 178
    Structure of the `returnstmt()` Function, 180
    Problems, 180

20   Constructing a Hybrid Interpreter Level 3, 182

    Introduction, 182
    Parse Trees Versus ASTs, 182
    Representing an AST, 183
    Constructing an AST, 184
    Interpreting an AST, 189
    Problems, 191

21 Constructing a Compiler Level 3, 192

    Introduction, 192
    Representing Dynamically-Typed Variables, 193
    Translating Multiplication, 197
    Translating Addition/Concatenation, 199
    Handling Strings in a Compiler, 202
    Capstone Project, 204
    Problems, 205

Appendix A: An Introduction to Python, 206

    Dynamic Typing, 206
    Multiline Statements, 206
    Code Blocks, 207
    Arithmetic Operations, 207
    Strings, 208
    Concatenation, 209
    Assignment Operator, 209
    Functions, 209
    Global and Local Variables, 212
    `print` Statement, 213
    `input()` Function, 214
    `if` Statement, 214
    `while` Statement, 216
    Files, 217
    Classes, 218
    Exceptions, 220
    Lists, 221
    `splitlines()` Method, 222
    Dictionaries, 222
    Accessing Command-Line Arguments, 223
    `len()` Function, 224
    `isalpha()`, `isdigit()`, `isalnum()`, and `issspace()` Methods, 224
    Date and Time, 224
    Problems, 224

Appendix B: Decimal, Binary, and Hexadecimal, 227

Appendix C: Answers to Selected Problems, 228

Index, 234

Preface

If you want to learn how to write interpreters and compilers, and at the same time learn how Python, Python bytecode, assembly language, and dynamic typing work, this is the book for you. The only prerequisites are some experience with any programming language and a computer on which you can install Python 3 (or Python 2 if you prefer). A Raspberry Pi is *not* required. Included in the software package for the book is an interpreter that allows you to run ARM/Raspberry Pi assembly language programs on your Windows, Linux, or Mac OS X systems. If you have not yet learned Python or assembly language, so much the better. You will get the added bonus of learning Python and assembly language while you learn all about interpreters and compilers. Two chapters on assembly language and an appendix on Python cover everything you need to know to start writing interpreters and compilers.

This book covers three types of language processors: pure interpreters, hybrid interpreters, and compilers. Rather than covering each type in depth before going on to the next type, the book initially covers all three at a very introductory level. So the presentation is easy to follow, and the interpreters and compilers are easy to implement. The book then repeats the cycle but at a higher level, and again at an even higher level. If you call it quits after the first cycle, you will have already benefited from a complete albeit introductory course on language processors. If you want more, you can continue with the more advanced cycles. If, instead, you want to take the depth-first approach, you can do that also. To do pure interpreters in depth, do chapters 1-7 (basic concepts and theory), then chapters 8, 14, 15, 16, and 19. To do hybrid interpreters in depth, do chapters 1-7, then chapters 9, 10, 14, 15, 17, and 20. To do compilers in depth, do chapters 1-7, then chapters 11-15, 18, and 21.

The entire book is Python oriented. Using Python, you will implement interpreters and compilers that process various subsets of the Python 3 language. In addition, the principal hybrid interpreter you will implement is structured like the Python interpreter. In particular, it generates and interprets the same intermediate language (Python bytecode).

Modern interpreter and compiler construction is based on some computer science theory. Sometimes theory is of little practical value. But the theory that underlies interpreters and compilers is, in fact, *very* practical. It provides us with a step-by-step procedure for designing and implementing interpreters and compilers. We present this theory informally so you should not have trouble understanding or applying it.

Here is what you can expect to learn if you study this book:

- Python
- Python bytecode
- Raspberry Pi assembly language
- how to implement dynamic typing
- how to define languages with regular expressions and context-free grammars
- how to construct a parser based on a context-free grammar
- how to construct a tokenizer
- how to construct a pure interpreter
- how to construct a hybrid interpreter
- how to construct a compiler
- how to construct an optimizing compiler
- how to construct abstract syntax trees
- how to interpret abstract syntax trees

The book provides much, but not all, of the code that you will need for your interpreters and compilers. It provides enough of the code so that implementing your interpreters and compilers will be an enjoyable and rewarding task rather than a hair-pulling mission impossible. Developing expertise in writing language processors is like learning how to drive a stick-shift car: You have to do it to learn how to do it. Simply reading a complete implementation of a language processor is like watching someone drive a stick-shift car—it is helpful in the learning process, but it is not going to make you an expert.

A compiled program generally executes much faster than an equivalent interpreted program. Thus, to implement a professional interpreter or compiler, you would certainly want to use a compiled language such as C. However, if your objective is to learn how to write interpreters and compilers, the best implementation language is one that is easy to learn and fun to use. I believe at the present time Python is the language that best meets that description. That is why Python is the implementation language used in this book. Once you can write interpreters and compilers using Python, you can easily transfer that skill to other programming languages.

In this edition, the typos in the the first edition have been corrected, the occasional too brief explanation has been expanded, additional code has been provided for the particularly complex functions, and more end-of-chapter problems have been included. In addition, PowerPoint slides are now included in the software package for this book.

For a Java-oriented book on compilers and interpreters, see my book *Compiler Construction Using Java, JavaCC, and Yacc*. It nicely complements this book. It covers language theory in depth, bottom-up parsing (as well as top-down parsing), and compiler-generating tools (JavaCC and Yacc).

Enjoy the book, and feel free to let me know how you like it. To get the software package, send an email to `wicrpi2@gmail.com`. You will then receive an automatic reply with a link to the site at which you can download the software package (click on the down-pointing arrow in the upper right corner).

I would like to thank Bruce Mardle, HyeSoo Choi (Heh-Soo Choi, 최혜수), Jinsoo Choi (최진수), Kristin Mayo, Cameron Pardo, Andy Pletch, and Dennis Vranjesevic for providing me with suggestions on the content of the book and for proofreading the manuscript.

Anthony J. Dos Reis
Department of Computer Science
SUNY New Paltz

1 Basic Concepts

Creating Your Work Directory

The standard way of invoking a program is to click on the program's icon with your mouse. However, there is another way to invoke programs: via the *command line*. In all the examples in this book, we use the command line. So let's become familiar with it.

To use the command line, you have to start the *command line program*. To do this on a Raspberry Pi running the Raspbian OS (operating system), click on the `Terminal` icon (it is a black rectangle with a blue border on top) on the task bar at the top of the startup screen. On Linux Ubuntu, click on the search icon in the upper left corner and search for "terminal." On a Mac, click on

```
Go
Utilities
Terminal
```

The easiest way to get to the command line program on any Windows system is to search for "command prompt." Alternatively, on a Windows 10 system, click on the start button in the lower left corner of the Desktop screen, then on

```
Windows System
Command Prompt
```

When you invoke the command line program, you will see on your screen the *command line prompt*, which indicates the system is waiting for you to enter a command. On a Raspbian system, the prompt looks like this:

```
pi@raspberrypi:~ $
```

The prompts on Linux and on a Mac are similar. On a Windows system, it looks something like this:

```
C:\Users\a>
```

Before starting your study of language processors, you should create a work directory to hold all your interpreter and compiler programs. Let's call it `wic` for "writing interpreters and compilers" (or you can call it whatever you like). To create a directory named `wic` on your desktop, start the command line program (`Command Prompt` or `Terminal` depending on your system) and then enter

```
cd Desktop          (position OS on Desktop directory)
mkdir wic           (create wic directory)
```

Next, you should unzip and copy the contents of the software package for this book into your `wic` directory. To get the software package, send an email to `wicrpi2@gmail.com`. You will then receive an automatic reply with a link to the site at which you can download the software package. Click on the down-pointing arrow in the upper right corner. Unzip the downloaded file and copy its files and directoriess into the `wic` directory.

Installing Python 3

The Python code we show in this book is Python 3 code. However, the corresponding Python 2 code is almost identical. So if you want to use Python 2, by all means, do so. However, if you use Python 2, you will have to make minor adjustments to the `print` statements in the code we provide: Replace the parentheses in the `print` statements with spaces, delete `end = ''` (but not the preceding comma) where it appears as the last argument in a `print` statement, and have the entire statement on one line.

As of this writing, the standard installs of the Raspbian operating system on the Raspberry Pi and Linux Ubuntu have both Python 2 and Python 3 preinstalled. The Mac currently comes with only Python 2 installed. To install Python 3 on a Mac, download the installer program for the latest version of Python 3 from `www.python.org`. Click on the installer program and follow the directions to complete the install. To install Python 3 on a Windows system, download the installer program for the latest version of Python 3 from `www.python.org`. Click on the installer program and *check the box labeled with* "Add Python 3.x to PATH." Then follow the directions to complete the install. If you do not check this box, then the operating system will not be able to find the Python interpreter when you invoke it from the command line. If you have already installed Python and did not check this box, go to the Control Panel, click on `Uninstall a program`, right click on the Python 3 entry, then click on `Change`, `Modify`, and `next`. Check the box labeled with "Add Python to environment variables." Then click on `Install`.

Starting Your Work

Whenever you want to work on your interpreters and compilers, turn on your computer, start the command line program, and then use the `cd` command to make your work directory the current directory. To do this, assuming your work directory is named `wic` and is on your desktop, start the command line program and enter

```
cd Desktop              (use a capital "D")
cd wic
```

The command line prompt on a Raspbian system then becomes

`pi@raspberrypi:~/Desktop/wic $`

The inclusion of "`wic`" before the dollar sign in the prompt indicates that `wic` is now the current directory. The prompts on the Linux, Mac and Windows systems are affected similarly. Once your work directory is the current directory, you are ready to start working on your compilers and interpreters.

You at times may want to see a list of the files in your work directory. To do this, make your work directory the current directory if you have not already done so. Then on a Raspbian, Linux, or Mac OS X system, enter on the command line

```
ls
```

On a Windows system, enter

```
dir
```

Which Text Editor to Use

You can use any text editor to create your interpreter and compiler programs. Here are two that are particularly easy to use: On a Raspbian, Linux, or Mac OS X system, `nano` is a simple text editor you invoke from the command line. For example, to create the file `program1.py` in your work directory, first make your work directory the current directory if you have not already done so. Then enter on the command line

```
nano program1.py
```

Next, enter your program. Then hit `Ctrl-x`, then `y` and `Enter` to save and exit. The file is then saved in your work directory. When `nano` is invoked, it displays at the bottom of the screen the various commands you can use. For example, it displays "`^X Exit`" which indicates that `Ctrl-x` triggers an exit from the `nano` program (the caret symbol, "`^`", represents the Ctrl key). On a Windows system, you can use the `notepad` program to create Python programs. For example, to create the file `program1.py` in your work directory, make your work directory the current directory, and then enter on the command line

```
notepad program1.py
```

After entering your program with `notepad`, save it by clicking on `File`, then on `Save as`. When you save a file with `notepad`, be sure to select the "`All Files`" option in the "`Save as type`" window. Otherwise, `notepad` appends "`.txt`" to the name of the file you are saving.

Running Python 3

Let's now try running a Python program. Make your `wic` work directory the current directory. Run the Python program in `sample.py` (which is in the software package for this book) by entering on the command line,

```
python sample.py
```

If this command does not work or if it invokes Python 2 (in which case you will get a syntax error because the program contains a Python 3 `print` statement), then try running `sample.py` by entering

```
python3 sample.py
```

On a Raspbian system, `python` and `python2` invoke Python 2; `python3` invokes Python 3. In all the examples in this book, We invoke the Python 3 interpreter with the `python` command. You, of course, should invoke the Python interpreter with the command that is appropriate for your system—the one that invokes Python 3.

Difference between Interpretation and Compilation

The language processors that are used by software developers fall into two categories: interpreters and compilers. An interpreter executes the program it is provided. A compiler, on the other hand, translates the program it is provided. For example, suppose you have the two programs in Fig. 1.1 *in the current directory of your computer*—the first program (a Python program) in the file `sample.py`, the second (a C program) in the file `sample.c` (these programs are available in the software package for this book).

```
sample.py

print('hello')
```

```
sample.c

#include <stdio.h>
int main(void)
{
    printf("hello\n");
    return 0;
}
```

Figure 1.1

If on the command line you invoke the Python interpreter with

```
python sample.py
```

the interpreter responds by executing the Python program in `sample.py`. Thus, it displays "hello". If, instead, you compile the program in `sample.c` with a C compiler, the compiler does not execute the program in `sample.c`. Instead, it translates `sample.c` to machine language instructions. *Machine language instructions* are the type of instructions the machine hardware (i.e., the computer hardware) can directly execute. To compile `sample.c` with the `gcc` C compiler, enter

```
gcc sample.c -o sample
```
                                   (output file name)

The translated program is written to the file specified by the `-o` switch (`sample` in this example).
    Windows does not have a C compiler preinstalled. However, you can download and install on Windows the Embarcadero `bcc32c` C/C++ compiler (see `rpi.txt` for installation directions). To compile `sample.c` with the Embarcadero compiler, enter

```
bcc32c sample.c
```
                          (be sure to include the ".c" extension)

The `bcc32c` compiler outputs to a file with the same base name as the input file but with the extension ".exe". Thus, the `bcc32c` command above outputs to a file named `sample.exe`. You can also download and install the `gcc` compiler on Windows (see `rpi.txt` for installation directions). For either compiler, to execute the machine language program in the output file, enter on the command line:

```
sample
```
        (on non-Windows systems, you may have to enter `./sample`)

The operating system responds by loading the machine language program into memory and giving it control. The computer then executes the program, which displays "hello." Do not be concerned if you do not have a C compiler available. You will be using Python for your interpreters and compilers.
    Try entering the `python`, `gcc` or `bcc32c`, and `sample` commands given above. On a Raspbian, Linux, or Mac OS X system (but not Windows), you may encounter a problem when you enter

```
sample
```

to execute the compiled program in the file `sample`. The operating system may not be able to find the `sample` file, in which case it will display the message

```
sample: command not found
```

The `gcc` command given above creates the `sample` file in the current directory on your computer. But on a Raspbian, Linux, or Mac OS X system, the operating system does not search the current directory by default when you enter a command on the command line, so it will not find the `sample` file. Note that this problem does not occur on a Windows system because Windows by default searches the current directory whenever a command is entered on the command line. So, on a Raspbian, Linux, or Mac OS X system, how do you invoke programs in the current directory? You prefix the program's name you enter with "`./`". For example, to invoke `sample`, enter

```
./sample
```

The period before the slash represents the current directory. It tells the operating system to search the current directory for the specified program. Use the "`./`" prefix *only* for programs in the current directory. Do *not* prefix the `python` or `gcc` commands with "`./`".

You can also configure Raspbian, Linux, or Mac OS X so that prefixing commands with "`./`" is unnecessary. To do this, position your operating system on your home directory (not your `wic` work directory) by entering on the command line

```
cd
```

Then using a text editor, modify or create a file named `.bashrc` so that it contains the following two lines:

```
PATH=.:$PATH
export PATH
```

If the `.bashrc` file already exists, then insert the two lines above at the beginning of the file. Note that the name of the `.bashrc` file starts with a period. If the `.bashrc` file did not already exist and you created it, enter the following command on the command line to make it executable:

```
chmod 755 .bashrc
```

Then exit and restart the `Terminal` program. If "`./`" is still required, then repeat but for the file `.bash_profile`.

Incidentally, on a Raspbian, Linux, or Mac system, a leading period in a file name makes the file hidden. A *hidden file* is not listed by the normal `ls` command. If you want to see all the files in the current directory, including the hidden files, enter on the command line

```
ls -al
```

Here is some terminology on the input and output files of language processors: The program in `sample.py` (the file inputted to the Python interpreter) and the program in `sample.c` (the file inputted to the C compiler) are called *source programs* (see Fig. 1.2). They are so called because they are at the "source" (i.e., beginning) of the language interpretation or compilation process. The language in which the source program is written is called the *source language*. The program to which a compiler translates the source program is called the *target program*. The language of the target program is called the *target language*. The language in which an interpreter or compiler is written is called the *implementation language*. For the interpreters and compilers that we will write, our implementation language will be Python 3. The source language will be a range of subsets—from simple to substantial—of Python 3.

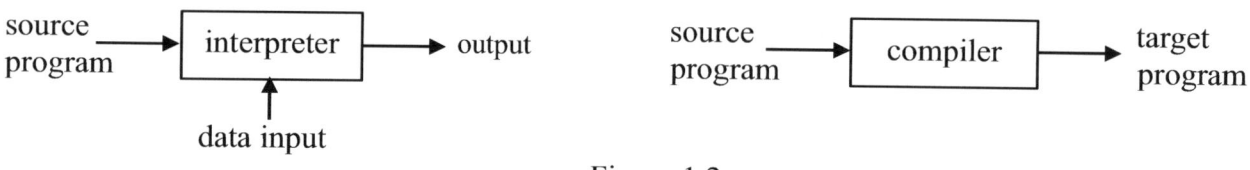

Figure 1.2

What Happens When an Interpreter Interprets

When we desk-check a program (i.e., mentally execute it to see if it works correctly), we are interpreting—not translating—the program. To get a sense of what an interpreter program does, let's examine what we do when we desk-check a program. Consider the Python program in Fig. 1.3.

```
1 firstnumber = 10
2 secondnumber = 20
3 if firstnumber == secondnumber:
4     print('equal')
5     print('good')
6 else:
7     print('not equal')
```

Figure 1.3

When we desk-check this program, we see a sequence of characters. We see "f", then "i", then "r", and so on. When we reach the space after the final "r" in "firstnumber", it registers in our minds that "firstnumber" is a meaningful unit of program. We also do this when we read a book. Our eyes scan individual letters. But our minds break up the sequence of letters into meaningful units. For a book, we call the meaningful units *words*. But for a computer program, we call them *tokens*.

At the end of every line in a text file, there is an invisible character. We call this character the *newline character* or the *end-of-line character*. When you create a text file, every time you hit the Enter key, you inject a newline character into the file you are creating. Python uses the newline character to mark the end of a statement. For example, in Python the following line is a complete statement

x = 1 + 2 + 3 ← newline character is here

Although the newline character is invisible, it nevertheless, is a token (i.e., a meaningful unit) in a Python program. It marks the end of a statement. The programming language C, on the other hand, uses the semicolon to mark the end of a statement. For example, in the following C assignment statement,

```
    x = 1
      + 2
      + 3;
```

we know we have reached the end of the statement when we reach the semicolon. Thus, in a C program the newline character is not a token.

In Python, an indentation preceded by a newline marks the beginning of a *code block*—a block of code to be treated as a unit. A *dedentation* (i.e., a change in indentation toward the left margin) marks the end of a code block. Thus, in Python, indentations and dedentations are also tokens but not in C. In C, braces delimit code blocks.

The list of all the tokens in the Python program in Fig. 1.3 is given in Fig. 1.4. In this listing, we represent the invisible newline character with NEWLINE, the end-of-file marker with EOF, an indentation with INDENT, and a dedentation with DEDENT. Note that a code block starts with a NEWLINE immediately followed by an INDENT and ends with a DEDENT.

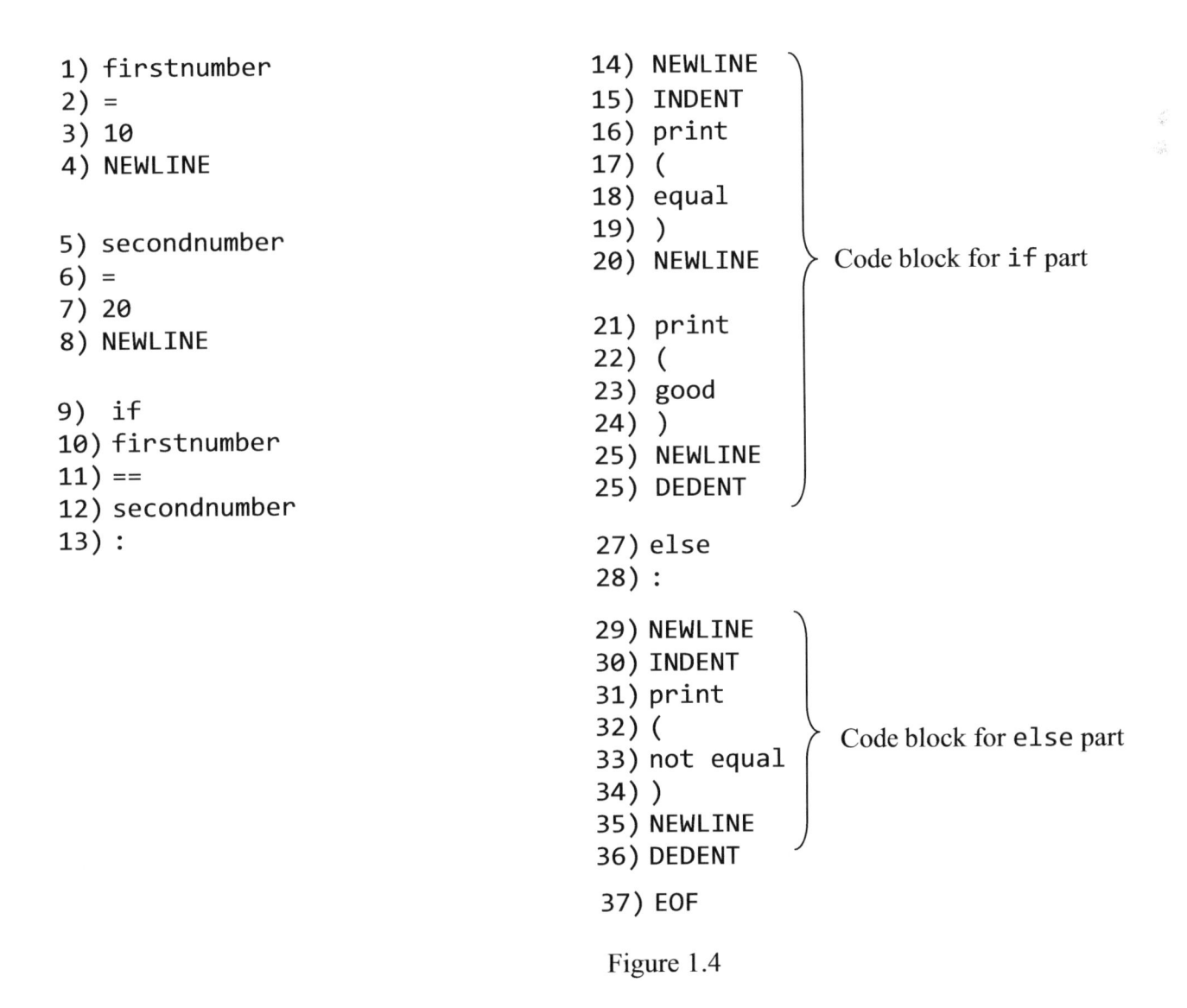

```
1)  firstnumber              14) NEWLINE
2)  =                        15) INDENT
3)  10                       16) print
4)  NEWLINE                  17) (
                             18) equal
5)  secondnumber             19) )
6)  =                        20) NEWLINE        Code block for if part
7)  20
8)  NEWLINE                  21) print
                             22) (
9)  if                       23) good
10) firstnumber              24) )
11) ==                       25) NEWLINE
12) secondnumber             25) DEDENT
13) :
                             27) else
                             28) :

                             29) NEWLINE
                             30) INDENT
                             31) print
                             32) (                Code block for else part
                             33) not equal
                             34) )
                             35) NEWLINE
                             36) DEDENT

                             37) EOF
```

Figure 1.4

For us to determine what the program in Fig. 1.3 does, we not only have to determine its tokens, but also determine its structure. For example, we have to identify the if and else subparts of the if statement. If the true/false expression in the `if` statement is true, we execute the `if`-part. Otherwise, we execute the `else`-part. Thus, obviously, we have to know which is the `if`-part and which is the `else`-part to do this. We call this process of determining a program's structure *parsing*.

Thus, to desk-check the program in Fig. 1.3, we start by tokenizing and parsing the first line. The parsing process tells us this is an assignment statement, and it isolates the left and right sides. With this information, we can "execute" this line. That is, we record somewhere that `firstnumber` now has the value 10. For example, on a piece of paper, we might draw a box labeled with `firstnumber` and place 10 inside the box:

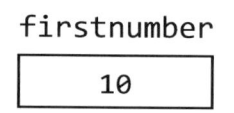

```
firstnumber
┌─────┐
│ 10  │
└─────┘
```

That box with 10 inside it represents the effect of the assignment statement. We similarly process the second line after which we have on our paper

```
firstnumber    secondnumber
┌─────┐        ┌─────┐
│ 10  │        │ 20  │
└─────┘        └─────┘
```

After tokenizing and parsing the `if` statement, we execute it by comparing the values of `firstnumber` and `secondnumber`, and then executing the `else`-part (because the numbers in the `firstnumber` and `secondnumber` are not equal). Thus, we display "`not equal`". We do this by writing on our piece of paper "`not equal`" in a box labeled "display monitor":

```
firstnumber    secondnumber        display monitor
┌─────┐        ┌─────┐              ┌ ─ ─ ─ ─ ─ ─ ─ ┐
│ 10  │        │ 20  │                  not equal
└─────┘        └─────┘              └ ─ ─ ─ ─ ─ ─ ─ ┘
```

Note that we did not translate the program in Fig. 1.3. Instead we executed it (after tokening and parsing it). This is precisely what a pure interpreter does.

There are two types of interpreter programs: pure interpreters and hybrid interpreters. *Pure interpreters* interpret the given source program or something very close to it, as we did above with the program in Fig. 1.3. In contrast, *hybrid interpreters* first translate the source program to an intermediate program that can easily and quickly be interpreted. It then interprets the intermediate program. Thus, hybrid interpreters consist of two components: a compiler that translates the source program to the intermediate program, and an interpreter that interprets the intermediate program (see Fig. 1.5). We call the language of the intermediate program the *intermediate language* (IL).

Hybrid Interpreter

source program → compiler → intermediate program → interpreter → output
                                                        ↑
                                                   data input

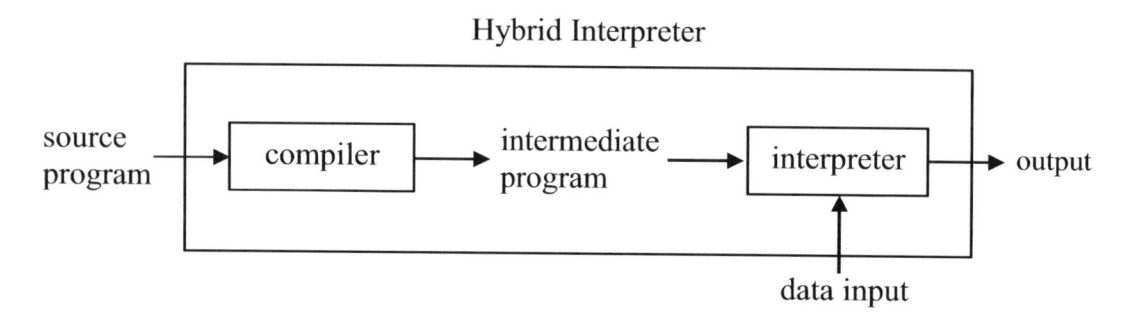

Figure 1.5

Python is an example of a hybrid interpreter. It first translates the Python source program to an intermediate program consisting of *Python bytecode* instructions. It then interprets this bytecode. Java takes the same approach, but with Java the compiler and interpreter components are separate programs. For example, to interpret a Java program in the file `T.java` that contains the Java class T, we first have to compile `T.java` with the `javac` compiler:

```
javac T.java
```

The `javac` compiler translates the Java code in `T.java` to Java bytecode, and outputs this bytecode to a file named `T.class`. We then interpret the Java bytecode in `T.class` by invoking the Java interpreter, specifying the class name T when we invoke the `java` interpreter:

```
java T
```

If the source language is relatively simple in structure, the pure interpretation approach works well. But if the language is more complex, then the hybrid approach is better. The original BASIC language was quite simple. In fact, it was designed so that you could learn the entire language in less than an hour. So its interpreters were more on the pure side of the spectrum. For more complex languages—for example, Java and Python—their interpreters are on the hybrid side of the spectrum.

Advantages of Interpreters over Compilers

Interpreters have several advantages over compilers. First, interpreting a program is a one-step procedure (Java's approach is an exception). In contrast, compiling requires an extra step: running the compiled program. Second, interpreters generally provide better error messages at run time. This is because interpreters work more directly with the source program. Thus, an interpreter can more easily generate error messages that identify the location of the error in the source program. Compiled code, on the other hand, consists of machine language instructions. When an error occurs at run time, the location of the error in the machine code can be displayed. But how does a programmer determine the location of the error in the source program given the error location in the machine code? Third, interpreters are portable. For example, a Python program can be run on any computer system that has a Python interpreter. But a C compiler produces a machine language program for a specific system. Thus, such a program must be run of that system. For example, a C compiler that runs on a Windows system typically produces machine language instructions for the Windows system. Thus, the machine language program it produces can run on only a Windows system. Fourth, an interpreter properly designed can prevent the interpreted program from doing any harm to the host computer (such as erasing the host computer's hard disk)—an important requirement for programs that are embedded in web pages. Fifth, to write an interpreter does not require intimate knowledge of the computer on which it is to run, but to write a compiler does, as you will see in chapter 13.

We should also mention the disadvantages of interpreters. Their principal disadvantage is that they are slow. Interpreted code always takes longer (generally a lot longer) than compiled code.

Problems

1. On a Raspbian, Linux, or Mac OS X system, why might a problem occur if you invoke the `sample` program without the "./" prefix but not if you invoke the `gcc` program without the "./" prefix?

2. Write a C program that does not output anything, whose execution time is 1 second (use nested loops). Then convert the program to Python, and run it using the Python interpreter. How long does the Python version take?

3. If you do not already know Python, read appendix A. Write a Python program that reads the file `p0103.txt` (it is in the software package for this book) and first displays the words it contains, then the numbers. The file `p0103.txt` contains the following line:

   ```
   Honesty is 123 the 456 best policy 789
   ```

4. Compile `p0104.c` with a C compiler and run it. Also run `p0104.py` using the Python 3 interpreter. The files `p0104.c` and `p0104.py` are in the software package for this book. Which one—the C compiler or the Python 3 interpreter—provides a better error message?

5. Some web pages have embedded Java programs. When you visit such a page, the Java program is downloaded to your computer and executed by the Java interpreter embedded in your web browser. Why would it be a bad idea to have compiled C programs embedded in web pages?

6. If `sample.c` is compiled with

   ```
   gcc sample.c
   ```

   what is the name of the executable file produced by the `gcc` compiler?

7. What are the advantages and disadvantages of a hybrid interpreter relative to a pure interpreter?

8. The *tokenizer* is the part of an interpreter that determines the tokens that make up the source program and provides them to the parser. In addition to the token itself, what might the tokenizer provide to the parser? *Hint*: If an interpreter detects an error in the source program, what should the error message contain?

9. In a Python program, does a completely blank line or a line with only a comment contain any tokens?

10. List all the tokens in the following Python and C code:

    ```
    # Python code              // C code
    x = 5                      x = 5;
    while x > 0:               while (x > 0) {
        print('hello')             printf("hello");
        x = x - 1                  x = x - 1;
    print('bye')               }
                               printf("bye");
    ```

11. When positioned on the directory that contains the software package for this book, enter on the command line

    ```
    python sample.py > ch1p11.txt
    ```

    Then examine with a text editor the file `ch1p11.txt`. What is the effect of "`> ch1p11.txt`"?

12. How do the files created by a text editor and a word processing program differ?

13. Why do you see "garbage" if you edit a executable file produced by a C compiler with a text editor? *Hint*: A text file represents each character with an eight-bit code.

14. What is the Python 2 equivalent of the Python 3 statement

    ```
    print('hello', end ='')
    ```

15. Python statements generally do not span multiple lines. Why?

16. What data structures does a pure interpreter need to execute the source program?

17. A program created from Java can be distributed to a user without distributing the source code (simply distribute only the class file created by the compiler). Is there some way to similarly distribute a Python program without distributing its source code?

2 Defining Languages with Regular Expressions

Introduction

Interpreters and compilers have embedded in them complete knowledge of the source language they process. Otherwise, they would not be able to do what they do. In a very real sense, the interpreter or compiler for a source language is what defines the source language. It is the ultimate arbiter of a source language's syntax and semantics. In this chapter, we start our discussion of language-defining mechanisms that can easily be embedded in a language processor.

Basic Language Concepts

An *alphabet* for a language is a finite set of symbols used to form strings in that language. For example, the alphabet of Python is the set of all the characters we can use when we write a Python program. Thus, it includes all the letters, the digits, and the special symbols that can be entered via a keyboard. To keep our discussion simple, in this section we will use only very small alphabets, such as {a, b}.

A *string over an alphabet* is a finite sequence of characters from that alphabet. For example, if our alphabet is {a, b}, then some strings over this alphabet are aaa, aba, bb, a, and b. Every string over the alphabet {a, b} has zero or more a's, zero or more b's, and no other characters. In Python, we have to surround a string with quotes. But in this chapter, we omit the quotes. But by omitting the quotes, we run into a problem: How do we represent on paper the *null string*—the string that has zero characters? To represent the null string in Python, we simply write two adjacent single quotes (' ') or two adjacent double quotes (" "). But we need something to write on a paper to represent the null string if we do not use quotes. Let's use the Greek letter lambda (λ) to represent the null string.

We now can define a language: A *language* over an alphabet is any set of strings—finite or infinite—over that alphabet. For example, suppose our alphabet is {a, b}. Then each of the following sets is a language over {a, b}: {a, aa}, {b}, {ab, a}, {λ}, and { }. Note that according to our definition, even the empty set, { }, is a language. Incidentally, {λ} and { } are not the same language. {λ} contains one string, but { } contains no strings.

If we use a non-negative integer exponent in a string, the exponent represents the repetition of the preceding character. For example, a^2 is shorthand for aa. In ab^3, the 3 applies to the preceding b. Thus, ab^3 represents the string abbb. But in $(ab)^3$, the 3 applies to the substring inside parentheses. Thus, $(ab)^3$ represents ababab. By definition any string to the zero exponent is the null string. For example, $(ab)^0$ is λ.

One way to specify a language is to use *set-builder notation*. For example, consider the language given by {$a^i | i \geq 1$}. Read this as "the set of strings a^i for all *i* greater than or equal to 1." When $i = 1$, a^i is a^1 which is just a; when $i = 2$, a^i is a^2, which is aa. Since *i* can be any integer greater than or equal to 1, a^i can be any string of one or more a's. Thus, this is the infinite language {a, aa, aaa, ...}.

Here is another example using set-builder notation: {$a^i b^i | i \geq 0$}. For any value of *i*, a^i and b^i have the same number of characters. Thus, this language is {λ, ab, aabb, aaabbb, ...}. Each string in this language has zero or more a's followed by the SAME number of b's.

Operations on Strings and Languages

Given two strings, we can *concatenate* them—that is, we can place them next to each other to form a new string. For example, if we concatenate aa and ab, we get aaab. The concatenation of any string with the null string does not produce a new string. For example, if we concatenate abb with λ, we get back abb.

We can also concatenate sets of strings. For example, the concatenation of {a, ab} and {bb, bbb} is the set of strings that can be obtained by concatenating a string from the first set with a string from the second set. Thus, the result of concatenating {a, ab} with {bb, bbb} is {abb, abbb, abbbb}. To indicate we want to concatenate two sets of strings, we simply place the two sets next to each other. For example {a}{a, ab} is the concatenation of {a} with {a, ab}.

We can also concatenate a string with a set of strings. For example, a{b, bb}, the concatenation of a and {b, bb}, is the set of strings obtained by concatenating a with each string in {b, bb}. Thus, a{b, bb} = {ab, abb}.

Concatenation with λ has no effect. That is, λx = xλ = x for any string x or any set x. For example, λab = abλ = ab, and λ{a, ab} = {a, ab}λ = {a, ab}.

An asterisk following a character means "zero or more." For example, b* is the set of strings consisting of zero or more b's. Zero b's by definition is λ. Thus, b* = {λ, b, bb, bbb, ...}. b*aa is the set of strings consisting of zero or more b's followed by a single instance of aa. Thus, b*aa = {aa, baa, bbaa, bbbaa, ...}. Note that the asterisk here applies to b, the character that precedes the asterisk. Think of b*aa as representing the concatenation of the set b* = {λ, b, bb, bbb, ...} with the set {aa} or the string aa. We call the asterisk the *star operator*.

a*b* is an important example. This language is the concatenation of a* = {λ, a, aa, aaa, ...} and b* = {λ, b, bb, bbb, ...}. To concatenate these two sets, we take any string in a* and any string in b* and concatenate them. a*b* contains all the strings that can obtained in this way. For example, we can take aa from a* and bbbb from b*. Then concatenate them to get aabbbb. Thus, aabbbb is one of the strings in a*b*. Let's describe this language using English: It is the set of all strings consisting of zero or more a's followed by zero or more b's. The language defined by a*b* is NOT the same as the language defined by $\{a^i b^i \mid i \geq 0\}$. In both languages, all the a's precede all the b's. In $\{a^i b^i \mid i \geq 0\}$, the number of a's in each string is the same as the number of b's. But in a*b*, the number of a's does not have to equal the number of b's. Compare the shortest strings in the two sets:

$\{a^i b^i \mid i \geq 0\}$ = {λ, ab, aabb, aaabbb, ...}
a*b*   = {λ, a, b, aa, ab, bb, ...}

In a*, we are applying the star operator to the single character a. We can also apply the star operator to a multi-character string by using parentheses. For example, in (ab)*, we are applying the star operator to the string ab. Thus, (ab)* = {λ, ab, abab, ababab, ...}. We can also apply the star operator to a set of strings. For example, {a, b}* is the set of strings that can be obtained by using zero or more a's and zero or more b's in any order. Note that if we take zero a's and zero b's, we get λ. That is why λ is in {a, b}*. Because we can take any number of a's and b's in *any* order, {a, b}* contains EVERY string over the alphabet {a, b}. For this reason, we call {a, b}* the *universe of strings* for the alphabet {a, b}. Here is another example that uses the star operator: {aa, ab, ba, bb}*. This is the set of all strings of even length over the alphabet {a, b}.

The plus operator is similar to the star operator. The *plus operator* means "one or more" whereas the star operator means "zero or more." For example, b+ = {b, bb, bbb, ...}. Note that bb* is the set of strings consisting of b followed by zero or more b's. It is the set of strings consisting of one or more b's. Thus, b+ = bb*. Similarly, b+ = b*b.

Square brackets around an item means the item is optional (i.e., there can be zero or one of that item)

For example, a[b] is an a optionally followed by b. Thus, a[b] represents two strings: a, and ab. We call a set of square brackets used in this way the *square-bracket operator*.

Because languages are sets, we can use the standard set operations—union, intersection, and complementation—on languages. We will represent the union operation with "|", intersection with "∩" and complementation with "~". Let's look at a few examples. Suppose our alphabet is {a, b}, A = {a, ab}, and B = {ab, bb}. Then

- $A|B$, the *union* of A and B, is the set of the strings in A or in B or in both. Thus, $A|B$ = {a, ab, bb}. We will sometimes refer to the union operator ("|") as the "*or*" operator or the *vertical bar operator*. The union operator is usually represented with the symbol "∪", but we use "|" because it is available on the standard keyboard.

- $A \cap B$, the *intersection* A and B, is the set of the strings that are in both A and B. Thus, $A \cap B$ = {ab}.

- ~A, the *complement* of A, is the set of all strings in the universe {a, b}* that are not in A. Thus, ~A contains λ, b, aa, ba, bb, and every string over {a, b} of length 3 or more.

Regular Expressions

A *regular expression* is a well-formed finite-length expression in which we are allowed to use only

- ∅ (which represents the empty set)
- λ (which represents the null string)
- any symbol in our alphabet
- the star, concatenation, and union operations
- parentheses (to show the scope of an operation)

For example, a*|(ab)* is a regular expression. It represents the language that is the union of a* and (ab)*.

Every regular expression defines a language. For example, the regular expression a represents the language {a}. Suppose our alphabet is {a, b}. Here is a list of some of the regular expressions for this alphabet and the languages they define:

Regular expression	Language defined
∅	{ }
λ	{λ}
a	{a}
b	{b}
ab	{ab}
a*	{λ, a, aa, aaa, ...}
b*	{λ, b, bb, bbb, ...}
a*b*	{λ, a, b, aa, ab, bb, ...}
a*|b*	{λ, a, b, aa, bb, aaa, bbb, ...}

Any language that can be represented by a regular expression is called a *regular language*.

An interesting question to consider is whether there are some languages that cannot be represented by a regular expression. Unfortunately, there are. One such language is $\{a^i b^i \mid i \geq 0\} = \{\lambda, ab, aabb, aaabbb, ...\}$. We can capture with a regular expression the requirement that all the a's precede all the b's (a*b* does this). But we cannot capture the requirement that all the a's precede the b's *and* the number of a's equal the number of b's. This is bad news for the writer of a language processor. Programming languages typically contain structures like the language $\{a^i b^i \mid i \geq 0\}$, and therefore cannot be defined by a regular expression. For example, in an arithmetic expression, the number of left parentheses must match the number of right parentheses. No regular expression can capture that requirement. Thus, regular expressions are not powerful enough to define the typical programming language. However, we can generally use regular expressions to define the tokens of a programming language. For example, suppose a variable name is any string that starts with a letter and is followed by zero or more letters and/or digits. The regular expression that defines this type of token is letter(letter|digit)*.

Regular expressions by definition are limited to the operations of star, concatenation, and union. However, because an expression that also uses the plus or square-bracket operators can always be converted to an equivalent regular expression (i.e., to a regular expression that defines the same language), we will allow the use of the plus and square-bracket operators in our regular expressions. For example, strictly speaking, ab+ and a[b] are not regular expressions. But we nevertheless consider them regular expressions because we can define the same languages they define with genuine regular expressions: ab+ is equivalent to abb*, and a[b] is equivalent to a|ab. Think of [b] as λ|b. Thus, a[b] = a(λ|b) = a|ab. We call regular expressions that use the plus or square-bracket operators *extended regular expressions*.

Problems

1. Using set builder notation, define the language a*b*.

2. Does a*|b* = (a|b)*? That is, does the left side define the same language as the right side?

3. Write a regular expression that defines the same language as a*b* ∩ b*c*.

4. Write a regular expression that defines the same language as ~(a*). Assume the alphabet is {a, b}. *Hint*: What must be true if a string over {a, b} is not in a*?

5. Same as problem 4, but assume the alphabet is {a}.

6. Write a regular expression that defines the language over {a, b} that consists of all strings that have exactly one b.

7. Convert [a]b+ to a genuine regular expression.

8. Define an unsigned decimal integer using a regular expression.

9. Write a regular expression that defines C-type multi-line comments (/* ...*/). Assume the alphabet is {/, *, a, b}.

10. Define a floating-point constant using an extended regular expression. A floating-point constant consists one or more digits and exactly one period. Examples: 1., .1, .12, 12., 1.2, 12.3, and 1.23.

3 Defining Languages with Context-free Grammars

Introduction

To detect syntax errors, a language processor obviously must have complete knowledge of the syntax of the source language. Thus, we need some way to represent the syntax of our source language that we can embed in a language processor. The representation we use should be concise and precise. It also should be complete. That is, it should capture all the syntax rules of the language. Finally, the representation should have an associated algorithm that uses the representation to efficiently perform syntax checking. On all four counts, context-free grammars are almost perfect.

Context-free grammars were introduced in the 1950s as a mechanism for describing natural languages such as English. Because the syntax of natural languages is so complex and irregular, context-free grammars turned out to be not particularly useful in the study of natural languages. However, they are great for defining programming languages.

Context-free Grammars Defined

A *context-free grammar* (CFG) is a set of replacement rules. Each replacement rule is called a *production* because it "produces" its right side from its left side. For example, the production

    A → aAb

indicates that A can be replaced by aAb. The arrow in a production means "can be replaced by." The symbols that can be replaced are called *nonterminal symbols*. We use capital letters for the nonterminal symbols. The symbols that cannot be replaced are called *terminal symbols*. We use lowercase letters for the terminal symbols.

The left side of a production should be a single nonterminal symbol. The right side can contain any combination of terminal symbols and nonterminal symbols. The right side can also be the null string. The following are all legal CFG productions:

A → bc		right side all terminals
A → BCD		right side all nonterminals
A → B		right side one nonterminal
A → a		right side one terminal
A → aBc		right side terminals and nonterminals
A → aABAb		left side also on right side
A → λ		right side lambda

The productions of a CFG are replacement rules. The replacement process always starts with a particular nonterminal symbol. We call this special nonterminal symbol the *start symbol*. By convention, when we list the productions of a grammar, we always list the productions for the start symbol first. For example, in the grammar in Fig. 3.1, the first production listed has S on its left side. Thus, S is the start symbol for the grammar. The nonterminal symbols are S, A, and B (the capital letters). The terminal symbols are a and b (the lowercase letters). The set of terminal symbols in a grammar is called its *terminal alphabet*. For example, the grammar in Fig. 3.1 has the terminal alphabet {a, b}.

1) S → AB
2) A → aA
3) A → λ
4) B → bb

Figure 3.1

A string that contains only the terminal symbols in a CFG or is equal to λ is called a *terminal string* for that grammar. For example, for the grammar in Fig. 3.1, bb and abb are terminal strings. We view the null string λ as a terminal string because it has no nonterminal symbols.

Using the CFG in Fig. 3.1, we start the replacement process with the start symbol S:

S

In our grammar in Fig. 3.1, there is only one production that replaces S (production 1). Using it to replace S, we get AB. Let's list horizontally the strings we get from the application of productions, with the symbol "⇒" separating the successive strings. Then, after our first replacement, we have

S ⇒ AB

If we now replace A using production 2 (A → aA), we get aAB from AB:

S ⇒ AB ⇒ aAB

The effect of production 2 is to insert an a at the beginning of the string. If we now replace A using production 3, the effect is to delete A (because A gets replaced by the null string). We get

S ⇒ AB ⇒ aAB ⇒ aB

Because the right side of production 3 is the Greek letter lambda (which represents the null string), we call production 3 a *lambda production*. Next, let's use production 4, which replaces B with bb. We get

S ⇒ AB ⇒ aAB ⇒ aB ⇒ abb   (this is a derivation of abb from S)

The resulting string, abb, has no nonterminals, so the replacement process ends.

We call a sequence of strings obtained by applying productions in a CFG a *derivation*. The derivation above shows that in this grammar abb can be derived from S. We say that S *generates* abb. We can derive other terminal strings from S using the grammar in Fig. 3.1. For example, here are the derivations for bb and aabb:

S ⇒ AB ⇒ B ⇒ bb
S ⇒ AB ⇒ aAB ⇒ aaAB ⇒ aaB ⇒ aabb

In the derivation of bb, we use productions 1, 3, and 4 in that order. In the derivation of aabb, we use productions 1, 2, 2, 3, 4 in that order. Each time we use production 2, we inject an a into the string we are deriving. Thus, to derive the string a^5bb (i.e., aaaaabb), we would use production 2 five times.

The *language defined by a context-free grammar* is the set of all the terminal strings that can be derived from its start symbol. For example, the grammar in Fig. 3.1 defines the language {bb, abb, aabb, aaabb,

...} = a*bb = {a^{i}bb | $i \geq 0$}. How do we know this? The B nonterminal creates a bb at the end of any terminal string derived from S. Each time production 2 is used, it injects an a. We can use it any number of times. So we can have any number (including zero) of a's followed by bb. Each string in a*bb is derivable from S. Moreover, no other terminal strings are derivable from S. Thus, this set is the language defined by the grammar.

Examples of Context-free Grammars

We learned in chapter 2 that the language {a^{i}b^i | $i \geq 0$} cannot be defined by a regular expression. But it can easily be defined with the following CFG:

1) S → aSb
2) S → λ

Each time we use the first production, we produce an a and a matching b. Thus, the number of a's ultimately produced will always equal the number of b's. In this grammar, we have two S productions. *Either one can be used first*. If we use the second production first, we get the derivation

S ⇒ λ

which shows that the null string is in the language defined by the grammar. To get a terminal string from S, we use production 1 zero or more times and then use production 2 once. Each time we use production 1, we get an a and a matching b. Thus, to get the string aabb, we use production 1 twice and then production 2:

S ⇒ aSb ⇒ aaSbb ⇒ aabb

To get the string a^{n}b^n where *n* is some non-negative integer, we use production 1 *n* times and then production 2 once.

Two grammars for a* are

1) S → aS   1) S → Sa
2) S → λ   2) S → λ

Each time we use production 1 in either grammar, an a is generated. When we use production 2, S is eliminated, and we are left with a terminal string. The grammar on the left generates the terminal string from left to right. The grammar on the right generates the terminal string from right to left. For example, the derivation of aa using the left grammar is

⎯⎯ this character generated first
↓
S ⇒ aS ⇒ aaS ⇒ aa

The first character in the terminal string is generated first. Then the second character is generated. But if we use the grammar on the right, the last character in the terminal string is generated first:

── this character generated first

S ⇒ Sa ⇒ Saa ⇒ aa

We have several grammars for a+ (i.e., one or more a's):

1) S → aS	1) S → Sa	1) S → aA	1) S → Aa
2) S → a	2) S → a	2) A → aA	2) A → Aa
		3) A → λ	3) A → λ

The first and second grammars above are similar, but they generate their terminal strings in different directions: The first grammar generates its terminal string left to right; the second, right to left:

S ⇒ aS ⇒ aaS ⇒ aaa   first grammar generates strings left to right
S ⇒ Sa ⇒ Saa ⇒ aaa   second grammar generates strings right to left

In the third and fourth grammars, the nonterminal A generates a list of zero or more a's. But in both grammars, the S production necessarily generates a single a. Thus, every terminal string derivable from S must have at least one a.

Grammars for Arithmetic Expressions

Let's write a grammar that defines arithmetic expressions restricted to the + (addition) and * (multiplication) operators. To keep our grammar simple, let's say that the only operands allowed are a, b, and c. Here are some of the strings in this language:

a
(a)
a+b
a*a
a*(b+c)

Note that in these strings, * and + are terminal symbols. They denote multiplication and addition, respectively. They are NOT the star (zero or more) and plus (one or more) operators. Fig. 3.2 shows a grammar for this language.

1) S → S+S
2) S → S*S
3) S → (S)
4) S → a
5) S → b
6) S → c

Figure 3.2

Because all the productions in Fig. 3.2 have the same nonterminal on the left side, we can represent them in a much shorter form: We specify the left side S only once and then list all the right sides separating each from the previous one with "|". We get

$$S \to S+S \mid S*S \mid (S) \mid a \mid b \mid c$$

Read the vertical bar as "or."

Let's show that the grammar in Fig. 3.2 can generate the string a+b:

$$S \Rightarrow S+S \Rightarrow a+S \Rightarrow a+b$$

Another way to show that S can generate a+b is to construct a *parse tree* for a+b that shows the substitutions that occur in the derivation of a+b. Here is the parse tree for a+b:

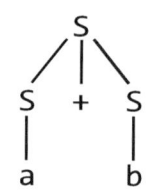

```
      S
    / | \
   S  +  S
   |     |
   a     b
```

The top S has three "children": S, +, and S. This structure indicates that a production used in the derivation replaced the top S with S+S. The second-level S on the left has one child, an a, which indicates that a production replaced this S with a. Similarly, the S to the right has one child, b. This indicates that a production replaced this S with b.

Here are two parse trees for the string a+b+c based on the grammar in Fig. 3.2:

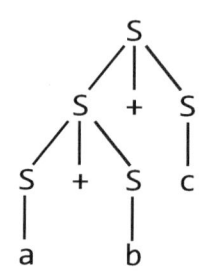

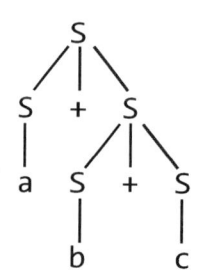

```
         S                        S
       / | \                    / | \
      S  +  S                  S  +  S
    / | \   |                  |    / | \
   S  +  S  c                  a   S  +  S
   |     |                         |     |
   a     b                         b     c
```

If there is at least one terminal string for which there is more than one parse tree, we say that the grammar is *ambiguous*. Thus, the grammar in Fig. 3.2 is ambiguous. Generally, when we are a designing language processor, we want to base its design on an unambiguous grammar. Note that the left parse tree above implies that the left addition should be performed first (because it is lower in the tree). But the right parse tree implies the right addition should be done first. We have a similar ambiguity in strings with a mixture of + and *. For example, the string a+b*c has two parse trees. In one, the + is lower (implying the addition should be done first). In the other, the * is lower (implying the multiplication should be done first).

The parse tree structure of a terminal string reflects its meaning. So if a terminal string has more than one parse tree, it has more than one meaning. Such an ambiguity is not acceptable in a programming language. We have the same kind of ambiguities in English. For example, consider the following sentence:

Time flies like arrows.

The meaning of this sentence depends on which word is the verb. If "flies" is the verb, it means that time passes by swiftly. If "like" is the verb, then it means that a type of fly called a "time fly" has an affection for arrows. Finally, if "Time" is the verb, it means you should measure the flight time of flies the way you would measure the flight time of arrows.

For arithmetic expressions, we need a grammar that is not ambiguous. Moreover, its parse trees should imply the correct order of evaluation. For example, in the parse tree for a+b+c and a*b*c, the left operator should be lower, implying the order of evaluation should be left to right. For a+b*c, the asterisk should be lower in the tree than the plus sign, implying the multiplication should be done before the addition.

Fig. 3.3 shows an unambiguous grammar for arithmetic expressions.

1) S → S+T
2) S → T
3) T → T*F
4) T → F
5) F → a | b | c | (S)

Figure 3.3

Here are the only possible parse trees for a+b+c and a+b*c using the grammar in Fig. 3.3:

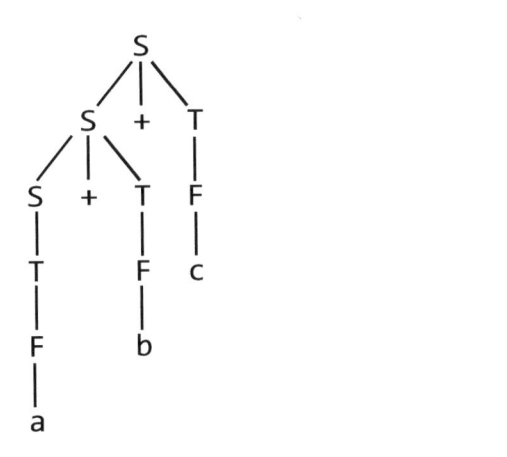

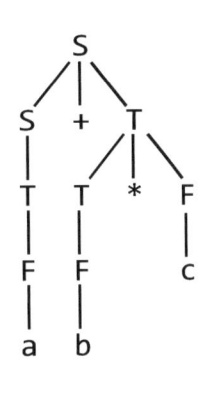

The left parse tree implies that the additions are performed in left-to-right order (because the left + is lower in the tree than the right +). The right parse tree implies that the multiplication is performed before the addition (because the * is lower in the tree than the +). This grammar not only unambiguously defines arithmetic expressions, it also captures the correct rules on the order in which operations should be performed.

Fig. 3.4 shows another unambiguous grammar for arithmetic expressions.

1) S → TL
2) L → +TL
3) L → λ
4) T → FM
5) M → *FM
6) M → λ
7) F → a | b | c | (S)

Figure 3.4

Here is the parse tree for **a+b+c** in the grammar in Fig. 3.4:

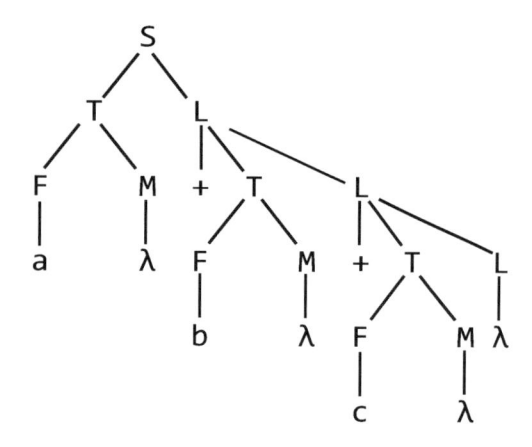

```
              S
           /     \
          T       L
         / \    / | \
        F   M  +  T   L
        |   |    / \  /|\
        a   λ   F   M + T  L
                |   |   /\  |
                b   λ  F  M λ
                       |  |
                       c  λ
```

Let's focus on the S and L productions in this grammar:

1) S → TL   (generates a leading T)
2) L → +TL   (each time used, generates one occurrence of "+T")
3) L → λ   (eliminates L)

Production 1 generates a leading T followed by L. Production 2 generates one occurrence of "+T" each time it is used. Production 3 eliminates L. The number of times we use production 2 determines the number of occurrences of "+T" that are generated. Thus, using the L productions, we can generate as many occurrences—zero or more—of "+T" that we want. To illustrate this, here are the derivations that start with L that generate zero, one, and two occurrences of "+T":

L ⇒ λ   (use production 3 once)
L ⇒ +TL ⇒ +T   (use production 2 once then production 3 once)
L ⇒ +TL ⇒ +T+TL ⇒ +T+T   (use production 2 twice then production 3 once)

The S production tells us that S consists of a leading T followed by L, where L is a list of zero or more occurrences of "+T". Thus, using the star operator, we can write the S production as

S → T(+T)*   (* is zero or more operator—not a termimal symbol)

If we do this, we do not need the L productions in our grammar.

By production 4 in Fig. 3.4, T consists of a leading F followed by M. The M productions generate a list of zero or more occurrences of "*F". Thus, we can write the T production as

T → F(*F)*   (* is zero or more operator—not a termimal symbol)

in which case, we do not need the M productions in our grammar. Simplifying our grammar using these new productions, we get the grammar in Fig. 3.5.

1) S → T(+T)*
2) T → F(*F)*
3) F → a | b | c | (S)

Figure 3.5

But now we have a problem: Each parenthesis can be interpreted two ways: as a terminal symbol in the grammar or as a special symbol to show the scope of the star operator. Similarly, each asterisk can be interpreted in two ways: as a terminal symbol or as the star operator. For example, if we interpret both asterisks in production 2 in Fig. 3.5 as the star operator, then this production generates an F followed by zero or more left parentheses (because of the star operator that follows the left parenthesis) followed by another F followed by zero more right parentheses. If, instead, we regard the first asterisk as a terminal symbol in the grammar, the second asterisk as the star operator, and the parentheses as indicating scope, then production 2 generates an initial F followed by zero or more occurrences of "*F". From the grammar itself, it is not clear which symbols are the terminal symbols and which symbols are the regular expression operators. We can fix this problem easily by adopting the following convention: Simply quote the terminal symbols. Let's also separate the components on the right side of each production with spaces wherever it makes the grammar easier to read. We then get the grammar in Fig. 3.6.

```
1) S → T('+' T)*
2) T → F('*' F)*
3) F → 'a' | 'b' | 'c' | '(' S ')'
```

Figure 3.6

Grammars for real programming languages require quite a few nonterminal symbols. By using a single capital letter for each nonterminal, we limit ourselves to 26 nonterminals. Moreover, we cannot use meaningful names for our nonterminals (such as "expr" in place of S in our grammars for arithmetic expressions). So let's allow the use of descriptive names for our nonterminals. But if a single nonterminal symbol can be a sequence of characters, how do we know if a sequence of characters is a single nonterminal symbol or a sequence of nonterminal symbols. For example, consider the production

A → XYZ

If a nonterminal can be a sequence of symbols, then how do we know if XYZ is one nonterminal or more than one. It might be three consecutive nonterminals: X, Y, and Z. The fix for this problem is simple: Enclose every nonterminal in angle brackets. Then if XYZ is a single nonterminal, the production above is written as

⟨A⟩ → ⟨XYZ⟩

If it is three consecutive nonterminals, it is written as

⟨A⟩ → ⟨X⟩⟨Y⟩⟨Z⟩

Let's rewrite the grammar in Fig. 3.6 using this convention, replacing S with ⟨expr⟩, T with ⟨term⟩, and F with ⟨factor⟩. Let's also separate the component parts of the right side of each production with spaces. We get the grammar in Fig. 3.7.

```
1) <expr>      → <term> ('+' <term>)*
2) <term>      → <factor> ('*' <factor>)*
3) <factor>    → 'a' | 'b' | 'c' | '(' <expr> ')'
```

Figure 3.7

For the rest of the book, we will write grammars in the form illustrated by the grammar in Fig. 3.7 That is, we will delimit terminal symbols with quotes and nonterminals symbols with angle brackets. We will separate component parts of the right sides of productions with spaces to improve readability. We will use meaningful names for the nonterminals. We will also use the star (zero or more), plus (one or more), and square-bracket (zero or one) operators whenever they can simplify the specification of a grammar.

Problems

1. Write a CFG that defines a*|b*.

2. Write a CFG that defines a*b*.

3. Write two CFGs that defines $\{(ab)^i c^i \mid i > 2\}$.

4. Write a CFG that defines the set of all strings over the alphabet {a, b} that have exactly one b.

5. Write a CFG that defines the set of all strings over the alphabet {a, b} that have at least one b.

6. Write a CFG that defines the set of all strings over the alphabet {a, b} that have exactly two b's.

7. Extend our CFG for arithmetic expressions in Fig. 3.3 to include the subtraction operator (-) and the division operator (/). *Hint*: Subtraction has the same precedence as addition, and division has the same precedence as multiplication.

8. Write a CFG that defines the set of all palindromes over the alphabet {a, b}. *Hint*: Be sure to consider palindromes of odd length (for example, aabaa).

9. Write a Python program that inputs a string and determines if it is in the language given in problem 6.

10. Write a Python program that inputs a string and determines if it is in the language given in problem 8.

11. Show that the following CFG is ambiguous:

    <S> → <S><S> | 'a'

12. Draw the parse tree for a*b+c corresponding to the grammars in Fig. 3.3 and Fig. 3.4.

13. A *regular grammar* is a context-free grammar in which the right side of each production is either a single terminal, a single terminal followed by a single nonterminal, or λ. Give regular grammars that define the same languages as a*, aa*, a*b*, a*|b*, a*bcc*, (a|b)*, and (b*ab*ab*ab*)*

4 Recursive-Descent Parsing

Introduction

To parse a string means to determine or construct its parse tree. There are two general categories of parsers: top down and bottom up. A *top-down parser* determines the parse tree starting with the top of the parse tree (i.e., from the start symbol), working down to the terminals. A *bottom-up parser* starts from the bottom of the parse tree (i.e., from the terminals), working up to the start symbol. In this book, we will construct top-down parsers only. Although bottom-up parsers have some advantages over top-down parsers, they are difficult to implement by hand, generally requiring special software tools.

There are essentially two ways to implement a top-down parser: one way uses an explicit stack; the other way uses a technique called *recursive-descent parsing*. In this book, we will use the latter approach. Recursive-descent parsing is easier to implement than the stack approach. Moreover, it can easily be extended to perform translation as well as parsing.

In this chapter, we will construct a parser for a language in which each character is a separate token. Thus, the *tokenizer* (the component of an interpreter or compiler that provides tokens to the parser) is quite minimal in structure: It simply provides to the parser each character of the input string as a separate token.

Implementing a Recursive-Descent Top-down Parser

Let's implement in Python a recursive-descent top-down parser for the grammar in Fig. 4.1.

```
1) <S> → <A><C>
2) <A> → 'a' 'b'
3) <C> → 'c' <C>
4) <C> → 'd'
```

Figure 4.1

Before we start, let's determine what terminal strings <A> itself and <C> itself can generate. Let's call any terminal string <A> can generate an "<A>-string." Similarly, let's call any terminal string <C> can generate a "<C>-string." There is only one <A> production, and it can generate only ab. Thus, the only <A>-string is ab. The two <C> productions can generate zero or more c's followed by a single d. That is, it can generate any string in the language defined by the regular expression c*d. Each time we use production 3, we get one c. When we ultimately use production 4, we get one d. Thus, a <C>-string is a string with zero or more c's followed by a single d. For example, to generate the <C>-string d, we use production 3 zero times and production 4 once:

<C> ⇒ d

To generate the <C>-string ccd, we use production 3 twice and production 4 once:

<C> ⇒ c<C> ⇒ cc<C> ⇒ ccd

Suppose we have a function named A() that works in the following way: If the parser is positioned at the beginning of an <A>-string, and the A() function is called, the A() function will advance the parser in the input string so it ends up just beyond the <A>-string. For example, suppose A() is called when the parser is positioned as indicated by the caret symbol in the following:

    abccd   before A() is called
    ^

Then after A() is called, the parser is positioned on c, the character immediately after the <A>-string ab:

    abccd   after A() is called
      ^

If, on the other hand, the parser is not positioned at the beginning of an <A>-string when A() is called, then A() raises an exception.

    For the grammar in Fig. 4.1, each single character in a terminal string is a token. Thus, we call the character on which the parser is positioned at any given point in the parse the *current token*. For example, in the "after" display above of abccd, the current token (marked by the caret) is the first c.

    Suppose we also have a function named C() that works for <C>-strings the same way A() works for <A>-strings. That is, C() advances the parser over any <C>-string. If we have these two functions, A() and C(), we can then easily write an S() function that will advance the parser over any <S>-string. We can see from production 1 of the grammar (<S> → <A><C>) that an <S>-string is any <A>-string followed by any <C>-string. Thus, we can implement the S() function simply with a call of A() followed by a call of C(). The call of A() advances over the <A>-string portion of the <S>-string; the call of C() advances over the <C>-string portion of the <S>-string. Together the two calls advance over the <S>-string. Here is the code for the S() function (the line numbers are from the complete parser in Fig. 4.2):

```
41 def S():
42     A()
43     C()
```

Suppose we call S() when the parser is positioned at the beginning of the <S>-string abcd (ab is an <A>-string; cd is a <C>-string):

    abcd
    ^

Then S() calls A() (which advances past ab) and then C() (which advances past cd). Thus, when S() finishes, the parser is positioned just beyond the end of the <S>-string abcd:

    abcd
        ^

If the end-of-file marker is at this final position, then we know that our input string is an <S>-string, and therefore is a string in the language defined by the grammar.

    The S() function we constructed above, along with the A() and C() functions, is our recursive-descent parser. Let's now implement the A() and C() functions. Assume we have an advance() function that acts as the tokenizer for our parser. Each time it is called by the parser, its effect is to both advance to the next character in the input string and assign the character at that position to a variable named token. In the language defined by the grammar in Fig. 4.1, each character in the input string is a separate token. Thus, each time the advance() function is called, it provides the next token via the variable token. We call the character in the token variable the *current token*. It is the token on which the parser is positioned.

    Assume we also have a consume() function which, when called, is passed a character. If this character matches the current token (i.e., the character in the variable `token`), `consume()` calls `advance()`. Otherwise, it raises an exception. For example,

    consume('a')

first checks if the current token is a. If it is, then `consume()` calls `advance()`, which advances past the a. Otherwise, `consume()` raises an exception.

Using `consume()`, the implementation of the A() function is trivial:

```
45 def A():
46     consume('a')
47     consume('b')
```

The first call of `consume()` checks if the current token is a. If it is, `consume()` causes the parser to advance to the next character. Otherwise, it raises an exception. The second call of `consume()` repeats this process but for b. The effect of the two calls of `consume()` is to advance the parser over the <A>-string ab (or raise an exception if ab is not present). Incidentally, by convention, we always include a pair of empty parentheses when specifying a function name—for example, `consume()`. The empty parentheses do not imply that the function takes no arguments when it is called. `consume()`, for example, is always passed one argument when it is called. We use the empty parentheses simply to emphasize that the name refers to a function.

The C() function is more complicated, but still easy to implement. It first has to decide which <C> production to use. If the current token is c, then C() proceeds according to the production that generates a leading c (production 3 in Fig. 4.1). If the current token is d, then C() proceeds according to the production that generates a leading d (production 4 in Fig. 4.1). If the parser is not positioned at the beginning of a <C>-string when C() is called, then C() raises an exception. Here is the complete C() function. Recall that `token` is the variable that holds the current token.

```
49 def C():
50     if token == 'c':
51         # perform actions corresponding to production 3
52         advance()
53         C()                                    # recursive call
54     elif token == 'd':
55         # perform action corresponding to production 4
56         advance()
57     else:
58         raise RuntimeError('Expecting c or d')
```

If c is the current token when C() is called, then the call of `advance()` on line 52 advances past it. Following this initial c should be another <C>-string. We know this from the production 3 in Fig. 4.1 (<C> → c<C>). Thus, to advance past this embedded C-string, C() simply calls itself recursively (see line 53). If d is the current token when C() is called, then the call of `advance()` on line 56 advances past the d. In either case, the original call of C() has the effect of advancing the parser past the <C>-string component of the input string.

Note the similarity between the <S>, <A>, and <C> productions in the grammar in Fig. 4.1 and their corresponding functions in the parser. There is, in fact, such a close correspondence that writing this type of parser is a trivial task. A terminal symbol in the grammar corresponds to a call of `consume()` or `advance()`; a nonterminal symbol in the grammar corresponds to a call of the function for that nonterminal. If there is more than one production with the same nonterminal on the left side, then the function for that nonterminal uses an `if` statement (which tests the current token) to determine which production to apply.

Fig. 4.2 shows the complete parser for the grammar in Fig. 4.1. It is in the file `sp.py` ("sp" is for "simple parser"). In this parser, the input string is provided via the second command line argument. For example, to run the parser against the input string abcd, enter on the command line

python sp.py abcd ← second command line argument

The parser then accesses the second command line argument (using `sys.argv[1]`) and uses it as the input string. If no second argument is given on the command line, or if the parser is at the end of the input string, the `advance()` function sets the `token` variable to `' '` (the null string), which signals the end of the input (see lines 23 and 24 in Fig. 4.2). Thus, if a second argument on the command line is not specified, the input string is the null string. The `advance()` function (which acts as the tokenizer in `sp.py`) provides the next token (in the variable `token`) each time it is called.

```
1  # sp.py parser
2  # Grammar:
3  #      <S> -> <A><C>
4  #      <A> -> 'a''b'
5  #      <C> -> 'c'<C>
6  #      <C> -> 'd'
7  import sys    # needed to access command line arg
8
9  #global variables
10 tokenindex = -1
11 token = ''
12
13 def main():
14     try:
15         parser()           # call the parser
16     except RuntimeError as emsg:
17         print(emsg)
18
19 def advance():
20     global tokenindex, token
21     tokenindex += 1      # move tokenindex to next token
22     # check for null string or end of string
23     if len(sys.argv) < 2 or tokenindex >= len(sys.argv[1]):
24         token = ''        # signal the end by returning ''
25     else:
26         token = sys.argv[1][tokenindex]
27
28 def consume(expected):
29     if expected == token:
30         advance()
31     else:
32         raise RuntimeError('Expecting ' + expected)
```

```
33
34 def parser():
35     advance()    # prime token with first character
36     S()          # call function for start symbol
37     # test if end of input string
38     if token != '':
39         print('Garbage following <S>-string')
40
41 def S():
42     A()
43     C()
44
45 def A():
46     consume('a')
47     consume('b')
48
49 def C():
50     if token == 'c':
51         # perform actions corresponding to production 3
52         advance()
53         C()
54     elif token == 'd':
55         # perform action corresponding to production 4
56         advance()
57     else:
58         raise RuntimeError('Expecting c or d')
59
60 main()
```

Figure 4.2

The `emsg` variable on line 16 receives the string passed when a `RuntimeError` exception is raised. For example, if the statement

```
58         raise RuntimeError('Expecting c or d')
```

is executed, then the `emsg` variable on line 16 receives the string `'Expecting c or d'`, which is then displayed by line 17.

If the parse is successful, the parser simply terminates. If the parse is unsuccessful, it displays an error message. If the input string is an `<S>`-string followed by some garbage, the parse completes. That is, `S()` returns control to `parser()`. `parser()` then detects the garbage and displays "`Garbage following <S>-string`" (line 39).

The parser in Fig. 4.2 is an example of a *recursive-descent parser*. Parsers of this type usually use recursion at some point (for example on line 53 in Fig. 4.2)—hence, the use of the term "recursive" in "recursive-descent." As the parser processes the input string, it in effect moves down the parse tree—from the start symbol to the terminals—hence, the use of the term "descent" in "recursive-descent." The `C()` function in the parser in Fig. 4.2 has a choice of `<C>` productions it can apply (because there is more than one `<C>` production). However, it can always "predict" the correct production to apply by examining the current token. If the current token is `'c'`, it applies the production `<C>` → `'c'<C>`; if the current token is 'd, it applies the production <C> → 'd'. We call this type of parser—that can predict which production to use—a *predictive recursive-descent parser.*

At the beginning of this chapter we defined parsing as a process in which the parse tree is determined or constructed. But does the parser in Fig. 4.2 do this? Yes, it does. Follow the sequence of function calls that occurs during the parse. For example, for the input string abcd, S() calls A(). That call corresponds to the construction of the beginning of the top part of the parse tree:

```
  <S>
  /
<A>
```

A() then calls consume('a'), and then consume('b'), which corresponds to adding 'a' and 'b' nodes under the <A> node of our tree. We get

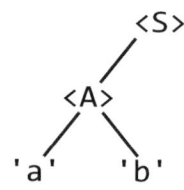

```
     <S>
     /
   <A>
   / \
 'a' 'b'
```

After A() returns to S(), S() calls C(), which in turn calls advance() (to advance past 'c') and C(). These calls correspond to the adding 'c' and <C> nodes under the <C> node that is under the <S> node:

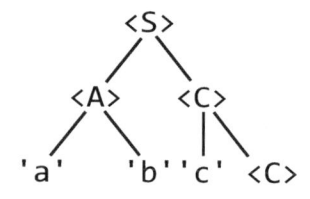

```
       <S>
      /   \
    <A>   <C>
    / \   | \
  'a' 'b' 'c' <C>
```

Finally, C() calls advance() which corresponds to adding a 'd' node under the lower <C> node, after which we have the complete parse tree:

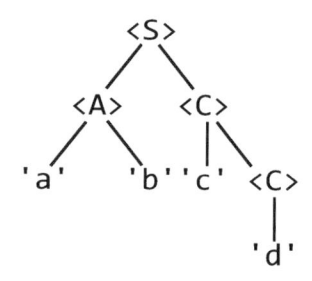

```
       <S>
      /   \
    <A>   <C>
    / \   | \
  'a' 'b' 'c' <C>
               |
              'd'
```

As this example illustrates, a recursive-descent parser does, indeed, determine the parse tree.

To see how our parser works, enter the following commands:

    python sp.py abd
    python sp.py abccd
    python sp.py
    python sp.py abdd

If the parse succeeds, sp.py simply terminates (generally, a parser generates messages *only* when it detects an error). If the parse fails, `sp.py` generates an error message and terminates.

When Not to Use Recursion

The grammar in Fig. 4.1 has two C productions:

    `<C> → 'c' <C>`   (these productions generate c*d)
    `<C> → 'd'`

The first `<C>` production in Fig. 4.1 has `<C>` on both the left and right sides. As a result, the corresponding code in the parser has a recursive call of `C()`. That is, the `C()` function calls itself (see line 53 in Fig. 4.2).

    Recursion tends to be inefficient. Calling and returning from a recursive method requires more time and memory space than the repetitive mechanism in a loop. Can we replace the recursion in the `C()` function with a more efficient loop? Note that the `<C>` productions generate a list of zero or more c's followed by a d. We can specify a list of zero or more c's using the star operator. If we do this, we can then combine the two `<C>` productions into a single production:

    `<C> → ('c')* 'd'`

In this form, we do not have `<C>` on the right side of a `<C>` production. Thus, the corresponding `C()` function does not have a recursive call. The production, however, has the star operator, which corresponds to a loop in the parser that advances over the list of c's. Here is our modified `C()` function, now considerably simplified and more efficient, that corresponds to our new `<C>` production:

```
1 def C():
2     while token == 'c':
3         advance()           # advance over the c's
4     consume('d')            # check for d at end
```

    Computer programs generally contain many lists—for example, lists of arguments, lists of parameters, and lists of statements. It is common practice to define these lists with a CFG that uses *recursive productions* (i.e., productions in which the left side also appears on the right side). The corresponding code then uses recursive calls, which are inefficient. So here is a good rule to follow: Never define lists in a programming language using recursive productions. Instead, use productions with the star or plus operator. If you do this, the corresponding parser code will be simpler and more efficient.

    Suppose in a grammar, we have the following production:

    `<A> → ('a')+`

What is its corresponding parser function? We implement the function for this production as if it were written this way:

    `<A> → 'a' ('a')*`

from which we get the following parser code:

```
1 def A():
2     consume('a')
3     while token == 'a':
4         advance()
```

Recursion is not always to be avoided. For nested structures, recursion is the preferred approach. The non-recursive alternative in such cases is usually considerably more complicated and not much more efficient than the recursive approach. For example, consider the following productions:

    <X> → 'a' <X> 'b' 'c'
    <X> → 'd'

These productions create a nested structure: a's on one side, bc's on the other side, with d in between. They define the language $\{a^i d(bc)^i \mid i \geq 0\}$. Because of the nested structure, the best approach is to implement the X() function according to the two X() productions above. We get the following recursive function:

```
 1 def X():
 2     if token == 'a':
 3         advance()
 4         X()
 5         consume('b')
 6         consume('c')
 7     elif token == 'd':
 8         advance()
 9     else:
10         raise RuntimeError('Expecting a or d')
```

Note that production 3 in Fig. 4.1 does not correspond to a nested structure because the <C> on the right side has nothing to its right in the production. Thus, for the <C> productions Fig. 4.1, the loop approach would be better than the recursive approach.

Using Grammars with the *, +, |, and [] Operators

Context-free grammars often use the "*" (zero or more), "+" (one or more), "|" (or), and "[ ]" (zero or one) operators, as in the following productions:

    <A> → 'a'* 'b'   (zero or more a's followed by b)
    <B> → 'a'+   (one or more a's)
    <C> → 'a'('b'|'c')   (a followed by b or c)
    <D> → 'a'['b']   (a optionally followed by b)

These productions can easily be converted to their corresponding parsing functions. The star and plus operators map to while statements; the "or" and square-bracket operators map to if statements. Here is the parsing code for these four productions:

```
1 # <A> → 'a'* 'b'
2 def A():
3     while token == 'a':
4         advance()
5     consume('b')
```

```
1 # <B> → 'a'+
2 def B():
3     consume('a')
4     while token == 'a':
5         advance()
```

```
1 # <C> → 'a'('b'|'c')
2 def C():
3     consume('a')
4     if token == 'b':
5         advance()
6     elif token == 'c':
7         advance()
8     else:
9         raise RuntimeError('Expecting b or c')
```

```
1 # <D> → 'a'['b']
2 def D():
3     consume('a')
4     if token == 'b':
5         advance()
```

Problems

1. Write a parser based on the following grammar:

   <S> → 'a' <S> 'b'
   <S> → 'c'

   Test your parser with c, acb, aacbb, λ, ca, ab, acbb, aacb, and bca.

2. Write a parser based on the following grammar:

   <S> → 'a' <B> 'd'
   <B> → ('b''b')* ['c']

   Test your parser with ad, acd, abbcd, abbd, abbbbd, abbbbcd, λ, abd, abcd, adc, and accd.

3. Write a parser based on the following grammar:

   <S> → 'a'* <B>
   <B> → 'b'* <C>
   <C> → 'c'['d'|'e']'f'

   Test your parser with cf, cdf, cef, aabbcf, acf, bcf, λ, cdef, cff, and abc.

4. Write a parser based on the following grammar after you simplify it with the star operator:

   <S> → 'a' <B> <S>
   <S> → 'e'
   <B> → 'b' 'c' 'd'

   Test your parser with e, abcde, abcdabcde, λ, abcdex, and abcdabcd.

5. Why is the grammar,

    ```
    <S> → 'a' <S>
    <S> → 'a' 'a' 'a' 'd'
    ```

    not suitable for a recursive-descent parser like the one described in this chapter? Convert it to a suitable grammar that generates the same language.

6. Copy sp.py to p0406.py. Then modify p0406.py so that it obtains the input string from a file whose name is specified on the command line.

7. Copy sp.py to p0407.py. Then modify p0407.py so that it parses without using recursion.

8. Why is consume('a') on line 46 in Fig. 4.2 used instead of advance()? Why is advance() on line 52 in Fig. 4.2 used instead of consume('c')?

9. Why is the following grammar not suitable for the type of parser discussed in this chapter? Convert it to a suitable grammar. *Hint*: Combine the two <S> productions into a single <S> production that contains a new nonterminal <X>. One <X> productions should generate <B>. The other should generate <C>. Implement the parser. Test your parser with abbb, accc, λ, abbc, accb, bbbb, and cccc.

    ```
    <S> → 'a' <B>
    <S> → 'a' <C>
    <B> → 'b' 'b' 'b'
    <C> → 'c' 'c' 'c'
    ```

10. Combine the S() and X() functions from problem 9 into a single S() function by replacing the call of X() in S() with the code from X(). Write a production that corresponds to your new S() function. *Hint*: It should have an interior "|" operation. Test your modified parser as specified in problem 9.

11. Why is the following grammar not appropriate for recursive-descent parsing:

    ```
    <S> → <S> 'a'
    <S> → 'b'
    ```

    Modify the grammar so that it works with recursive-descent parsing. Implement the parser. Test with b, ba, baa, aba, bab, baab, and λ.

12. Can the grammar in question 11 be made to work in a recursive-descent parser if it looks ahead in the token stream produced by the tokenizer? If so, how far ahead does it have to look?

5 Predict Sets

Introduction

When we design a parser, we base it on a context-free grammar. But not all grammars are suitable. In this chapter, we learn how to determine if a grammar is suitable for a parser (specifically for a predictive recursive-descent parser).

Analyzing Grammars for Predictive Recursive-Descent Parsing

Consider the grammar in Fig. 5.1.

```
1) <S> → <A>
2) <S> → <C>
3) <A> → 'a' 'b'
4) <A> → 'b' 'b'
5) <C> → 'c' 'c'
6) <C> → 'd' 'd'
```

Figure 5.1

Here is the A() function for the grammar in Fig. 5.1:

```
1 def A():
2     if token == 'a':   # use production 3
3         advance()
4         consume('b')
5     elif token == 'b': # use production 4
6         advance()
7         consume('b')
8     else:
9         raise RuntimeError('Expecting a or b')
```

The A() function compares the current token with the leading terminals on the right sides of the <A> productions to determine which <A> production to use. The C() function is constructed similarly. But we have a problem with the S() function. The two <S> productions have right sides that do not start with terminal symbols. How then does the S() function decide which <S> production to use?

To determine how to implement the S() function for the grammar in Fig. 5.1, we have to analyze the <A> and <C> nonterminals. Specifically, we have to determine the terminals symbols that can start an <A>-string, and the terminal symbols that can start a <C>-string. From productions 3 and 4, we can see that an <A>-string can start with either a or b. A <C>-string starts with either c or d. Thus, if the current token is either a or b when S() is called, the S() function should call A() since the parser is positioned at the beginning of an A-string. If, on the other hand, the current token is c or d, then the S() function should call C() since the parser is positioned at the beginning of a <C>-string. Here is the S() function:

```
1  def S():
2      if token == 'a' or token == 'b':
3          A()
4      elif token == 'c' or token == 'd':
5          C()
6      else:
7          raise RuntimeError('Expecting a, b, c, or d')
```

Note that S() does not call advance() or consume() because the <S> productions do not generate any terminals. The <A> and <C> productions, however, generate terminals. So the A() and C() functions do the advancing by calling advance() or consume().

Let's repeat the grammar in Fig. 5.1, adding to the right of each production the set of terminal symbols that the right side can produce as leading terminals. For example, <A>, the right side of the production <S> → <A> in the grammar in Fig. 5.1, can generate either a leading a or b. Thus, we show the set {'a', 'b'} to the right of this production:

   1) <S> → <A>   {'a', 'b'}

If we do this for the entire grammar, we get the grammar in Fig. 5.2.

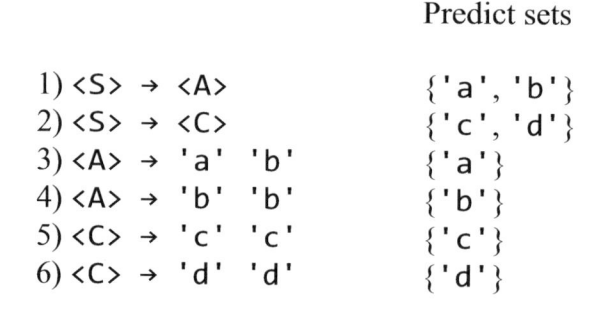

                                                    Predict sets
            1) <S> → <A>   {'a', 'b'}
            2) <S> → <C>   {'c', 'd'}
            3) <A> → 'a' 'b'   {'a'}
            4) <A> → 'b' 'b'   {'b'}
            5) <C> → 'c' 'c'   {'c'}
            6) <C> → 'd' 'd'   {'d'}

                        Figure 5.2

We call the sets to the right of each production in Fig. 5.2 *predict sets* or *selection sets* because they allow the parser to "predict" or "select" which production it should use. For example, the predict set for the first production, {a, b}, indicates that the S() function should use the first production if the current token at that point is either a or b.

Now suppose production 5 in Fig. 5.2 is

   <C> → 'a' 'c'

Then <C> can generate either a leading a with this production or a leading d with production 6. Thus, the predict set for production 2 becomes {a, d}, in which case, we have a problem: Both productions 1 and 2 have the terminal symbol a in their predict sets (see productions 1 and 2 in Fig. 5.3).

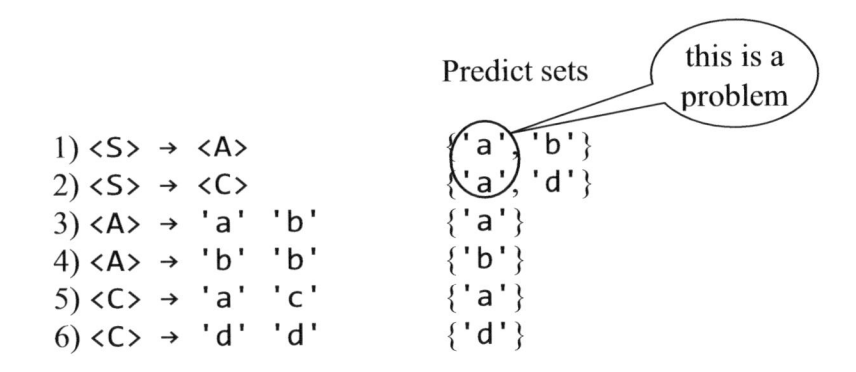

```
                                         Predict sets    ⎛ this is a ⎞
                                                         ⎝ problem   ⎠
     1) <S> → <A>                         {'a', 'b'}
     2) <S> → <C>                         {'a', 'd'}
     3) <A> → 'a' 'b'                     {'a'}
     4) <A> → 'b' 'b'                     {'b'}
     5) <C> → 'a' 'c'                     {'a'}
     6) <C> → 'd' 'd'                     {'d'}
```

Figure 5.3

Now, when the `S()` function is called, if the current token is a, the `S()` function cannot determine from the current token alone which `<S>` production to apply—it could be either production 1 or production 2. The problem with the grammar in Fig. 5.3 is that it has two productions (productions 1 and 2) with the *same* left side whose predict sets have an element in common. For predictive recursive-descent parsers, we do *not* want grammars that have this property. The two A productions in Fig. 5.3 are okay (their predict sets have no elements in common), and so are the two `<C>` productions. But the two `<S>` productions have a in common. So this is not a good grammar. Note that the first `<A>` production and the first `<C>` production have a in common. But this is *not* a problem because the productions have different left sides. We have a problem only if productions with the *same* left side have predict sets with an element in common.

We have three possible solutions for the problem with the `<S>` productions in Fig. 5.3:

1. Rewrite the grammar so this problem does not occur.

2. Have the parser look ahead in the token stream to determine which production to apply. For this grammar if a is followed by b, then the parser is positioned at the beginning of an `<A>`-string, in which case `A()` should be called. If, on the other hand, a is followed by c, then the parser is positioned at the beginning of a `<C>`-string, in which case `C()` should be called.

3. Use the first `<S>` production. If it does not work (i.e., the parse fails), then backtrack to the current point in the token stream and try the second `<S>` production.

Approach 3 involves a lot of programming complexity and runtime overhead (see problem 9). So we definitely want to avoid using it. Approach 1 is the best but not always possible. So we will use approach 1, and when necessary approach 2.

We call the grammar in Fig. 5.2 an *LL(1) grammar*. The 1 in this designation indicates that no more than one token (the current token) is ever needed for the parser to determine which production to apply. But the grammar in Fig. 5.3 is not LL(1)—to decide between productions 1 and 2, the parser needs two tokens (the current token and the next). Thus, the Fig. 5.3 grammar is LL(2) (for an explanation of "LL", see answer for problem 12 on page 230).

Figuring out predict sets can be difficult. But for the grammars we use in this book, the predict sets are more or less obvious. So it is not important for our purposes for you to be able to compute predict sets for complicated grammars. If you know only what predict sets are and how they are used by the parser, you are in good shape. But if you are curious about how to compute predict sets, by all means read the remainder of this section.

Let's now determine the predict sets for the grammar in Fig. 5.4.

Chapter 5: Predict Sets

$$
\begin{array}{lll}
1) & \text{<S>} \rightarrow \text{<A><B>} & \{\text{'a', 'b'}\} \\
2) & \text{<S>} \rightarrow \text{<C>} & \{\text{'c'}\} \\
3) & \text{<A>} \rightarrow \text{'a'} & \{\text{'a'}\} \\
4) & \text{<A>} \rightarrow \lambda & \{\text{'b'}\} \quad \textit{why 'b'?} \\
5) & \text{<B>} \rightarrow \text{'b'} & \{\text{'b'}\} \\
6) & \text{<C>} \rightarrow \text{'c' 'd'} & \{\text{'c'}\}
\end{array}
$$

Figure 5.4

This grammar is a little tricky because of the lambda production (production 4). An <A>-string in this grammar can be the null string because of production 4. But if it is not null, then it has to start with a (because of production 3). A <B>-string has to start with b (because of production 5). What then is the predict set for production 1? The <A> nonterminal can generate a leading a. So a is in the predict set for production 1. But <A> is *nullable*. That is, it can generate the null string, in which case whatever leading terminal <B> generates would be the leading terminal of the right side of production 1. The following derivations show that from <A><B>, we can get either a leading a or a leading b:

<A><B> ⇒ a<B>   (use production 3)

<A><B> ⇒ <B>   (use production 4 to eliminate <A>)
         ⇒ b   (use production 5)

Thus, the predict set for production 1 is {a, b}. What about the predict set for production 4, the lambda production? Its right side cannot generate any terminal symbol, so what is its predict set? Recall what the A( ) function is supposed to do: advance over an <A>-string. If the <A>-string is the null string, then there is nothing to advance over. The A( ) function in that case should simply return to its caller. But that means the current token has to be generated by something in the grammar that *follows* the <A> nonterminal. Examining the parse trees for the strings ab and b in Fig. 5.5 may make this idea easier to understand.

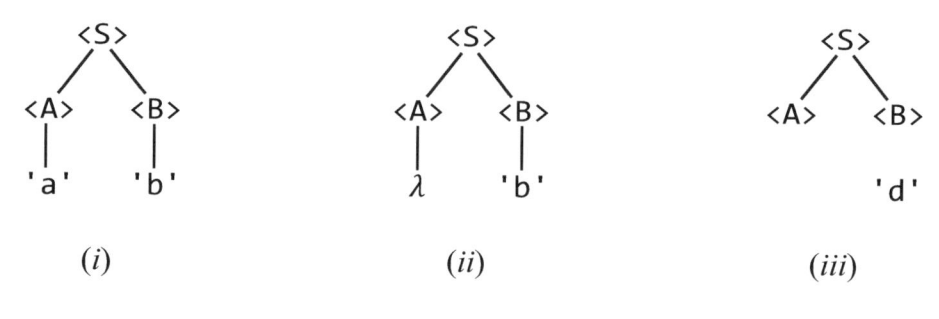

```
      <S>                    <S>                    <S>
     /   \                  /   \                  /   \
   <A>   <B>              <A>   <B>              <A>   <B>
    |     |                |     |                      
   'a'   'b'               λ    'b'                    'd'

    (i)                    (ii)                   (iii)
```

Figure 5.5

Suppose the parser has just called S( ), and the input string is ab (Fig. 5.5*i*). Then S( ) calls A( ) which advances past the a and returns to S( ) which then calls B( ), which advances past the b. If, however, the input string is b (Fig. 5.5*ii*), then A( ) immediately returns to S( ) (because it is proceeding according to the lambda production). But then the current token, b, has to be generated by something that follows <A> in the parse tree. You can see from the parse tree that <B> follows <A>. So <B> has to generate the current token b. Because <B> can generate a leading b, it makes sense for the parser to use the lambda production for <A>—*because what follows <A> can generate the current token*. What if the input string is a single d

(Fig. 5.5*iii*)? Then it does not make sense for the parser to use the lambda production because what follows <A> (the <B> nonterminal) cannot generate the d. From this analysis, we can conclude that the predict set for production 4 contains only b.

Here are the S() and A() functions corresponding to the productions in Fig. 5.4:

```
1  def S():
2      if token == 'a' or token == 'b':
3          A()
4          B()
5      elif token == 'c':
6          C()
7      else:
8          raise RuntimeError('Expecting a, b, or c')
9
10 def A():
11     if token == 'a':    # test if <A> -> a should be applied
12         advance()
13     elif token == 'b'   # test if <A> -> lambda should be applied
14         pass            # Python stmt that does nothing
15     else:
16         raise RuntimeError('Expecting a or b')
```

Note that the parser does nothing (i.e., it executes a `pass` statement) when it applies a lambda production on line 14 in the A() function above. This makes sense. When the parser applies a production, it is supposed to move in the input string past the substring that the production generates. Thus, if the production is a lambda production, there is nothing to move past.

Here are the rules for computing the predict set for the production

<A> → *rightsideofproduction*

1) The predict set for this production includes all the leading terminals in the strings that can be derived from *rightsideofproduction*. We refer to this set as FIRST(*rightsideofproduction*). Suppose the production is

    <A> → <B><C><D>

   Then FIRST(*rightsideofproduction*) = FIRST(<B><C><D>). FIRST(<B><C><D>) includes everything in FIRST(<B>). But if <B> is nullable, then FIRST(<B><C><D>) *also* includes everything in FIRST(<C>). If both <B> and <C> are nullable, then FIRST(<B><C><D>) *also* includes everything in FIRST(<D>).

2) If *rightsideofproduction* is λ or nullable (i.e., it can generate the null string), then the predict set *also* includes the set of terminal symbols that can follow the left side of the production. We refer to the set of terminal symbols that can follow <A> as FOLLOW(<A>).

3) There is always some kind of end-of-input marker at the end of the string we are parsing. Thus, the FOLLOW set of the start symbol *always* contains that marker. Let's use EOF to represent the end-of-input marker. Consider the following grammar:

```
<S> → 'a'<S>        {'a'}
<S> → λ             {EOF}
```

The predict set for the first production is FIRST('a'<S>) = {'a'}. The predict set for the second production is FIRST(λ), which is the empty set, and in addition, FOLLOW(<S>) = {EOF}. Thus, its predict set is {EOF}.

4) Suppose in a grammar, FOLLOW(<A>) includes the terminal symbol x. Thus, in some string derived from the start symbol, x follows <A>:

$$<S> \Rightarrow \cdots \Rightarrow \_\_<A>x\_\_ \Rightarrow \cdots$$

If one of the <A> productions is <A> → <B><C>, and we replace <A> with <B><C> in the preceding derivation, we get:

$$<S> \Rightarrow \cdots \Rightarrow \_\_<A>x\_\_ \Rightarrow \_\_<B><C>x\_\_ \Rightarrow \cdots$$

Now x follows <C>. Thus, FOLLOW(<C>) also includes x. Moreover, if <C> is a nullable nonterminal (i.e., it can generate the null string), we can get the following derivation (by nulling out <C>):

$$<S> \Rightarrow \cdots \Rightarrow \_\_<A>x\_\_ \Rightarrow \_\_<B><C>x\_\_ \Rightarrow \cdots \Rightarrow \_\_<B>x\_\_ \Rightarrow \cdots$$

Now x follows <B>. Thus, FOLLOW(<B>) also includes x. These observations give us the following rule on computing FOLLOW sets:

> Whatever follows the left side of a production follows any symbol on the right side that is either rightmost or has only nullables to its right.

For example, this rule tells us that given the following production,

```
<A> → <B><C><D>
```

whatever follows <A> also follows <D>. If <D> is nullable, then whatever follows <A> also follows <C>. If both <C> and <D> are nullable, then whatever follows <A> also follows <B>.

Let's apply these rules to the grammar in Fig. 5.6.

```
                                        Predict sets
     1) <S> → <A><B>                    {'a', 'b', EOF}
     2) <A> → 'a'                       {'a'}
     3) <A> → λ                         {'b', EOF}
     4) <B> → 'b'                       {'b'}
     5) <B> → λ                         {EOF}
```

Figure 5.6

Productions 2 and 4 each start with a terminal symbol so their predict sets contain just that terminal symbol. From the right side of production 1, we can get a leading a and a leading b, as the following derivations demonstrate:

$$\langle S \rangle \Rightarrow \langle A \rangle \langle B \rangle \Rightarrow a \langle B \rangle \cdots \quad \text{(can get leading a)}$$
$$\langle S \rangle \Rightarrow \langle A \rangle \langle B \rangle \Rightarrow \langle B \rangle \Rightarrow b \langle B \rangle \Rightarrow \cdots \quad \text{(can get leading b)}$$

Thus, the FIRST set of the right side of production 1 is {'a', 'b'}. But the right side of production 1 is nullable, so the predict set of production 1 also includes FOLLOW(<S>)—the follow set of the left side of production 1. FOLLOW(<S>) = {EOF}. Thus, the predict set for production 1 is {'a', 'b', EOF}.

The predict set for production 3 is FOLLOW(<A>). What is FOLLOW(<A>)? The terminal symbol b can follow <A>, as the following derivation demonstrates: <S> ⇒ <A><B> ⇒ <A>b ⇒ ···
So b is in FOLLOW(<A>). <A> has only nullables to its right in production 1. Using rule 4 above on FOLLOW sets, we get that whatever follows <S> also follows <A>. EOF follows <S>. Thus, EOF also follows <A>. Thus, the FOLLOW(<A>)—the predict set of production 3—is {'b', EOF}.

The predict set for production 5 is FOLLOW(<B>). <B> appears rightmost in production 1. Again, using rule 4, we get that whatever follows <S> follows <B>. EOF follows <S>. Thus, FOLLOW(<B>)—the predict set of production 5—is {EOF}.

In our simple parser sp.py in chapter 4 (see Fig. 4.2), the tokenizer (the advance() function) returns the null string when the parser is at the end of the input string. Assuming we are using the same tokenizer, then the recursive-descent parsing function for <A> in the grammar in Fig 5.6 is

```
1  def A():
2      if token == 'a':
3          advance()
4      elif token = 'b' or token = '':      # '' represents EOF
5          pass                              # do nothing
6      else:
7          raise RuntimeError('Expecting a or end-of-input marker')
```

Productions with a Choice

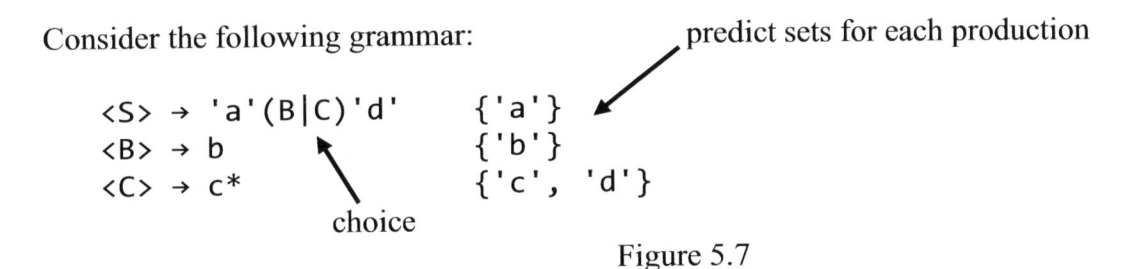

Consider the following grammar: predict sets for each production

$$\langle S \rangle \rightarrow \text{'a'}(B|C)\text{'d'} \quad \{\text{'a'}\}$$
$$\langle B \rangle \rightarrow b \quad \{\text{'b'}\}$$
$$\langle C \rangle \rightarrow c^* \quad \{\text{'c'}, \text{'d'}\}$$

choice

Figure 5.7

The predict set for the <S> production is {'a'}. However, within this production there is a choice—between <B> and <C>. Associated with the <B> choice *is another predict set*. Similarly, associated with the <C> choice *is a third predict set*. The predict sets for <B> and <C> choices determine which function—B() or C()—the parser calls after it advances past the initial 'a'.

Here is the corresponding S(), B() and C() functions:

```
def S():
    consume('a')           ← predict set for <S> production
    if token == 'b':       ← predict set for <B> choice
        B()                ← predict set for <C> choice
    elif token in ['c', 'd']:
        C()
    else:
        raise RuntimeError("Expecting 'b', 'c', or 'd'")
    consume('d')
def B():
    advance()  # token is 'b' here so no need to use consume('b')
def C():
    while token == 'c': # structure for a starred item (see page 33)
        advance()
```

Figure 5.8

After advancing pass the initial `'a'`, if the current token is `'b'`, then the parser should apply the `<B>` production (since `<B>` generates a leading `'b'`). Thus, the predict set for the `<B>` choice is `{'b'}`. But for which current tokens should the parser apply the `<C>` production? `<C>` can generate a leading `'c'`. But `<C>` *can also generate the null string* (because its right side is starred), in which case the current token would be `'d'` at the choice point. If the current token is `'d'`, it make sense for the parser to apply the `<C>` production because its right side can be null, allowing what *follows* `<C>` to generate the `'d'`. So the predict set for the `<C>` choice is `{'c', 'd'}`.

If we wish to include the predict sets in a production, we place the predict set for the entire production at the end and the predict sets for the interior choices right after each choice. Using this convention, we get the following `<S>` production for the grammar above (the predict sets are within the curly braces):

<S> → 'a' (<B> {'b'} | <C> {'c', 'd'}) 'd'   {'a'}

Here is the rule for computing predict sets extended to handle choices within a production. In the production below, α and β represents arbitrary strings consisting of terminals and/or nonterminals that comprise the choices). "..." represents whatever precedes and follows the α|β choice in the production. For the production

<A> → ...(α|β)...

the predict set for the entire production is FIRST(production's right side). If its right side is nullable, then the predict set also includes FOLLOW(<A>). The predict set for the α choice is FIRST(α). If α is nullable, then the predict set *also* includes FOLLOW(α). Similarly, the predict set for the β choice is FIRST(β). If β is nullable, then the predict set *also* includes FOLLOW(β).

Problems

1. Implement the parser for the following grammar:

<S>	→ <A><B><C>	{'a', 'b', 'c', EOF}
<A>	→ 'a'	{'a'}
<A>	→ λ	{'b', 'c', EOF}
<B>	→ 'b'	{'b'}
<B>	→ λ	{'c', EOF}
<C>	→ 'c'	{'c'}
<C>	→ λ	{EOF}

   Test your parser with abc, ac, bc, a, b, c, λ, aaa, abcd, aba, and acb.

2. Implement the parser for the following grammar:

   ```
   <S> → 'a'(<B>|<C>)['d']'e'
   <B> → 'b'*
   <C> → 'c'+
   ```

   Test your parser with ae, ade, ace, acde, abe, abde, λ, abce, acbe, a, and ac. *Hint*: The predict set for the <B> productions includes 'b'. But it also includes what can follow <B> because <B> is nullable.

3. Determine the predict sets for the following grammar:

   ```
   <S> → <A><B>'d'
   <A> → 'a'<A>'c'
   <A> → λ
   <B> → 'b'<A>'e'
   <B> → λ
   ```

4. Implement the parser for the following grammar:

   ```
   <S> → <A><B>
   <A> → ('a')*
   <B> → ('b')+
   ```

   Test your parser with b, ab, aab, aabb, λ, aa, and ba.

5. Determine the predict sets for

   ```
   <S> → <S>'a'
   <S> → 'a'
   ```

   Why is this grammar not suitable for predictive recursive-descent parsing? Can looking ahead solve the problem with this grammar?

6. Modify the grammar in problem 5 so that it is suitable for recursive-descent parsing. Implement the

corresponding parser. Test your parser with a, aa, λ, ab, and abb.

7. The following `<S>` productions are not suitable for recursive-descent parsing as described in this chapter. Why? Fix the productions. *Hint*: Use the vertical bar operator to combine the two `<S>` productions into a single production. Write the `S()` function corresponding to your new `<S>` production. Assume `<C>` always generates a leading `'c'`.

    ```
    <S> → <A><C>
    <S> → <A>'d'
    ```

8. The following grammar is not suitable for recursive-descent parsing as described in this chapter. Why? Fix the grammar. *Hint*: Use the square-bracket operator to combine the two `<S>` productions into a single production. Write the `S()` function corresponding to your new `<S>` production.

    ```
    <S> → <A><C>
    <S> → <A>
    <A> → 'a'
    <A> → 'b'
    <C> → 'c'
    ```

9. Redo problem 1, but do not use predict sets. Instead, use a *backtracking* recursive-descent parser. Use `spbt.py` (the backtracking version of `sp.py`) as your model. Here is the essential idea behind the backtracking approach: Suppose there are five `<A>` productions. Then your parser should have an `A()` function and five additional functions—`A1()`, `A2()`, `A3()`, `A4()`, and `A5()`—one for each of the five `<A>` productions. Each of these five additional functions applies the right side of the corresponding production. If it succeeds, it returns `True`. Otherwise, it returns `False`. When the `A()` function is called, it saves the current position in the token stream. It then calls `A1()`. If `A1()` returns `True`, then `A()` returns `True` to its caller. However, if `A1()` returns `False`, then `A()` resets the current position in the token stream to the saved position. It then calls `A2()`. If `A2()` returns `True`, then `A()` returns `True` to its caller. If, however, `A2()` returns `False`, then `A()` again resets the current position in the token stream to the saved position. It then calls `A3()`. `A()` continues in this fashion, trying each production by calling the corresponding function until one returns `True`. If they all return `False`, then `A()` returns `False` to its caller. To distinguish this type of recursive-descent parser from the predictive type described in this chapter, we call this type a *backtracking recursive-descent parser*.

10. Implement the parser that corresponds to Fig. 5.7. Test with ad, abc, acd, accd, abbd, abcd, and λ.

11. Modify the grammar in Fig. 5.7 by replacing the choice in the `<S>` production with `<X>`. Then add two `<X>` productions, one generating `<B>`, the other generating `<C>`. Implement the corresponding parsing. Test your parser as specified in problem 10.

12. Implement a predictive recursive-descent parser based on the following grammar:

    ```
    <S> → 'a'<S>
    <S> → 'a' 'a'
    ```

    Test with aa, aaa, aaaa, a, ab, and λ. *Hint*: This grammar requires a lookahead in the token stream.

6 Constructing a Tokenizer for a Python Subset

Introduction

The front end of an interpreter or compiler is a tokenizer. Most interpreter and compiler books present a formal procedure based on computer science theory (specifically on finite automata theory) for the design and implementation of the tokenizer. However, tokenizers are easy to implement in an *ad hoc* manner. Thus, although the design-based-on-theory approach for a tokenizer is interesting, it is an unnecessary diversion for us.

The tokenizer we used in the preceding two chapters (the `advance()` function) simply returns the next character in the input string each time it is called. The tokenizer we need for our Python subset is necessarily more elaborate. It has to handle tokens that can consist of multiple characters, such as variable names and integer constants.

Tokenizer-Parser Interface

The input to a tokenizer in an interpreter or compiler is the source program. The tokenizer breaks up the source program into a sequence of meaningful units, called *tokens*, and provides these tokens to the parser. There are two approaches the tokenizer can take:

1. Tokenize the entire source program and then provide to the parser the complete list of tokens. In other words, the tokenizer finishes its job before the parser starts its job, or

2. Tokenize the source program on an as needed basis. In this approach, the parser initially gets control. Whenever it needs the next token from the source program, it calls the tokenizer, which then gets the next token and provides it to the parser.

What are the tradeoffs between these two approaches? Consider this: The specific actions a parser takes obviously depends on the sequence of tokens it is provided. Most of the time the action the parser takes depends only on the token it is currently parsing. However, sometimes it has to look ahead in the token stream to determine what it should do with the current token. If the tokenizer uses approach 1 above, these occasional look-ahead operations are simple to do. The entire list of tokens is available so the parser simply looks ahead in this list. Look ahead operations are also possible with approach 2 but are more difficult to implement. So approach 1 seems better. If, however, we want our source program to be executed *as it is keyed into the computer*, then obviously we have to use approach 2. Total run time is essentially the same for these two approaches. Because approach 1 is easier to implement, we will use it in our tokenizers.

When the parser detects an error in the token stream it is processing, it should generate an informative error message. For example, suppose the following statement is on line 7 of a Python program:

x = &23

A good error message should specify the location of the error in the source program. In this example, the error is the ampersand. A good error message should specify the location of the error: line 7, column 5.

To do this, the parser needs the source program location of the offending token. Thus, the tokenizer should not only provide the token itself to the parser, but also the token's location in the source program.

The actions the parser takes usually depend on the category of the token rather than the specific token itself. For example, suppose the parser has to call a particular function if the current token is a variable name. Thus, to determine if it should perform this action, the parser needs to know *only* the category of the token. The tokenizer can easily provide the category of a token to the parser along with the token itself and its source program location in one convenient bundle. With this information, the parser never has to examine the token itself to determine its category.

Based on our preceding discussion, the tokenizer should provide the parser with the following four items of information on each token:

1. the line number of the token in the source program
2. the column number in which the token starts in the source program
3. its category
4. the token itself (i.e., the string of characters that makes up the token). We call this string the *lexeme* of the token.

Our tokenizer uses an object created from the `Token` class to hold these four items of information for each token. The `Token` class is defined as follows (the line numbers are from Fig. 6.3):

```
4  class Token:
5      def __init__(self, line, column, category, lexeme):
6          self.line = line            # line number of the token
7          self.column = column        # column in which token starts
8          self.category = category    # category of the token
9          self.lexeme = lexeme        # token in string form
```

A `Token` object has four variables: `line`, `column`, `category`, and `lexeme`. To access a variable in a `Token` object, the name of the variable should be prefixed with the reference that points to the object's variables. For example, if `self` points to the variables of a `Token` object, then `self.category` references the `category` variable in that object.

`__init__()` in the `Token` class is the *initializer method*. It initializes the object when it is created. For example, the following statement creates and initializes a `Token` object, and assigns to `token` a pointer to the newly created object:

```
89         token = Token(line, column, None, '')
```

Specifically, this statement creates an object from the `Token` class, and then calls the initializer method, passing it five arguments: the pointer to (i.e., the address of) the object's variables, `line`, `column`, `None`, and `''`. These five arguments are received by the parameters `self`, `line`, `column`, `category`, and `lexeme`, respectively, on line 5. The initializer method uses these parameters to initialize the variables of the object. Because within the initializer method the parameter `self` points to the object's variables, to reference any one of the object's variables, we prefix the name of the variable with "`self.`". For example, the initializer method executes the following statement to assign the parameter `category` to the object variable `category`:

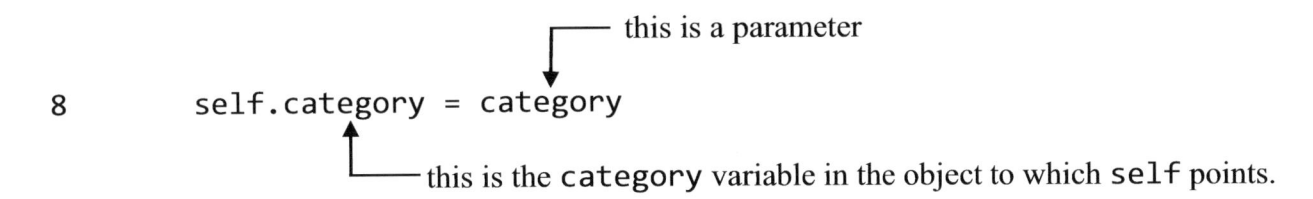

```
 8        self.category = category
```
— this is a parameter (pointing to `category` on the right)

— this is the `category` variable in the object to which `self` points.

The assignment statement on line 89 assigns the pointer to the object's variables to the variable `token`. Thus, outside the initializer method, we reference any one of the object's variables by prefixing its name with "`token.`". But inside the initializer, we use the prefix "`self.`". For example, the following statement, which is outside the initializer method, assigns UNSIGNEDINT to the `category` variable of the object:

```
92        token.category = UNSIGNEDINT   # set category of token
```

After creating the Token object for a token, our tokenizer then appends the Token object to a list named `tokenlist`. Thus, when the tokenizer finishes processing the source program, the entire stream of tokens for the source program is available to the parser in `tokenlist` (see Fig. 6.1).

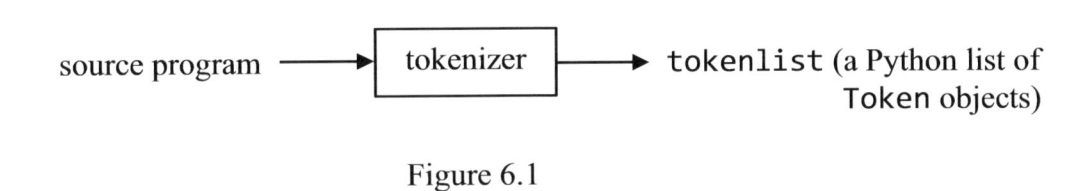

source program → tokenizer → `tokenlist` (a Python list of Token objects)

Figure 6.1

To represent the various token categories, our tokenizer uses arbitrary non-negative integers. For example, the integer representing the plus sign is 7. To improve the readability of our code, we give each category number a name, and use category names rather than numbers in our Python code. The following statements give a name to each category number:

```
21 # constants that represent token categories
22 EOF            = 0      # end of file
23 PRINT          = 1      # 'print' keyword
24 UNSIGNEDINT    = 2      # integer
25 NAME           = 3      # identifier that is not a keyword
26 ASSIGNOP       = 4      # '=' assignment operator
27 LEFTPAREN      = 5      # '('
28 RIGHTPAREN     = 6      # ')'
29 PLUS           = 7      # '+'
30 MINUS          = 8      # '-'
31 TIMES          = 9      # '*'
32 NEWLINE        = 10     # newline character
33 ERROR          = 11     # if not any of the above, then error
```

Some of the token categories correspond to multiple tokens. For example, the NAME category is the category for any name that is not a keyword. Other categories represent just a single token. For example, the PLUS category corresponds to the "+" token only.

Fig. 6.2 shows a simple Python program and the tokens our tokenizer produces from it.

Source code	Line	Column	Category	Lexeme
a = (-59 + 20*3)	1	1	NAME	a
	1	3	ASSIGNOP	=
	1	5	LEFTPAREN	(
	1	6	MINUS	-
	1	7	UNSIGNEDINT	59
	1	10	PLUS	+
	1	12	UNSIGNEDINT	20
	1	14	TIMES	*
	1	15	UNSIGNEDINT	3
	1	16	RIGHTPAREN	)
	1	17	NEWLINE	
print(a)	2	1	PRINT	print
	2	6	LEFTPAREN	(
	2	7	NAME	a
	2	8	RIGHTPAREN	)
	2	9	NEWLINE	
	3	1	EOF	

Figure 6.2

Try running the tokenizer yourself (see Fig. 6.3). It is in the file `t1.py` which is in the software package for this book. The source code shown in Fig. 6.2 is in the file `test.in`. To run the tokenizer against `test.in`, enter

```
python t1.py test.in
```

When `t1.py` is invoked, it displays on the screen the tokens it produces. If you want a text file that contains what `t1.py` displays, simply redirect the output produced by `t1.py` to a file. To do this, enter

```
python t1.py test.in > test.out
```
output redirected to test.out

This command redirects the output produced by `t1.py` to the file `test.out`. You can then examine the list of tokens in `test.out` with any text editor.

Structure of the t1.py Tokenizer

The `main()` function of the `t1.py` tokenizer opens and reads in the entire input file into the variable `source`:

```
53      infile = open(sys.argv[1], 'r')
54      source = infile.read()                      # read source program
```

Some text editors (for example, notepad) do *not* terminate the last line in a file with the newline character ('\n') unless you hit the Enter key. If you create the source program with such a text editor, and you do not hit the Enter key at the end of the last line, then the Python statement on that line will not be properly terminated with a newline character. To accommodate text editors that do this, main() checks for a newline character at the end of the source program. If one is missing, it adds one:

```
63          if source[-1] != '\n':
64              source = source + '\n'
```

It then calls tokenizer():

```
70          tokenizer()    # tokenize source code in source
```

Each time the tokenizer wants the next character in the source program, it calls the function getchar(). On each entry, getchar() checks prevchar, which contains the preceding character in source program. If it is the newline character, then the next character must be the start of a new line. In that case, getchar() adjusts the line and column numbers appropriately:

```
136     # check if starting a new line
137     if prevchar == '\n':    # signals start of a new line
138         line += 1           # adjust line number
139         column = 0          # reset column number
140         blankline = True    # initialize blankline
```

It also sets blankline to True. If later it determines that the new line is not blank, then it resets blankline to False (see line 151). getchar() accesses the next character in the source program using the index sourceindex, assigning the next character to the variable c. It then updates sourceindex and the column number:

```
147     c = source[sourceindex] # get next char in the source program
148     sourceindex += 1        # increment sourceindex to next char
149     column += 1             # adjust column number
```

If c is not whitespace, then the line is not a blank line. getchar() sets the variable blankline to False to indicate this:

```
150     if not c.isspace():     # if c not whitespace then line not blank
151         blankline = False   # indicate line not blank
```

Before returning the character in c, getchar() saves it in prevchar:

```
152     prevchar = c            # save current character
```

A blank line should not result in any tokens. But a NEWLINE token would be created if getchar() returned the newline character at the end of a blank line. To prevent this, getchar() returns a space in place of the newline character at the end of a blank line:

```
154         # if at end of blank line, return space in place of '\n'
155         if c == '\n' and blankline:
156             return ' '
157         else:
158             return c                    # return character to tokenizer()
```

When `tokenizer()` starts the processing of a token, it skips any whitespace, except for newline characters, that precedes the token (recall the newline character is a token in Python programs except for the newline character at the end of a blank line):

```
85          # skip whitespace but not newlines
86          while curchar != '\n' and curchar.isspace():
87              curchar = getchar() # get next char from source program
```

It then constructs and initializes a Token object with

```
89          # construct and initialize new token
90          token = Token(line, column, None, '')
```

The arguments `line` and `column` are variables the tokenizer uses to keep track of its current position in the source program. When the statement on line 90 is executed, `line` and `column` are the line and column numbers of the first character of the token the tokenizer is about to process. At this point, the `category` and `lexeme` variables of the token object are yet to be determined. Thus, line 90 initializes those fields with `None` and the null string, respectively.

Next, using an `if` statement, `tokenizer()` determines the type of token about to be processed based on the token's first character (which is in `curchar`). For example, the following segment checks if `curchar` is a digit. If it is, then it is the beginning of an unsigned integer token, in which case `tokenizer()` sets the `category` field of the Token object to UNSIGNEDINT. It then reads in each digit, appending each one to `token.lexeme`:

```
92          if curchar.isdigit():                  # start of unsigned int?
93              token.category = UNSIGNEDINT       # save category of token
94              while True:
95                  token.lexeme += curchar        # append curchar to lexeme
96                  curchar = getchar()            # get next character
97                  if not curchar.isdigit():      # break if not a digit
98                      break
```

If the current character is a letter or the underscore character, then it is the start of either a keyword or a name token. `tokenizer()` reads in each character of the token, appending each to `token.lexeme`:

```
100         elif curchar.isalpha() or curchar == '_':   # start of name?
101             while True:
102                 token.lexeme += curchar     # append curchar to lexeme
103                 curchar = getchar()         # get next character
104                 # break if not letter, '_', or digit
105                 if not (curchar.isalnum() or curchar == '_')
106                     break
```

The dictionary `keywords` contains each keyword in the source language and its corresponding token category (our source language has only one keyword):

```
41  keywords = {'print': PRINT}
```

If the lexeme of the current token is in `keywords`, then its category is obtained from the `keywords` dictionary. Otherwise, the lexeme is the name of a variable, in which case its token category is NAME:

```
108          # determine if lexeme is a keyword or name of variable
109          if token.lexeme in keywords:
110              token.category = keywords[token.lexeme]
111          else:
112              token.category = NAME
```

Note that after the processing an unsigned integer or a name token, `curchar` holds the character immediately *after* the end of the token just processed. For consistency sake, all tokens are processed so that this is true. This is the reason for the call of `getchar()` on line 117.

The `smalltokens` dictionary contains the one-character tokens that are not unsigned integers, keywords, or names. Each entry consists of a token lexeme and its category:

```
44  smalltokens = {'=':ASSIGNOP, '(':LEFTPAREN, ')':RIGHTPAREN,
45                 '+':PLUS, '-':MINUS, '*':TIMES, '\n':NEWLINE, '':EOF}
```

If the current character is in `smalltokens`, then its category is obtained from it:

```
114          elif curchar in smalltokens:
115              token.category = smalltokens[curchar]   # get category
116              token.lexeme = curchar
117              curchar = getchar()         # move to first char after the token
```

After completing the creation of the `token` object, tokenizer appends it to `tokenslist`:

```
124          tokenlist.append(token)         # append token to tokenlist
```

Thus, when `tokenizer()` is finished processing the source program, `tokenlist` will contain a Token object for every token in the input file. On line 125, if `trace` on line 12 is `True`, the tokenizer displays the four fields of the token:

```
125          if trace:                       # display token if trace is True
126              print("%3s %4s  %-14s %s" % (str(token.line),
127                  str(token.column), catnames[token.category], token.lexeme))
```

When we use this tokenizer or an extension of it in the interpreters and compilers we will construct, we will want the tokenizer to display the tokens it creates for debugging and testing purposes. But once our interpreter or compiler is working correctly, we will want to turn off the token display. We do this simply by setting the `trace` variable to `False`.

If an error is detected when the current token is the newline character, the `except` block that catches the exception displays a backslash-n sequence in place of the newline character:

```
73        lexeme = token.lexeme.replace('\n', '\\n')
74        print('\nError on '+ "'" + lexeme + "'" + ' line ' +
75            str(token.line) + ' column ' + str(token.column))
```

It does this because the newline character is invisible, and therefore not suitable for the error message.

Fig. 6.3 has the complete listing of the `t1.py` tokenizer. As we add more features to our source language, you will have to extend the `t1.py` tokenizer to handle them. Thus, it would be wise to thoroughly study Fig. 6.3 so that you can modify and extend it easily.

```
1  # t1.py tokenizer
2  import sys            # sys needed to access cmd line args and exit()
3
4  class Token:
5      def __init__(self, line, column, category, lexeme):
6          self.line = line         # source prog line number of the token
7          self.column = column     # source prog col in which token starts
8          self.category = category # category of the token
9          self.lexeme = lexeme     # token in string form
10
11 # global variables
12 trace = True            # controls token trace
13 source = ''             # receives entire source program
14 sourceindex = 0         # index into source
15 line = 0                # current line number
16 column = 0              # current column number
17 tokenlist = []          # list of tokens created by tokenizer
18 prevchar = '\n'         # '\n' in prevchar signals start of new line
19 blankline = True        # reset to False if line is not blank
20
21 # constants that represent token categories
22 EOF          = 0    # end of file
23 PRINT        = 1    # 'print' keyword
24 UNSIGNEDINT  = 2    # integer
25 NAME         = 3    # identifier that is not a keyword
26 ASSIGNOP     = 4    # '=' assignment operator
27 LEFTPAREN    = 5    # '('
28 RIGHTPAREN   = 6    # ')'
29 PLUS         = 7    # '+'
30 MINUS        = 8    # '-'
31 TIMES        = 9    # '*'
32 NEWLINE      = 10   # newline character
33 ERROR        = 11   # if not any of the above, then error
34
35 # displayable names for each token category
36 catnames = ['EOF', 'PRINT', 'UNSIGNEDINT', 'NAME', 'ASSIGNOP',
37             'LEFTPAREN', 'RIGHTPAREN', 'PLUS', 'MINUS',
38             'TIMES', 'NEWLINE','ERROR']
```

```python
39
40 # keywords and their token categories}
41 keywords = {'print': PRINT}
42
43 # one-character tokens and their token categories
44 smalltokens = {'=':ASSIGNOP, '(':LEFTPAREN, ')':RIGHTPAREN,
45             '+':PLUS, '-':MINUS, '*':TIMES, '\n':NEWLINE, '':EOF}
46
47 # main() reads input file and calls tokenizer()
48 def main():
49     global source
50
51     if len(sys.argv) == 2:    # check if correct number of cmd line args
52         try:
53             infile = open(sys.argv[1], 'r')
54             source = infile.read()  # read source program
55         except IOError:
56             print('Cannot read input file ' + sys.argv[1])
57             sys.exit(1)
58     else:
59         print('Wrong number of command line arguments')
60         print('format: python t1.py <infile>')
61         sys.exit(1)
62
63     if source[-1] != '\n':          # add newline to end if missing
64         source = source + '\n'
65
66     if trace:                       # for token trace
67         print('Line  Col Category       Lexeme\n')
68
69     try:
70         tokenizer()                 # tokenize source code in source
71     except RuntimeError as emsg:
72         # output slash n in place of newline
73         lexeme = token.lexeme.replace('\n', '\\n')
74         print('\nError on '+ "'" + lexeme + "'" + ' line ' +
75             str(token.line) + ' column ' + str(token.column))
76         print(emsg) # message from RuntimeError object
77         sys.exit(1)         # 1 return code indicates an error has occurred
78
79 # tokenizer tokenizes tokens in source code and appends them to tokens
80 def tokenizer():
81     global token
82     curchar = ' '                       # prime curchar with space
83
84     while True:
85         # skip whitespace but not newlines
86         while curchar != '\n' and curchar.isspace():
87             curchar = getchar()         # get next char from source program
```

```
 88
 89         # construct and initialize a new token
 90         token = Token(line, column, None, '')
 91
 92         if curchar.isdigit():               # start of unsigned int?
 93             token.category = UNSIGNEDINT    # save category of token
 94             while True:
 95                 token.lexeme += curchar     # append curchar to lexeme
 96                 curchar = getchar()         # get next character
 97                 if not curchar.isdigit():   # break if not a digit
 98                     break
 99
100         elif curchar.isalpha() or curchar == '_':   # start of name?
101             while True:
102                 token.lexeme += curchar     # append curchar to lexeme
103                 curchar = getchar()         # get next character
104                 # break if not letter, '_', or digit
105                 if not (curchar.isalnum() or curchar == '_'):
106                     break
107
108             # determine if lexeme is a keyword or name of variable
109             if token.lexeme in keywords:
110                 token.category = keywords[token.lexeme]
111             else:
112                 token.category = NAME
113
114         elif curchar in smalltokens:
115             token.category = smalltokens[curchar]   # get category
116             token.lexeme = curchar
117             curchar = getchar()             # move to first char after token
118
119         else:
120             token.category = ERROR          # invalid token
121             token.lexeme = curchar          # save lexeme
122             raise RuntimeError('Invalid token')
123
124         tokenlist.append(token)             # append token to tokens list
125         if trace:                           # display token if trace is True
126             print("%3s %4s  %-14s %s" % (str(token.line),
127                 str(token.column), catnames[token.category], token.lexeme))
128
129         if token.category == EOF:           # finished tokenizing?
130             break
131
132 # getchar() gets next char from source and adjusts line and column
133 def getchar():
134     global sourceindex, column, line, prevchar, blankline
135
136     # check if starting a new line
```

```
137     if prevchar == '\n':              # '\n' signals start of a new line
138         line += 1                     # increment line number
139         column = 0                    # reset column number
140         blankline = True              # initialize blankline
141
142     if sourceindex >= len(source):    # at end of source code?
143         column = 1                    # set EOF column to 1
144         prevchar = ''                 # save current char for next call
145         return ''                     # null str signals end of source
146
147     c = source[sourceindex]           # get next char in the source program
148     sourceindex += 1                  # increment sourceindex to next character
149     column += 1                       # increment column number
150     if not c.isspace():               # if c not whitespace then line not blank
151         blankline = False             # indicate line not blank
152     prevchar = c                      # save current char for next call
153
154     # if at end of blank line, return space in place of '\n'
155     if c == '\n' and blankline:
156         return ' '
157     else:
158         return c                      # return character to tokenizer()
159
160 main()                                # call main function
```

Figure 6.3

Our tokenizer breaks up the source code it reads into tokens. Thus, "tokenizer" is certainly a good name for it. However, you will find that tokenizers discussed elsewhere are often given different names. Other names that are commonly used are "token manager", "lexical analyzer", "lexer", and "scanner."

Problems

1. Tokenizing the source code can be done before or in parallel with parsing. From a user's perspective, how does the approach used affect the operation of a pure interpreter? What about a hybrid interpreter?

2. What happens if `getchar()` returns the null string, but then is called again?

3. `prevchar` is used only in `getchar()`, but it is global. Why?

4. Why is `curchar` initialized to a space (line 82 in Fig. 6.3) and `prevchar` to `'\n'` (line 18)?

5. If lines 133-137 are switched with lines 139-142 in Fig. 6.3, what is the effect?

6. Rewrite the tokenizer in the C programming language. Test your program with `t1.in`.

7. Copy `t1.py` to `p0607.py`. Then modify `p0607.py` so that is displays the number of occurrences of each token category. Test `p0607.py` with `t1.in`.

8. If all blank characters are removed from `t1.in`, will `t1.py` produce the same list of tokens? Can all blanks, with the exception of indentation and dedentation blanks, be removed from a Python program without affecting the operation of the program?

9. Copy `t1.py` to `p0609.py`. Then modify `p0609.py` so that it supports single or multi-line /*...*/ comments. Test p0609.py with `p0609.in`.

10. Copy `t1.py` to `p0610.py`. Then modify `p0610.py` so that the token tracing display, normally off, can be turned on with the command line argument `-traceon`. For example, either of the following commands turns on the token tracing display:

    ```
    python p0610.py t1.in -traceon
    python p0610.py -traceon t1.in
    ```

11. Copy `t1.py` to `p0611.py`. Then modify `p0611.py` so that each time the `tokenizer()` function is called, it returns only the next token. Modify `main()` so that it repeatedly calls `tokenizer()` and displays the returned token until it reaches the end of the input file. Test `p0611.py` with `t1.in`.

12. In place of the Python `pass` statement in the source program to be tokenized, can a blank line be used, in which case would the tokenizer have to be modified to handle blank lines differently.

7 Constructing a Parser for a Python Subset

Introduction

In chapters 3, 4, and 5, we learned some computer science theory. Specifically, we learned about context-free grammars and how to base the design of a parser on a suitable context-free grammar. In this chapter, we put the theory to good use: We use the theory to design a parser for a subset of the Python language. Our parser uses the tokenizer in the file `t1.py` that we discussed in the chapter 6.

Grammar for Our Python Subset

Let's construct a parser that can handle the simple Python program in Fig. 7.1 (also in the file `t1.in`). Our parser has to handle only a very small subset of the Python language: the assignment statement, the `print` statement, and arithmetic expressions with + (addition), * (multiplication), unary + and -, variable names, and integer numbers.

```
1 print(-59 + 20*3)
2 a = 2
3 bb_1 = -(a) + 12
4 print(a*bb_1 + a*3*(-1 + -1 + -1))
```

Figure 7.1

To construct our parser, we first need to write a grammar that defines the source language. Writing this grammar, for the most part, is straightforward. Let's start by developing productions for arithmetic expressions. Consider the following `print` statement:

`print(-59 + 20*3)`

Its argument is an arithmetic expression. An arithmetic expression is a list of one or more terms, with successive terms separated by +. The expression in the `print` statement above has two terms: -59 and 20*3. A term, in turn, is a list of one or more factors, with successive factors separated by *. Our expression has two terms. The first term, -59, has a single factor so it has no *. The second term, 20*3, has two factors 20 and 3. A factor is any one of the following possibilities:

- + followed by a factor
- - followed by a factor
- unsigned integer
- variable name
- '(' expression ')'

Now that we understand what an expression is, it is not too hard to write the productions for it (see Fig.

7.2). Note that the unquoted asterisks are star (zero or more) operators.

```
<expr>    → <term> ('+' <term>)*
<term>    → <factor> ('*' <factor>)*
<factor>  → '+' <factor>
<factor>  → '-' <factor>
<factor>  → UNSIGNEDINT
<factor>  → NAME
<factor>  → '(' <expr> ')'
```

Figure 7.2

Our tokenizer provides the parser with the list of tokens that make up the source program. In Fig. 7.2, UNSIGNEDINT represents any unsigned integer token, and NAME represents any name token. The quoted characters are tokens that represent themselves.

To make is easier to read our grammar, we separate the component parts of the right sides of productions with spaces wherever they make the grammar more readable. For example, the last `<factor>` production in Fig. 7.2 has three parts on its right side: `'('`, `<expr>`, and `')'`. The spaces between these parts do not mean that we have to have the same spacing in the language the grammar defines. There can be any number (zero or more) of spaces between the parentheses and the expression they enclose in the source program.

Now that we have written the productions for an expression (the hard part of the grammar), the rest is easy. Fig. 7.3 has the complete grammar for our subset language:

```
<program>         → <stmt>* EOF
<stmt>            → <simplestmt> NEWLINE
<simplestmt>      → <assignmentstmt>
<simplestmt>      → <printstmt>
<assignmentstmt>  → NAME '=' <expr>
<printstmt>       → 'print' '(' <expr> ')'
<expr>            → <term> ('+' <term>)*
<term>            → <factor> ('*' <factor>)*
<factor>          → '+' <factor>
<factor>          → '-' <factor>
<factor>          → UNSIGNEDINT
<factor>          → NAME
<factor>          → '(' <expr> ')'
```

Figure 7.3

A program consists of zero or more statements followed by the end-of-file marker This syntax is nicely captured by the starred expression in the `<program>` production in Fig. 7.3. EOF is the end-of-file marker. Our source language has only *simple statements*—as opposed to *compound statements* like `if` and `while` that we will introduce later on. Thus, for now `<stmt>` generates only `<simplestmt>`. We have two productions for `<simplestmt>` corresponding to the assignment and `print` statements.

Now that we have our grammar, we can implement our parser using the grammar as the basis of the parser's structure. Unlike the simple parsers in chapters 4 and 5, this parser will use the tokenizer from chapter 6. If you do not remember the details of this tokenizer, it would be a good idea to review chapter 6 before reading on.

The tokenizer from chapter 6 provides the tokens in a list named `tokenlist`. In our parser, we need an `advance()` function that advances in this list of tokens. We use the variable `tokenindex` to hold the index into `tokenlist` of the current token. When `advance()` is called, it increments `tokenindex` and then uses it to access the next token in `tokenlist` list. It assigns this token to a global variable named `token` so that the parser functions can access it. Here is the code for the `advance()` function:

```
1 def advance():
2     global token, tokenindex
3     tokenindex += 1                          # move to next token
4     if tokenindex >= len(tokenlist):
5         raise RuntimeError('Unexpected end of file')
6     token = tokenlist[tokenindex]    # token is the current token
```

> It is important to remember that any time during a parse, the variable `token` contains the current token, and `tokenindex` is the index of that token in `tokenlist`, the list of tokens created by the tokenzier. Also remember that `token` is an object that has the variables `line`, `column`, `category`, and `lexeme`.

Since `token` always holds the current token,

- `token.line` is the line number of the line in the source program in which the current token appears.
- `token.column` is the column number of the column in the source program in which the current token starts.
- `token.category` is the category of the current token.
- `token.lexeme` is the lexeme of the current token.

`consume()` in our parser is passed the category—not the lexeme—of the expected token. It compares it with `token.category` (i.e., the category of the current token) and either advances (if they match) or raises a `RuntimeError` exception (if they do not match). Here is the code for `consume()`:

```
1 def consume(expectedcat):
2     if token.category == expectedcat:
3         advance()                            # call advance() on a match
4     else:
5         raise RuntimeError('Expecting ' + catnames[expectedcat])
```

To make its decisions, the parser examines the categories of the tokens—not their lexemes. For example, at the start of a statement, the parser checks the current token. If its category is **NAME**, then the statement must be an assignment statement. So the parser does not need to examine lexeme of the current token to determine the type of the statement.

Let's look at some of the functions in the parser. They are all easy to implement—their structure matches the structure of the corresponding productions. Here the `program()` function. The `<program>` production contains a starred expression. Thus, `program()` is implemented with a `while` loop:

```
1  # <program> → <stmt>* EOF
2  def program():
3      while token.category in [NAME, PRINT]:
4          stmt()
5      if token.category != EOF:
6          raise RuntimeError('Expecting end of file')
```

A program consists of zero or more statements followed by the end-of-file marker. A statement can start with either a `NAME` token or a `PRINT` token. Thus, the `while` statement on line 3 tests if the category of the current token (in `token.category`) is `NAME` or `PRINT`. The `<program>` production shows that an `EOF` (i.e., end-of-file marker) follows the starred expression. Accordingly, line 6 in the `program()` function checks if the category of the current token is `EOF`. If it is not, it raises a `RuntimeError` exception.

`stmt()` calls `simplestmt()`. Because a newline character should follow every simple statement, `stmt()` checks for this newline character by calling `consume(NEWLINE)`:

```
1  def stmt():
2      simplestmt()
3      consume(NEWLINE)
```

`simplestmt()` calls the appropriate statement function, based on the category of the current token:

```
1  def simplestmt():
2      if token.category == NAME:
3          assignmentstmt()
4      elif token.category == PRINT:
5          printstmt()
6      else:
7          raise RuntimeError('Expecting statement')
```

The structure of `printstmt()` matches the structure of the `<printstmt>` production. The production is essentially pseudocode for the `printstmt()` function. For each terminal component of the production, `printstmt()` calls `consume()` or `advance()`. For `<expr>`, its one nonterminal component, `printstmt()` calls `expr()`:

```
1  def printstmt():
2      advance()            # advance past PRINT token
3      consume(LEFTPAREN)
4      expr()
5      consume(RIGHTPAREN)
```

`printstmt()` is called by `simplestmt()` only if the category of the current token is `PRINT`. Thus, when `printstmt()` is called, it does not need to test if the category of the current token is `PRINT`. It simply advances past it (see line 2 above). `consume()`, however, is needed to test the presence of the parentheses (see lines 3 and 5).

`assignmentstmt()`, like `printstmt()`, has a structure that closely matches the structure of its corresponding production. It consists of a call of advance(), consume(ASSIGNOP), and expr().

expr() uses a loop, reflecting the star operator in its production:

```
1  def expr():
2      term()
3      while token.category == PLUS:
4          advance()     # no need for consume() here
5          term()
```

term() has a similar structure.

Because there are several <factor> productions, factor() uses a nested if to determine which production to apply:

```
1  def factor():
2      if token.category == PLUS:
3          advance()
4          factor()
5      elif token.category == MINUS:
6          advance()
7          factor()
8      elif token.category == UNSIGNEDINT:
9          advance()
10     elif token.category == NAME:
11         advance()
12     elif token.category == LEFTPAREN:
13         advance()
14         expr()
15         consume(RIGHTPAREN)
16     else:
17         raise RuntimeError('Expecting factor')
```

For our parser, we need a modified main() function: It should call both the tokenizer and the parser within the try block (lines 30 and 31 in Fig. 7.4). In our parser, main() calls tokenizer(), then parser(). parser(), in turn, calls program() to start the parsing process.

```
1  def main():
2      global source
3
4      if len(sys.argv) == 2:    # check if correct number of cmd line args
5          try:
6              infile = open(sys.argv[1], 'r')
7              source = infile.read()   # read source program
8          except IOError:
9              print('Cannot read input file ' + sys.argv[1])
10             sys.exit(1)
11
12     else:
13         print('Wrong number of command line arguments')
```

```
14        print('Format: python p1.py <infile>')
15        sys.exit(1)
16
17    if source[-1] != '\n':   # add newline to end if missing
18        source = source + '\n'
19
20    if trace:
21        print('-------------------------------------------- Token trace')
22        print('Line  Col Category     Lexeme\n')
23
24    try:
25        tokenizer()    # tokenize source code in source
26        parser()
27
28    # on an error, display an error message
29    # token is the token object on which the error was detected
30    except RuntimeError as emsg:
31        # output slash n in place of newline
32        lexeme = token.lexeme.replace('\n', '\\n')
33        print('\nError on '+ "'" + lexeme + "'" + ' line ' +
34            str(token.line) + ' column ' + str(token.column))
35        print(emsg)      # message from RuntimeError object
36        sys.exit(1)
```

Figure 7.4

Problems

1. The file p1shell.py contains the tokenizer from chapter 6 and the shell of the parser described in this chapter. Copy p1shell.py to p1.py. Then fill in the missing parts of p1.py. Test your completed parser by entering

   python p1.py p1.in

   The file p1.in contains the Python program in Fig. 7.1. On a successful parse, your parser should simply terminate without generating any messages. Also run your p1.py parser on the following input files (each has an error) to check how your parser responds to errors in the source program: p0701a.in, p0701b.in, and p0701c.in.

2. Global variables can easily lead to hard-to-locate bugs. It also makes it difficult to test functions separately if they can access global variables. However, the use of global variables can reduce the complexity of your code and improve run-time efficiency. Copy your p1.py parser from problem 1 to p0702.py. Modify p0702.py so that it has as few global variables as possible. Which version do you like better?

3. Copy your p1.py parser from problem 1 to p0703.py. Modify p0703.py so that it supports the Python pass statement. Test your parser with the source code in p0703.in.

4. Copy your `p1.py` parser from problem 1 to `p0704.py`. Modify `p0704.py` so that it supports subtraction and division. Test your parser with the source code in `p0704.in`. *Hint*: Handle subtraction like addition, and handle division like multiplication.

5. Copy your `p1.py` parser from problem 1 to `p0705.py`. Modify `p0705.py` so that on a successful parse it displays the number of statements in the source program. Test your parser with the source code in `p1.in`.

6. Is the `raise` statement at the end of the `simplestmt()` function necessary?

7. Modify the grammar in Fig. 7.3 so that it generates expressions in postfix form. Copy your `p1.py` parser from problem 1 to `p0707.py`. Modify `p0707.py` so that it handles the same statements as in `p1.in` but with the expressions in postfix form. Test your parser with the source code in `p0707a.in` (which has no errors) and `p0707b.in` (which has an error).

8. Does your `p1.py` parser from problem 1 correctly parse the following legal statement:

   ```
   a = ++--++-----+--3    # a lot of unary plusses and minuses
   ```

9. If the current character is % and `expr()` is called, where in the `p1.py` parser is the error detected?

10. What is in `emsg` when line 41 in Fig. 7.4 is executed?

8 Constructing a Pure Interpreter

Introduction

In this chapter, we will learn how to extend the `p1.py` parser from problem 1 in chapter 7 so that it not only parses the source program but also interprets it. You will be surprised how few modifications are needed to turn your parser into a pure interpreter. Recall that a pure interpreter executes the source program directly—it does not first translate it to another form.

Structures Needed for a Pure Interpreter

One of the structures our interpreter needs is the *symbol table*. It is a table that holds the name of each variable and its corresponding value. A symbol table is easy to implement in Python. We simply use a Python dictionary. Our interpreter creates and initializes the symbol table dictionary with

```
symtab = {}
```

To update or add an entry to `symtab`, we use an assignment statement. For example, suppose `'x'` is not already in `symtab`. Then the statement

```
symtab['x'] = 1
```

creates an entry for `'x'` and associates with it the value 1. If we then execute

```
symtab['x'] = 7
```

The value associated with `'x'` is changed from 1 to 7. To access the value associated with `'x'`, we use `'x'` as the key into `symtab`. For example, the statement

```
print(symtab['x'])
```

displays the current value in `symtab` associated with `'x'`. To check if a symbol is in `symtab`, use the `in` operator in an `if` statement. For example, to determine if `'x'` is in `symtab`, use

```
if 'x' in symtab:
    ...
```

Another structure we need in our interpreter is the stack. A *stack* is a list structure with two sides: the bottom side and the top side. Adding or removing values from a stack always occurs on the top side of the stack. We call the operation that adds a value to the top of a stack a *push operation*. We call the operation that removes the value at the top of a stack a *pop operation*. A pop operation always removes the most recent value pushed. For this reason, a stack is commonly described as a *last-in-first-out* (LIFO) data structure. A stack is easily implemented in Python with a list. Our interpreter uses a stack named `operandstack`. It creates and initializes it with

```
operandstack = []
```

To push a value onto the stack, we use the `append()` method. For example, suppose `token.lexeme` is currently equal to `'x'`. The following statement pushes `symtab[token.lexeme]`, which is the value of x, onto the stack:

```
operandstack.append(symtab[token.lexeme])
```

To pop the top of the stack, we use the `pop()` method. For example, suppose `token.lexeme` is currently equal to `'x'`. Then the following statement pops the stack and assigns the popped value to x:

```
symtab[token.lexeme] = operandstack.pop()
```

Modifications to Our Parsing Functions

To extend our `p1.py` parser from problem 1 in chapter 7 so it interprets, we have to modify each parsing function. Each parsing function has to be modified so that it executes the source code it parses. Let's start with the code for the `assignmentstmt()` function:

```
1 def assignmentstmt():
2     left = token.lexeme   # save lexeme of the current token
3     advance()
4     consume(ASSIGNOP)
5     expr()
6     symtab[left] = operandstack.pop()
```

The `simplestmt()` function calls `assignmentstmt()` only if the current token is a name. Thus, on entry into `assignmentstmt()`, the current token is the name on the left side of the source code assignment statement. Line 2 in the `assignmentstmt()` function,

```
2     left = token.lexeme
```

saves the lexeme of the left side of the source code assignment statement in the local variable `left`. For example, if the source code assignment statement is

```
x = y
```

then `left` is assigned `'x'`. `assignmentstmt()` then advances past the variable name and the `'='` tokens, and calls `expr()`. The effect of `expr()` is to parse the expression on the right side of the source code assignment statement. But it also (because of the modifications we will make) has the effect of leaving the value of the expression on top of the stack. Thus, the next statement in `assignmentstmt()`,

```
6     symtab[left] = operandstack.pop()
```

pops the value of the right side of the source code assignment statement and assigns it to the variable on the left side. With these modifications, `assignmentstmt()` both parses and executes.

The `printstmt()` in the parser requires only one simple modification so that it both parses and executes. In `printstmt()` there is a call of `expr()`. With the modifications to `expr()` we will make, this call of `expr()` pushes the value of the expression onto `operandstack`. Thus, to execute as well as parse, `printstmt()` simply pops `operandstack` and displays the value popped:

```
1  def printstmt():
2      advance()
3      consume(LEFTPAREN)
4      expr()
5      print(operandstack.pop())
6      consume(RIGHTPAREN)
```

To modify `expr()` so that it leaves the value of the expression on the top of the stack is easy. Simply pop two values from the stack each time the right-side term of an addition has been parsed, add the two values, and push the sum onto the stack. Here is the code:

```
1  def expr():
2      term()                    # pushes value of term onto top of stack
3      while token.category == PLUS:
4          advance()
5          term()                # pushes value of term onto top of stack
6          rightoperand = operandstack.pop()
7          leftoperand = operandstack.pop()
8          operandstack.append(leftoperand + rightoperand)
```

Where do the two values that `expr()` pops off the stack on lines 6 and 7 come from? They come from the calls of `term()` on lines 2 and 5. `term()` is modified so it not only parses a term but also leaves the value of the term on top of the stack. Thus, the addition at the bottom of the `while` loop on line 8 adds the values of the two terms and pushes the sum onto the stack. This sum, in turn, becomes the left operand in the next iteration of the `while` loop if the expression has more terms.

The modifications to `term()` that are required are very similar to the modifications we made above to the `expr()` function, with one very important exception: `term()` initializes the global variable `sign` to 1 before each call of `factor()`:

```
1   def term():
2       global sign
3       sign = 1           # initialize sign before calling factor()
4       factor()           # leaves value of term on top of stack
5       while token.category == TIMES:
6           advance()
7           sign = 1       # initialize sign before calling factor()
8           factor()       # leaves value of term on top of stack
9           rightoperand = operandstack.pop()
10          leftoperand = operandstack.pop()
11          operandstack.append(leftoperand * rightoperand)
```

`factor()` uses `sign` to keep track of whether there are an even or odd number of unary minuses. When `factor()` parses a factor that starts with one or more unary minuses, `factor()` flips the sign of `sign` for each unary minus it parses by executing

```
        sign = -sign
```

Because `term()` initializes `sign` to 1 before it calls `factor()`, an even number of unary minuses leaves 1 in `sign`; an odd number of unary minuses leaves -1 in `sign`. Each pair of unary minuses cancel each other out. Thus, if the number of unary minuses is even (in which case the final value of `sign` is 1), they all cancel each other out. If the number is odd (in which case the final value of `sign` is -1), one unary minus remains in effect. For example, for the factor ---7, `factor()` changes `sign` three times resulting in a final value of -1. This value in `sign` indicates one unary minus remains in effect.

`factor()`, like `expr()` and `term()`, is modified so that it leaves the value of what it parses on top of the stack. Here is its code for `factor()`:

```
1  def factor():
2      global sign
3      if token.category == PLUS:
4          advance()
5          factor()
6      elif token.category == MINUS:
7          sign = -sign                    # flip sign for each unary minus
8          advance()
9          factor()
10     elif token.category == UNSIGNEDINT:
11         operandstack.append(sign*int(token.lexeme))
12         advance()
13     elif token.category == NAME:
14         if token.lexeme in symtab:
15             operandstack.append(sign*symtab[token.lexeme])
16         else:
17             raise RuntimeError('Name ' + token.lexeme + ' is not defined')
18         advance()
19     elif token.category == LEFTPAREN:
20         advance()
21         # save sign because expr() calls term() which resets sign to 1
22         savesign = sign         # sign is global but savesign is local
23         expr()                  # value of expr is pushed onto operandstack
24         if savesign == -1:      # use the saved value of sign
25             operandstack[-1] = -operandstack[-1] # change sign of expr
26         consume(RIGHTPAREN)
27     else:
28         raise RuntimeError('Expecting factor')
```

If the value of `sign` on line 11 is 1 (indicating the number of minus signs preceding a number is even) then the minus signs cancel each other out. Thus, the value of the factor is non-negative. But if the value of `sign` is -1 (indicating the number of minus signs is odd), the minus signs have the effect of a single minus sign. Thus, the value of the factor is negative. By multiplying the unsigned integer value of the number token by `sign` on line 11, we give the value appended to the `operandstack` the correct sign: non-negative for an even number of unary minuses, and negative for an odd number of unary minuses. We similarly use `sign` on line 15 to adjust the value of a variable, and `savesign` on line 24 to determine if the value of a parenthesized expression that is on top of `operandstack` needs to be negated. Note that `sign` *must* be declared global within `factor()`, but `savesign` is local. If `sign` is not declared global, then it is treated as a local variable because it is assigned a value (on line 7 in the code above).

Problems

1. Copy the `i1shell.py` to `i1.py`. Then extend `i1.py` so that it interprets as it parses, as described in this chapter. Test your interpreter by entering

    ```
    python i1.py i1.in
    ```

    The file `i1.in` contains the Python program in Fig. 7.1.

    The global variable `grade` in `i1shell.py` (and in `h1shell.py` and `p2shell.py`) is initialized to `False`. If it is set to `True`, then `i1.py` constructed from `i1shell.py` outputs to the display everything an instructor would likely want to see to evaluate your work (a heading with a time stamp, your name, the input and out file names, the output produced by `i1.in`, and the source code in `i1.py`). This output can be redirected to a file, which can then be submitted to an instructor for grading (see `projects.txt` for specific instructions). Unless you have to submit your projects to an instructor, keep `grade` set to `False`. In addition, keep `trace` (which controls the token trace) set to `False` unless for some reason you must see a token trace.

2. Modify your `i1.py` interpreter from problem 1 so that on a `RuntimeError` exception, it displays the line of the source program on which the error was detected (in addition to the error message), with a caret pointing to the token on which the error was detected. For example,

    ```
    Error on line 1 column 5
    a = b
        ^
    Name b is not defined
    ```

    Hint: Use the statement

    ```
    lines = source.splitlines()
    ```

    after reading the source code into `source`. Use the repetition operator to create a string of blanks you can use to position the caret on the offending token. Test your modified `i1.py` interpreter on the following files: `p0802a.in`, `p0802b.in`, and `p0802c.in`.

3. Create a source code file for each `RuntimeError` exception that can be raised by your interpreter that will raise that exception. Run your `i1.py` interprter on each source code file. Does all your error handling code work the way it should?

4. Would it be inherently easier or more difficult to write the pure interpreter in C compared to Python? Why? Would your answer depend on the source language?

5. Pure interpreters are particularly inefficient when processing loops. Why?

6. Why must the `savesign` variable in `factor()` be local?

7. Are the commands processed by the command line program interpreted or compiled?

8. Does your `i1.py` interpreter from problem 1 respond to an input file that contains only a single blank line in the same way the Python 3 interpreter responds?

9. A pure interpreter that supports a `while` loop must be able to jump forward right after the exit test (if the tested expression is false) and backward at the bottom of the loop (back to the exit test). How would a pure interpreter implement forward and backward jumps? Which is more difficult to implement—forward or backward jumps (justify your answer).

10. Implement the `i1` interpreter in C or Java.

11. Line 6 in the `expr()` function treats the first operand popped as the right operand. Why?

12. How would your interpreter behave differently if lines 16 and 17 in the `factor()` function were deleted?

13. Give a source program that would not execute correctly if line 24 in the `factor()` function tested `sign` rather than `savesign`.

14. Replace lines 3 to 9 in the `factor()` function with equivalent instructions that do not use recursion.

15. For source code that contains -123, our tokenizer returns two tokens: one for "-" and one for "123". Would it be possible for the tokenizer to return one token, "-123" with the category `INTEGER`?

⑨ Bytecode

Introduction

As we learned in chapter 1, the Python interpreter is a hybrid interpreter. It does not directly interpret the source program. Instead, it first compiles (i.e., translates) the source program to a form that can easily be interpreted called *bytecode*. It then interprets the bytecode (see Fig. 9.1).

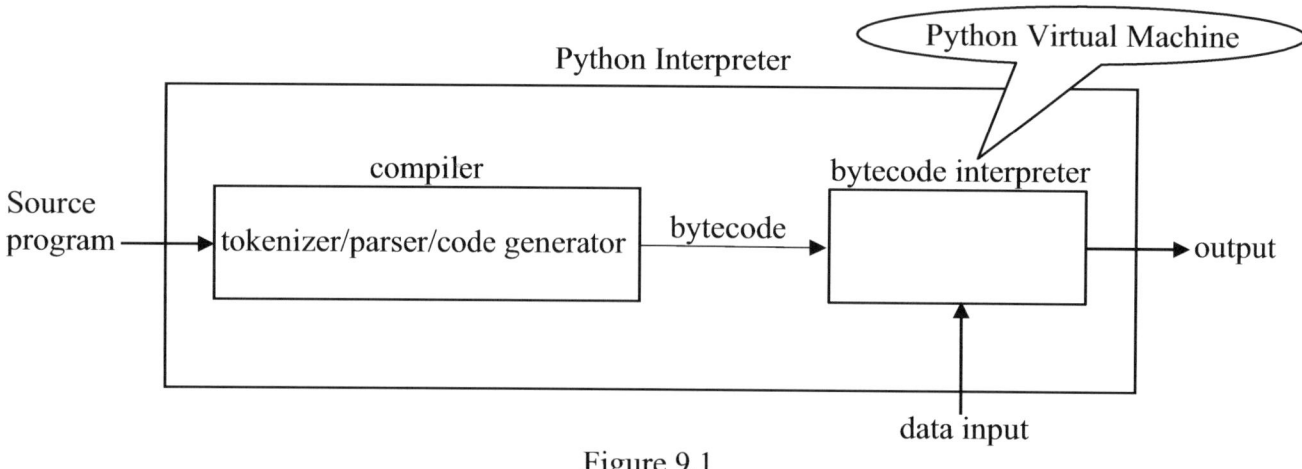

Figure 9.1

Hybrid interpreters, like pure interpreters, have a tokenizer and a parser. However, unlike a pure interpreter, they also have a code generator that produces the translated version of the source program.

Python's bytecode is designed so that it can be interpreted quickly—more quickly than the source code from which it is translated. Thus, the overhead associated with the compile step generally is more than compensated for by the increase in the speed of interpretation.

The bytecode interpreter, in a sense, is the "machine" that executes bytecode. But it, of course, is not a real machine (it is software). For this reason, the bytecode interpreter within the Python interpreter is called the *Python Virtual* (i.e., not real) *Machine*.

What is Python Bytecode

Each bytecode instruction consists of one or two numbers. The first number in a bytecode instruction is the *opcode* (i.e., operation code). The opcode specifies the operation to be performed. The second number, if there is one in the instruction, generally is an index into a table of variables or constants. Thus, via this index, the second number specifies a variable or a constant.

The opcode part of a Python bytecode instruction occupies just one byte (a *byte* is 8 bits; a *bit* is a 0 or 1 in a binary number). Because many of the bytecode instructions consist of just the opcode, the entire instruction is only one byte—hence, the name "bytecode instruction." The compiler component of the hybrid interpreter we will construct generates bytecode that is essentially the same as the bytecode generated by the Python 3 interpreter.

Structures Produced by the Parser in a Hybrid Interpreter

The front end of the hybrid interpreter we will construct—the compiler component—has a tokenizer and a parser. It also has a code generator that produces the bytecode instructions. The code generator is not a separate component. Rather, its code is embedded in the code for the parser. Thus, as the parser executes so does the code generator, the effect of which is to produce the bytecode.

The code generator produces three tables during the parsing of the tokenized source code:

1. co_code: the table in which the code generator stores the bytecode it generates.

2. co_names: the table that holds the names of the global variables in the source code.

3. co_consts: the table that holds the values of the constants in the source program.

These tables are implemented as Python lists, and are initialized with

```
co_code = []
co_names = []
co_consts = []
```

Incidentally, "co" in these names is for "code object."

Code Generation for a Small Program

Let's see how these tables are built as the code generator processes the program in Fig. 9.2.

sample2.py

```
x = 7
y = x
```

Figure 9.2

Initially the three tables are empty. When the parser parses x in the first statement, the code generator (i.e., the code generator embedded in the parser) adds 'x' to the co_names table:

co_names

0 | 'x'

When the parser then parses the 7, the code generator adds the value 7 to the co_consts table:

co_names

| 0 | 'x' |

co_consts

| 0 | 7 |

Because `'x'` is the first name added to `co_names`, its index is 0 in that table. Similarly, the index of the constant 7 in the `co_consts` table is 0. In addition to making entries into the `co_names` and `co_consts` tables, the code generator produces two bytecode instructions for the assignment statement. It stores this bytecode in the `co_code` table. After the first statement in `sample2.py` is parsed, we have the following structures:

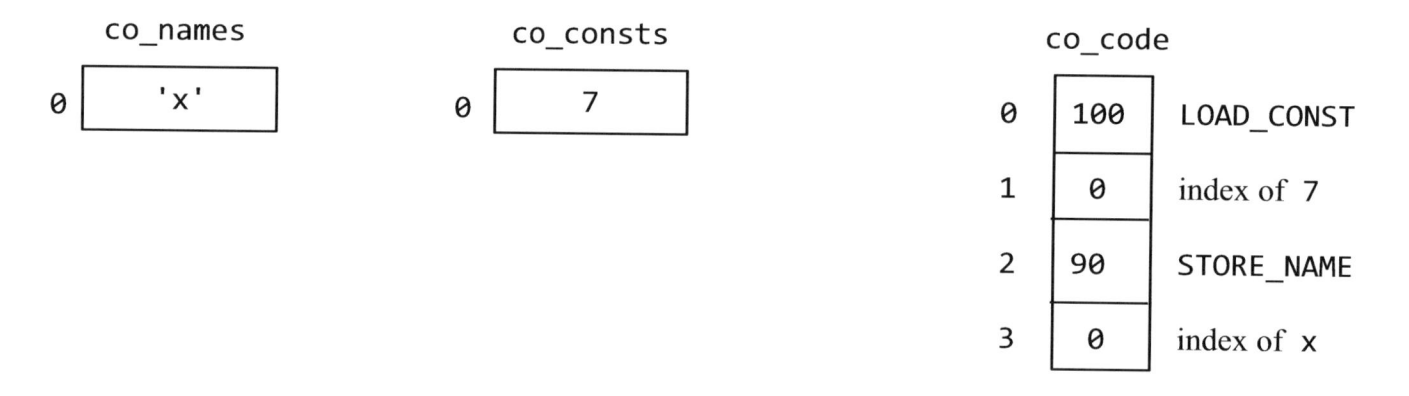

co_names

| 0 | 'x' |

co_consts

| 0 | 7 |

co_code

0	100	LOAD_CONST
1	0	index of 7
2	90	STORE_NAME
3	0	index of x

As the second assignment statement is processed, the name `'y'` is added to the `co_names` table, and two more bytecode instructions are stored in `co_code`:

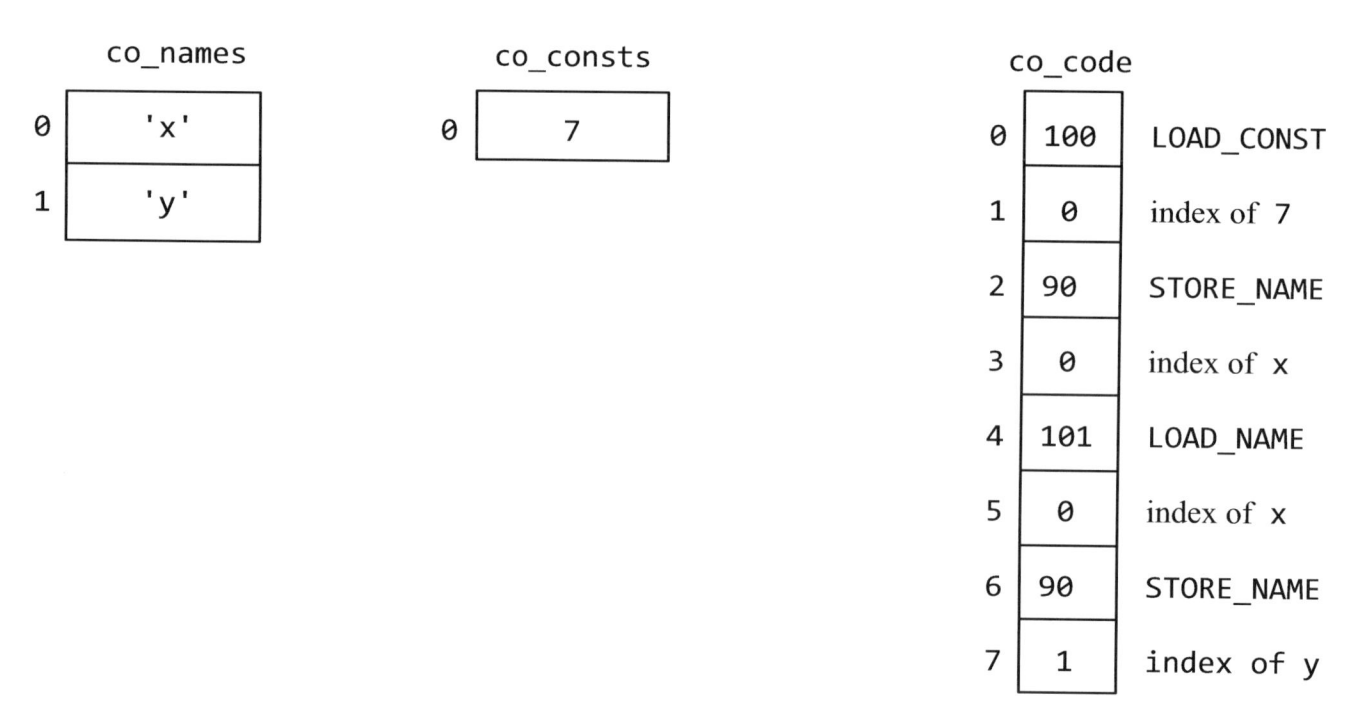

co_names

| 0 | 'x' |
| 1 | 'y' |

co_consts

| 0 | 7 |

co_code

0	100	LOAD_CONST
1	0	index of 7
2	90	STORE_NAME
3	0	index of x
4	101	LOAD_NAME
5	0	index of x
6	90	STORE_NAME
7	1	index of y

Bytecode Interpretation of a Small Program

When the compile phase of our hybrid interpreter ends, the bytecode interpreter takes over. The interpreter starts by creating another table, the `co_values` table, that holds the values of the variables in the co_names table. The value of each variable in the co_names table is in the corresponding position in the co_values table. Thus, the co_values table has the same size of the co_names table. The interpreter also creates a stack, which initially is empty. Fig. 9.3 shows the structures that exist as the bytecode interpreter is about to start.

	co_names		co_values		co_consts		co_code	
0	'x'	0	None	0	7	0	100	LOAD_CONST
1	'y'	1	None			1	0	index of 7
						2	90	STORE_NAME
						3	0	index of x
						4	101	LOAD_NAME
						5	0	index of x
						6	90	STORE_NAME
						7	1	index of y

created by bytecode interpreter

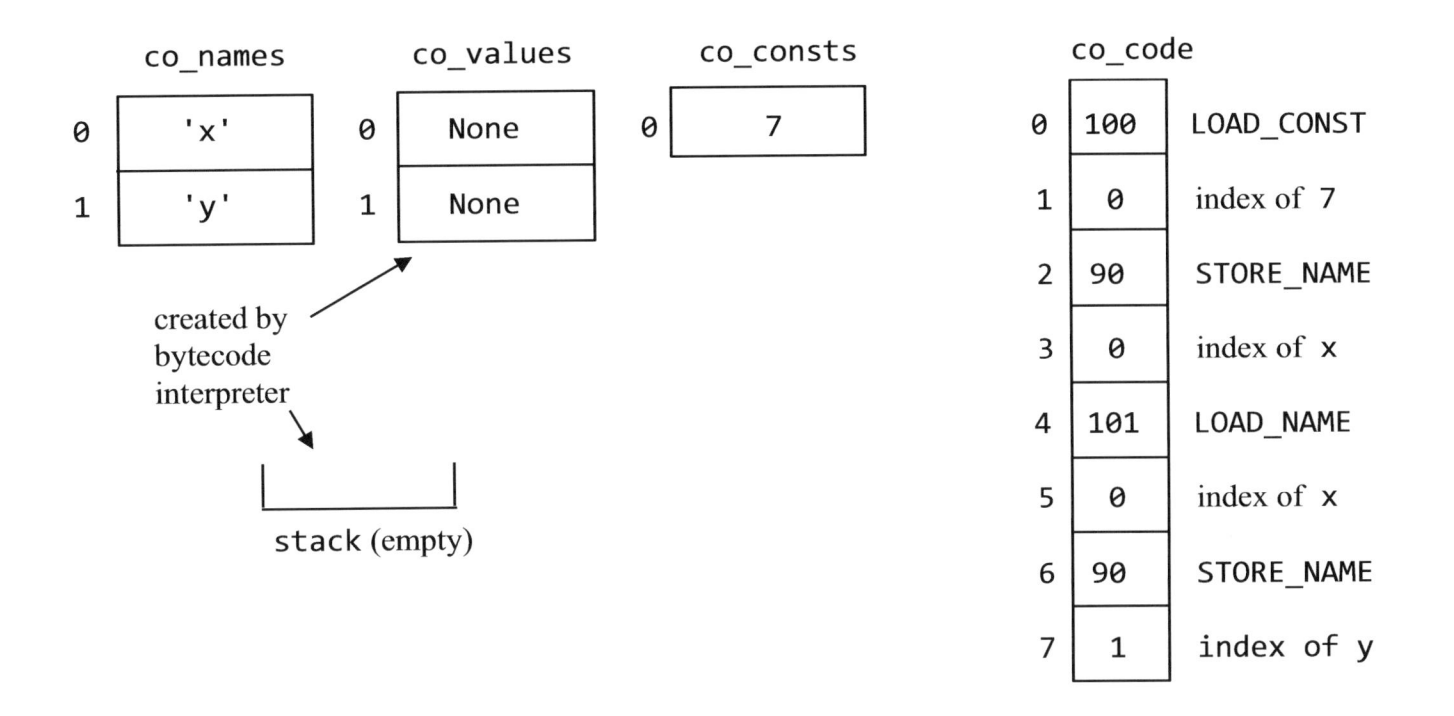

stack (empty)

Figure 9.3

The co_code table for our small program contains four instructions, each with two components: the opcode and an index. Each opcode has a name. For example, the name of the opcode 100 is LOAD_CONST (we show these names in Fig. 9.3 to the right of each opcode). The first instruction has the opcode 100, which is the opcode for the LOAD_CONST instruction, and the index 0. The effect of this instruction is the push onto the stack a copy of the constant whose index is 0. Note that in bytecode, "LOAD" means push. Thus, this instruction pushes the constant at index 0 in the co_consts table:

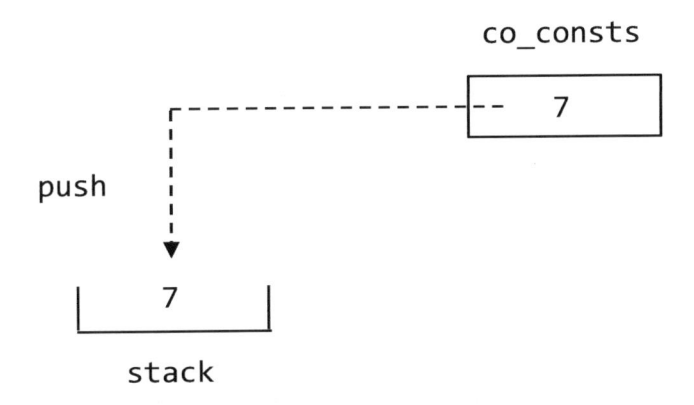

co_consts: 7

push

stack: 7

The next instruction, the STORE_NAME, pops the top item off the stack (in bytecode, "STORE" means pop) and stores it in the co_values table at the index 0 (the index specified in the instruction). Thus, this instruction pops 7 off the stack and stores it at index 0 (the location corresponding to the x variable). x now has the value 7:

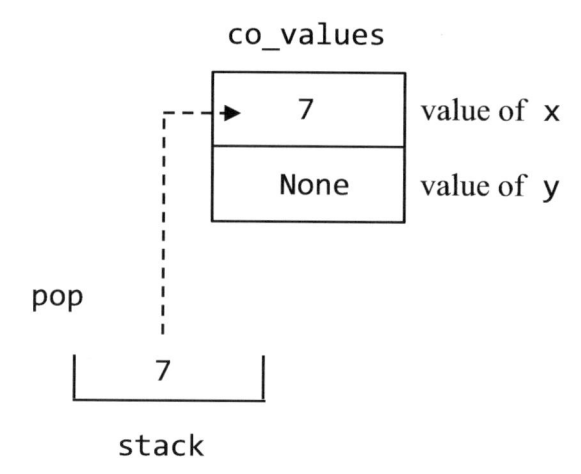

```
                co_values
          ┌─────────────┐
       ┌─▶│      7      │  value of x
       │  ├─────────────┤
       │  │    None     │  value of y
       │  └─────────────┘
  pop  │
       │
    ┌──┴──┐
    │  7  │
    └─────┘
     stack
```

The effect of the first two instructions is to assign 7 to x. The third instruction, the LOAD_NAME instruction, then pushes 7, the value of the variable at index 0 in the co_values table. Index 0 in the co_values table is where the value of x is located. Thus, this instruction pushes the value of x. The final STORE_NAME instruction pops the 7 off the stack and stores it at index 1 in the co_values table (which is the location of the value of y). Thus, the last two instructions assign the value of x to y. The final value of both x and y is 7:

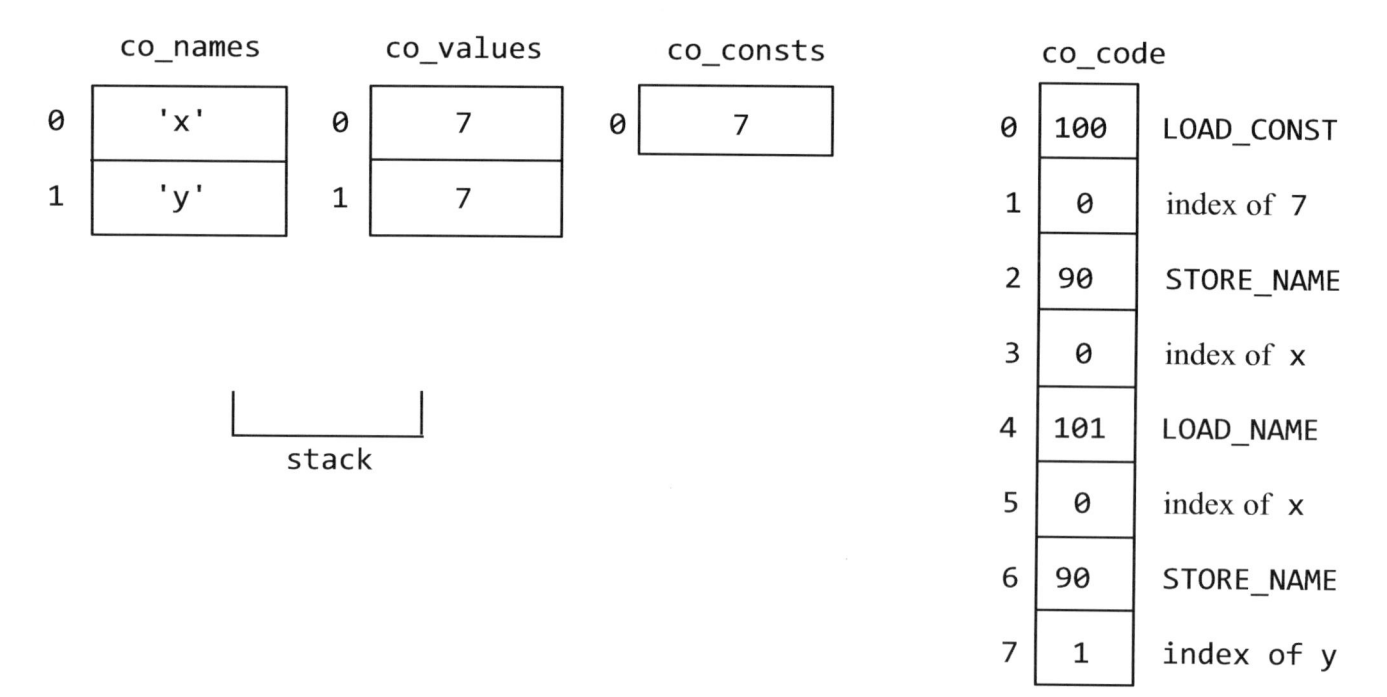

```
     co_names           co_values         co_consts              co_code
   ┌─────────┐         ┌─────────┐       ┌─────────┐       0 │ 100 │ LOAD_CONST
 0 │   'x'   │       0 │    7    │     0 │    7    │         ├─────┤
   ├─────────┤         ├─────────┤       └─────────┘       1 │  0  │ index of 7
 1 │   'y'   │       1 │    7    │                           ├─────┤
   └─────────┘         └─────────┘                         2 │ 90  │ STORE_NAME
                                                             ├─────┤
                                                           3 │  0  │ index of x
                                                             ├─────┤
         ┌─────────┐                                       4 │ 101 │ LOAD_NAME
         │         │                                         ├─────┤
         └─────────┘                                       5 │  0  │ index of x
            stack                                            ├─────┤
                                                           6 │ 90  │ STORE_NAME
                                                             ├─────┤
                                                           7 │  1  │ index of y
```

Displaying Bytecode

One nice way of displaying bytecode concisely is simply to display the co_names, co_consts, and co_code tables with a Python print() statement (for example, print(co_names)). Here is the bytecode corresponding to the source program in Fig. 9.2 displayed by print() statements:

```
['x', 'y']                          (print(co_names))
[7]                                 (print(co_consts))
[100, 0, 90, 0, 101, 0, 90, 1]      (print(co_code))
```

We call this form of bytecode the *list form*. Unfortunately, the list form is hard to read. It requires us to remember or look up what each opcode does. Fig. 9.4 shows a more readable form of bytecode.

Statement number	co_code index	Opcode name	Index	Item referenced
1	0	LOAD_CONST	0	(7)
	2	STORE_NAME	0	(x)
2	4	LOAD_NAME	0	(x)
	6	STORE_NAME	1	(y)

Figure 9.4

We call this form the *dis form* (for reasons to be explained below). "Statement number" in Fig. 9.4 is the line number of the source program statement that produces the corresponding bytecode. "co_code index" is the location of the instruction in the co_code table. "Opcode name" is the name that describes the effect of the opcode. "Index" is the contents of second part of the instruction. "Item referenced" is the constant referenced (by the LOAD_CONST instruction) or the variable referenced (by the LOAD_NAME and STORE_NAME instructions). This display of bytecode is more readable because it is in symbolic form. That is, it uses symbols (i.e., names) rather than numbers to represent the opcodes. It also tells us the values of the constants and the names of the variables referenced by each instruction.

It is easy to remember what an bytecode instruction does if we are given its name rather than its number. For this reason, we call the names of the opcodes—LOAD_CONST, STORE_NAME, LOAD_NAME—*mnemonics* (a mnemonic in general usage is any memory-aiding device).

Each bytecode instruction consists of one or two numbers. When we display these numbers, we usually display them in decimal. However, bytecode instructions in the computer are binary numbers (i.e., numbers that are represented with sequences of 0 and 1 only).

Symbolic instructions that correspond to binary instructions are commonly called *assembly language instructions*. Accordingly, we call the symbolic form of bytecode show in Fig. 9.4 *assembly language*. If we convert the symbolic form to binary, we are *assembling* the symbolic form. If we do the reverse—convert the binary form to symbolic form—we are *disassembling* the binary form (see Fig. 9.5).

symbolic form → assemble → binary form

symbolic form ← disassemble ← binary form

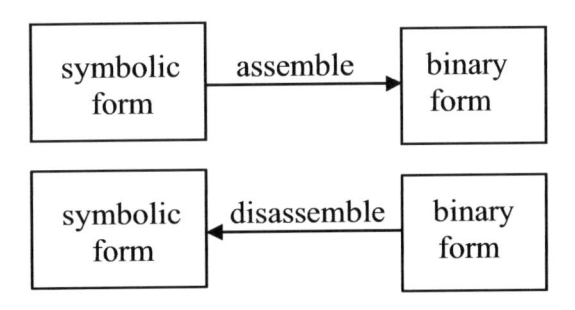

Figure 9.5

The symbolic form of the bytecode shown in Fig. 9.4 is the *dis*assembled form of the binary bytecode—hence the name "dis form."

After creating the `sample2.py` file in Fig. 9.2 (or getting it from the software package for this book), try entering the following command:

```
python -m dis sample2.py
```

The Python interpreter will then display the bytecode for `sample2.py` in the dis (i.e., disassembled) form.

Opcodes for Our First Hybrid Interpreter

Here are the opcodes we will need for the hybrid interpreter we construct in the next chapter:

Opcode	Index	Name	Effect
11		UNARY_NEGATIVE	Negates TOS
20		BINARY_MULTIPLY	Pops TOS, TOS1; pushes TOS1 * TOS
23		BINARY_ADD	Pops TOS, TOS1; pushes TOS1 + TOS
71		PRINT_ITEM	Pops and displays TOS
72		PRINT_NEWLINE	Outputs newline character
90	namei	STORE_NAME	Pops TOS into co_values[namei]
100	consti	LOAD_CONST	Pushes co_consts[consti]
101	namei	LOAD_NAME	Pushes co_values[namei]

TOS refers the item on top of the stack. TOS1 is the item just below the top of the stack. Thus, the effect of the BINARY_MULTIPLY instruction is to pop the top two items, multiply them, and push the result back onto the stack. UNARY_NEGATIVE negates the top of the stack. Fig. 9.6 shows the before and after pictures for the BINARY_MULTIPLY and UNARY_NEGATIVE instructions.

Before BINARY_MULTIPLY   After BINARY_MULTIPLY

```
| 5 |
| 3 |                      | 15 |
  stack                      stack
```

Before UNARY_NEGATIVE   After UNARY_NEGATIVE

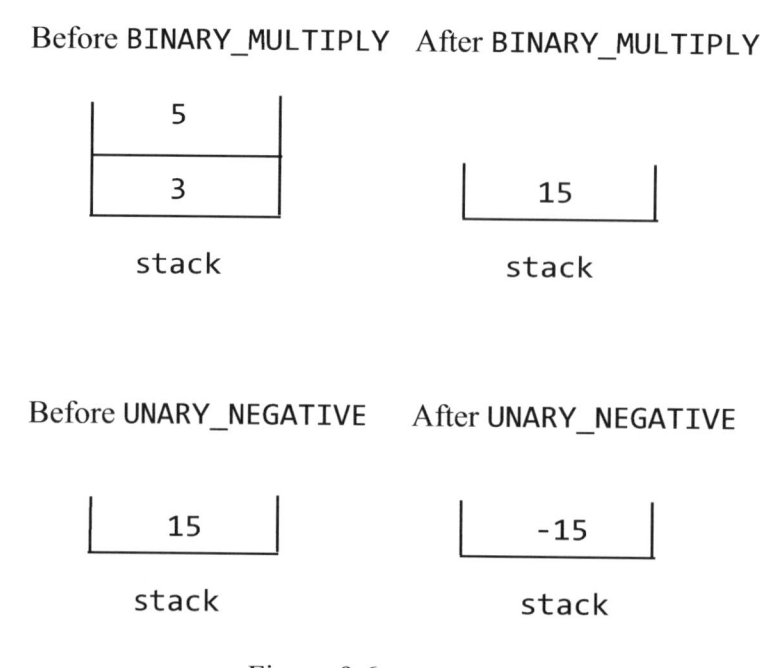

```
| 15 |                    | -15 |
  stack                     stack
```

Figure 9.6

Problems

1. Is the co_names table needed by the bytecode interpreter?

2. Translate the following program to bytecode:

   ```
   a = 1 + 2 + 3
   b = a + 4
   c = a + b
   ```

   Show the co_names, co_consts, and co_code tables as in Fig. 9.3.

3. Reverse compile (i.e., convert back to Python code) the following bytecode:

   ```
   co_names  = ['x']
   co_consts = [2, 3, 4]
   co_code   = [100, 0, 100, 1, 20, 100, 2, 23, 90, 0]
   ```

4. Reverse compile (i.e., convert back to Python code) the following bytecode:

   ```
   co_names  = ['x']
   co_consts = [2, 3, 4]
   co_code   = [100, 0, 100, 1, 20, 100, 2, 23, 90, 0, 101, 0, 71,
                72]
   ```

5. Show the changes in the stack when the following statement is interpreted by the bytecode interpreter:

   ```
   x = 1 + 2 + 3
   ```

6. Translate the statement in problem 5 to bytecode. Show the co_names, co_consts, and co_code tables as in Fig. 9.3.

7. Show the changes in the stack when the following statement is interpreted by the bytecode interpreter:

   ```
   x = 1 + 2*3
   ```

8. Translate the program in problem 7 to bytecode. Show the co_names, co_consts, and co_code tables as in Fig 9.3.

9. Convert your bytecode in problem 8 to the dis form. Check your answer by comparing it with the disassembled form produced by the Python 3 interpreter.

10. What does the "co" prefix in co_names, co_consts, and co_code, which is terminology originating from the Python 3 interpreter, stand for?

10 Constructing a Hybrid Interpreter

Introduction

In chapter 8, we saw that constructing a pure interpreter was quite easy. It required only a few modifications to the `p1.py` parser from problem 1 in chapter 7. However, constructing a hybrid interpreter is a little more difficult because a hybrid interpreter translates the source program to bytecode before the interpretation step, rather than directly interpreting the source program. Our starting point, as with our pure interpreter, will be the `p1.py` parser. The source language is the same as the source language for our `p1.py` parser in chapter 7 (see Fig. 7.1 for a source program and Fig. 7.3 for its grammar). Our first modification to our parser will be to add the globals that the parser and the bytecode interpreter need to share. Next, we will embed the code generator in the parser. Finally, we will add the code for the bytecode interpreter.

Global Constants and Variables in Our Hybrid Interpreter

Each bytecode opcode is an integer. To make our interpreter code more readable, we give a name to each opcode. We then use these names in our code instead of the numeric opcodes. Both the parser and the interpreter need these constants. Thus, we define them in the global section of our hybrid interpreter (see Fig. 10.1).

```
# bytecode opcodes
UNARY_NEGATIVE      = 11        # hex 0B
BINARY_MULTIPLY     = 20        # hex 14
BINARY_ADD          = 23        # hex 17
PRINT_ITEM          = 71        # hex 47
PRINT_NEWLINE       = 72        # hex 48
STORE_NAME          = 90        # hex 5A
LOAD_CONST          = 100       # hex 64
LOAD_NAME           = 101       # hex 65
```

Figure 10.1

The comments in Fig. 10.1 give the values of the opcodes in hexadecimal. For example, `BINARY_MULTIPLY` is 20 in decimal and 14 in hexadecimal (*hexadecimal* is the base-16 numbering system—see appendix B). The documentation that is available on Python bytecode typically lists opcodes in hexadecimal. So we provide their hexadecimal values in Fig. 10.1 for reference.

You may be wondering why the opcode for the `BINARY_MULTIPLY` instruction is 20, rather than some other number. The number 20 is arbitrary. The designers of Python bytecode just happen to pick 20 for the opcode for the `BINARY_MULTIPLY` instruction. Python bytecode opcodes run from 0 to 143 (0 to 8F in hexadecimal). For our first hybrid interpreter, we need only the eight listed in Fig. 10.1.

The parser and the interpreter both need access to the `co_names`, `co_consts`, and `co_code` tables.

So we make then global by initializing them in the global section of the interpreter with

```
co_code = []
co_names = []
co_consts = []
```

Embedding the Code Generator in the Parser

The *code generator* consists of those instructions in our hybrid interpreter that generate the bytecode instructions. The code generator is embedded in the parser—it is not a separate module.

Consider the parser code for `expr()`:

```
1 def expr():
2     term()
3     while token.category == PLUS:
4         advance()
5         term()
```

In `expr()` there are two calls of `term()`. We will modify `term()` and the function it calls (`factor()`) so that the effect of a call of `term()` is to generate bytecode (i.e., to append bytecode to the `co_code` table) that, when executed, pushes the value of the term it is parsing onto a stack (recall that the bytecode interpreter uses a stack). Thus, after the second call of `term()` (on line 5 in the `while` loop), `expr()` should generate a BINARY_ADD bytecode instruction that, when executed, pops and adds the two values pushed by the bytecode generated as a result of the two calls of `term()`. Here's the modified `expr()`:

```
1 def expr():
2     term()     # generates bytecode that pushes term's value
3     while token.category == PLUS:
4         advance()
5         term()   # generates bytecode that pushes term's value
6         co_code.append(BINARY_ADD) # generate the add instruction
```

For example, suppose the expression parsed by `expr()` is

```
    2 + 3
```

The first call of `term()` in `expr()` calls `factor()` which generates a LOAD_CONST instruction that, when executed, pushes 2 onto the stack. The second call of `term()` calls `factor()` which generates a LOAD_CONST instruction that, when executed, pushes 3 onto the stack. So `expr()` should generate a BINARY_ADD instruction that, when executed, pops the 2 and 3, adds them, and then pushes 5 back onto the stack. For example, suppose 2 and 3 are at indices 0 and 1, respectively, in the `co_consts` table. Then when `expr()` parses 2 + 3, it (along with `term()` and `factor()`) generates the following bytecode:

```
        LOAD_CONST  0     (when executed, pushes 2)
        LOAD_CONST  1     (when executed, pushes 3)
        ADD_BINARY        (when executed, pops 2, 3, adds, pushes 5)
```

The ADD_BINARY instruction is generated by `expr()`; the LOAD_CONST instructions are generated by `factor()` in response to calls by `term()`. Keep in mind that these bytecode instructions are not executed during the parse. The parser/code generator simply appends the bytecode instructions to the `co_code` table. In contrast, `expr()` in a pure interpreter executes code. That is a big difference—the difference between execution and translation.

The `term()` function is modified the same way the `expr()` function is modified, except a MULTIPLY_BINARY instruction is used rather than an ADD_BINARY instruction at the bottom of the `while` loop. In addition, the `sign` variable is initialized to 1 before each call of `factor()`:

```
1  def term():
2      global sign
3      sign = 1        # initialize sign
4      factor()
5      while token.category == TIMES:
6          advance()
7          sign = 1    # initialize sign
8          factor()
7          co_code.append(BINARY_MULTIPLY)
```

`factor()` uses `sign` to keep track of whether there are an even or odd number of unary minuses. When `factor()` parses a factor that starts with one or more unary minuses, `factor()` flips the sign of `sign` for each unary minus it parses. Because `term()` initializes `sign` to 1 before it calls `factor()`, an even number of unary minuses leaves 1 in `sign`; an odd number of unary minuses leaves -1 in `sign`. Each pair of unary minuses cancel each other out. Thus, if the number of unary minuses is even (in which case the final value of `sign` is 1), they all cancel each other out. If the number is odd (in which case the final value of `sign` is -1), one unary minus remains in effect. For example, for the factor ---7, `factor()` changes `sign` three times resulting in a final value of -1. This value in `sign` indicates one unary minus remains in effect.

The `factor()` function is modified so that it generates LOAD_CONST instructions for constants and LOAD_NAME instructions for variable names. `factor()` generates a LOAD_NAME instruction followed by a UNARY_NEGATIVE instruction if the variable is preceded by an odd number of unary minuses or just a LOAD_NAME instruction if the factor is preceded by an even number of unary minuses.

What should `factor()` do when it parses a constant, say 7? It should generate a bytecode instruction which, *when executed*, pushes 7 on the stack. In our pure interpreter, `factor()` pushes the value of 7 onto a stack. But `factor()` in our hybrid interpreter generates a bytecode instruction that, *when executed later*, pushes the value of 7 on a stack. Here is the code for `factor()`:

```
1  def factor():
2      global sign
3      if token.category == PLUS:
4          advance()
5          factor()
6      elif token.category == MINUS:
7          sign = -sign      # change sign for each unary minus
8          advance()
9          factor()
10     elif token.category == UNSIGNEDINT:
11         v = sign*int(token.lexeme)
12         if v in co_consts:
```

```
13            index = co_consts.index(v)
14        else:
15            index = len(co_consts)   # get index of next available slot
16            co_consts.append(v)      # add value to co_consts
17        co_code.append(LOAD_CONST)
18        co_code.append(index)
19        advance()
20    elif token.category == NAME:
21        if token.lexeme in co_names:
22            index = co_names.index(token.lexeme)
23        else:
24            raise RuntimeError('Name ' + token.lexeme + ' is not defined')
25        co_code.append(LOAD_NAME)
26        co_code.append(index)
27        if sign == -1:
28            co_code.append(UNARY_NEGATIVE)
29        advance()
30    elif token.category == LEFTPAREN:
31        advance()
32        # expr() calls term() which sets sign to 1 so must save sign
33        savesign = sign
34        expr()
35        if savesign == -1:                      # use saved value of sign
36            co_code.append(UNARY_NEGATIVE)      # negate expr
37        consume(RIGHTPAREN)
38    else:
39        raise RuntimeError('Expecting factor')
```

Suppose factor() parses 7. Then line 11 above assigns 7 to v. If 7 is already in co_consts, factor() executes line 13. Otherwise, it executes lines 15 and 16, which append 7 to co_consts. In either case, index is assigned the index of 7 in co_consts. factor() then generates a LOAD_CONST instruction whose second component is the index of 7. Thus, this instruction, when executed, pushes 7 onto the stack.

If a number that is parsed is preceded by an odd number of unary minus signs, the sign variable will be -1 when line 11 is executed. Thus, the value assigned to v will be negative (or zero if the number is zero). If, on the other hand, the number of unary minuses is even, then v should be assigned a non-negative value (because an even number of unary minuses cancel each other out). For an even number of unary minuses, sign will be 1, in which case v on line 11 will, indeed, be assigned a non-negative value.

For a variable name, factor() generates a LOAD_NAME instruction followed by the co_names index of the variable. If sign is -1 (which means a unary minus is in effect), factor() also generates a UNARY_NEGATIVE instruction following the LOAD_NAME instruction (line 28). The UNARY_NEGATIVE instruction negates the value on top of the stack. Thus, the combined effect of the LOAD_NAME and the UNARY_NEGATIVE is to push the negated value of the variable onto the stack. factor() also generates a UNARY_NEGATIVE instruction on line 36 to negate the value of a parenthesized expression if savesign is -1.

Note that len(co_consts) on line 15 above is the index of the next available slot in the co_consts table. For example, if len(co_consts) is 5, then the slots with indices 0 to 4 are already occupied. Thus, the slot with index 5 is the next available slot.

Modifying the printstmt() Function

How should we modify the `printstmt()` function:

```
1 def printstmt():
2     advance()
3     consume(LEFTPAREN)
4     expr()
5     consume(RIGHTPAREN)
```

What happens when `printstmt()` calls `expr()`? For example, suppose `printstmt()` is parsing

```
print(2 + 3)
```

Then the call of `expr()` in `printstmt()` parses the expression 2 + 3, which as we saw above, generates the bytecode

    LOAD_CONSTANT 0   when executed, pushes 2 (0 is index of 2 in the `co_consts` table)
    LOAD_CONSTANT 1   when executed, pushes 3 (1 is index of 3 in the `co_consts` table)
    ADD_BINARY   when executed, pops 2, 3, adds, pushes 5

When this code is ultimately executed, the value to be displayed is on top of the stack. Thus, after calling `expr()`, `printstmt()` should generate the bytecode instruction that, when executed, pops and displays the top of the stack, and then outputs a newline character to move the cursor on the screen to the beginning of the next line. We have two bytecode instructions that do just that: PRINT_ITEM and PRINT_NEWLINE. Here is our modified `printstmt()`:

```
1 def printstmt():
2     advance()
3     consume(LEFTPAREN)
4     expr()
5     co_code.append(PRINT_ITEM)        # pop stack and display
6     co_code.append(PRINT_NEWLINE)     # output a newline char
7     consume(RIGHTPAREN)
```

Modifying the assignmentstmt() Function

The `assignmentstmt()` function first gets the index of the variable on the left side of the assignment statement it is parsing. Then, after parsing the expression on the right side of the assignment statement (which generates bytecode which when executed leaves the value of the expression on top of the stack), `assignmentstmt()` generates a STORE_NAME instruction followed by the index of the variable on the left side:

```
1 def assignmentstmt():
2     if token.lexeme in co_names:
3         index = co_names.index(token.lexeme)
4     else:
5         index = len(co_names)           # get index of next available slot
6         co_names.append(token.lexeme)   # add lexeme to co_names
7     advance()
8     consume(ASSIGNOP)
9     expr()
10    co_code.append(STORE_NAME)
11    co_code.append(index)
```

When the STORE_NAME instruction is ultimately executed, the top of the stack will have the value of the expression on the right side of the assignment statement. The STORE_NAME instruction pops this value and stores it in co_values at the location corresponding to the index in the second half of STORE_NAME instruction (which is the index of the variable on the left side of the assignment statement).

Implementing a Bytecode Interpreter

We are now done embedding the code generator into the parser. All that remains to do is to implement the required bytecode interpreter, sometimes called the *Python Virtual Machine*. Sounds difficult, but it is not.

The main function in our hybrid interpreter first calls the tokenizer and then the parser. If the tokenizer and parser succeed, main then calls the interpreter:

```
1 def main():
2     ...
3     try:
4         tokenizer()
5         parser()
6     except RuntimeError as emsg
7         ...
8     interpreter()
```

The first action of the bytecode interpreter is to create a co_values table that has the same size as the co_names table. Each slot of the co_values table holds the value of the variable whose name is in the corresponding slot of the co_names table. For example, suppose x is in the first slot of co_names and has the value 3. Its value, 3, would then be in the first slot of the co_values table (see Fig. 10.2).

co_names   co_values

  'x'   3 ←———— This is the value of x

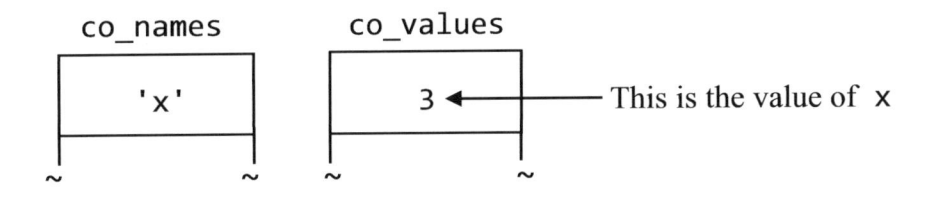

Figure 10.2

Initially, none of the variables have values. Accordingly, the `co_values` table is initialized with `None` (a variable in Python that is assigned `None` indicates that the variable has no value). The right side of the following statement creates the list `co_values` with `len(co_names)` elements, each set to `None`:

```
co_values = [None] * len(co_names)      # * is the repetition op
```

Thus, the `co_values` list has the same size as the `co_names` list. The asterisk here is not the multiplication operator but the repetition operator. Its right operand indicates how big the list should be. Its left operand indicates that the list should be initialized with all its elements set to `None`.

The interpreter also creates a stack, which initially is empty:

```
stack = []
```

and initializes a variable named `pc` to 0:

```
pc = 0
```

`pc` holds the address (i.e., the index into the `co_code` table) of the bytecode instruction to be executed next by the interpreter. Execution always starts with the first bytecode instruction in the `co_code` table, which is at index 0. Thus, `pc` is initialized to 0. Think of `pc` as "pointing to" the slot corresponding to the index it holds. For example, if `pc` holds the index 2, think of `pc` as pointing to the slot in `co_code` with index 2 (see Fig. 10.3).

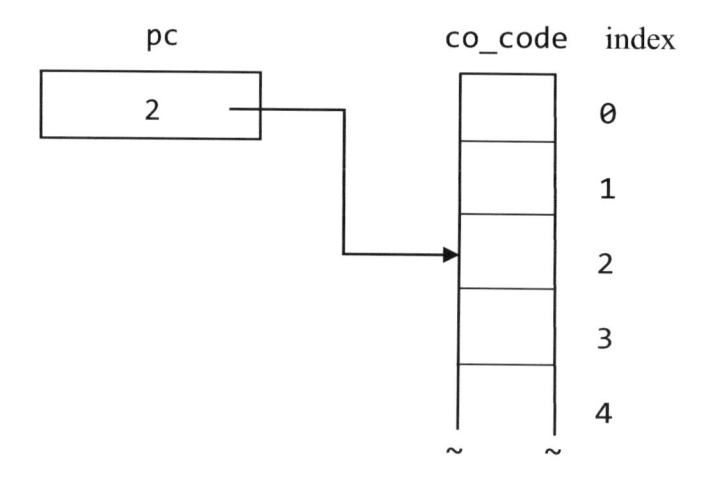

Figure 10.3

Using the pointer metaphor, we describe the function of `pc` by saying that it "points to" the bytecode instruction to be executed next.

After the initialization of `co_values`, `stack`, and `pc`, the interpreter executes a `while` loop. Each iteration of the `while` loop interprets one bytecode instruction—the bytecode instruction to which `pc` points. Each iteration also increments `pc`, so on the next iteration of the `while` loop, `pc` points to the next instruction, resulting in the execution of that instruction. The `while` loop continues interpreting the bytecode instructions in a sequential fashion until all the bytecode instructions have been interpreted. Fig. 10.4 shows the structure of the bytecode interpreter.

```
1  # bytecode interpreter
2  def interpreter():
3      co_values = [None] * len(co_names)
4      stack = []
5      pc = 0
6
7      while pc < len(co_code):
8          opcode = co_code[pc]         # get opcode from co_code
9          pc += 1                      # increment pc past the opcode
10
11         if opcode == UNARY_NEGATIVE:
12             stack[-1] = -stack[-1]
13         elif opcode == BINARY_MULTIPLY:
14             right = stack.pop()
15             left = stack.pop()
16             stack.append(left * right)
17         elif opcode == BINARY_ADD:
18             ...                      # missing instructions
19         elif opcode == PRINT_ITEM:
20             ...                      # missing instructions
21         elif opcode == PRINT_NEWLINE:
22             ...                      # missing instructions
23         elif opcode == STORE_NAME:
24             ...                      # missing instructions
25         elif opcode == LOAD_CONST:
26             index = co_code[pc]      # get index from inst
27             pc += 1                  # increment pc to next inst
28             value = co_consts[index] # get value from co_consts
29             stack.append(value)      # push value onto stack
30         elif opcode == LOAD_NAME:
31             index = co_code[pc]      # get index of variable
32             pc += 1                  # increment pc to next inst
33             value = co_values[index] # get value of variable
34             if value == None:
35                 print('No value for ' + co_names[index])
36                 sys.exit(1)
37             stack.append(value)      # push value onto stack
38         else:
39             break
```

Figure 10.4

The incrementation of pc on line 9 changes pc so that it points to just after the opcode of the current bytecode instruction. This incrementation of pc causes it to point to the next instruction if the current instruction consists of just the opcode, or to an index if the current instruction is a two-component instruction. The code that interprets a two-component instruction must increment pc a second time so that pc points to the next instruction before the next iteration of the while loop occurs. For example, the LOAD_CONST instruction is a two-component instruction: It contains an opcode and an index. Thus, the code that interprets this instruction must increment pc a second time (see line 27 in Fig. 10.4) so that pc points to the instruction that follows it (see Fig. 10.5). In contrast, the BINARY_MULTIPLY instruction is just an opcode, so pc is not incremented by the code that interprets this instruction (lines 14-16).

What does it mean to "interpret" a bytecode instruction? It means to do the operation specified by the instruction. For example, the BINARY_MULTIPLY instruction is supposed to pop the top two items from the stack, multiply them, and then push the result back onto the stack. Thus, to interpret this instruction, we need the following code:

```
14          right = stack.pop()
15          left = stack.pop()
16          stack.append(left * right)
```

After incrementation of pc on line 9   After incrementation of pc on line 27

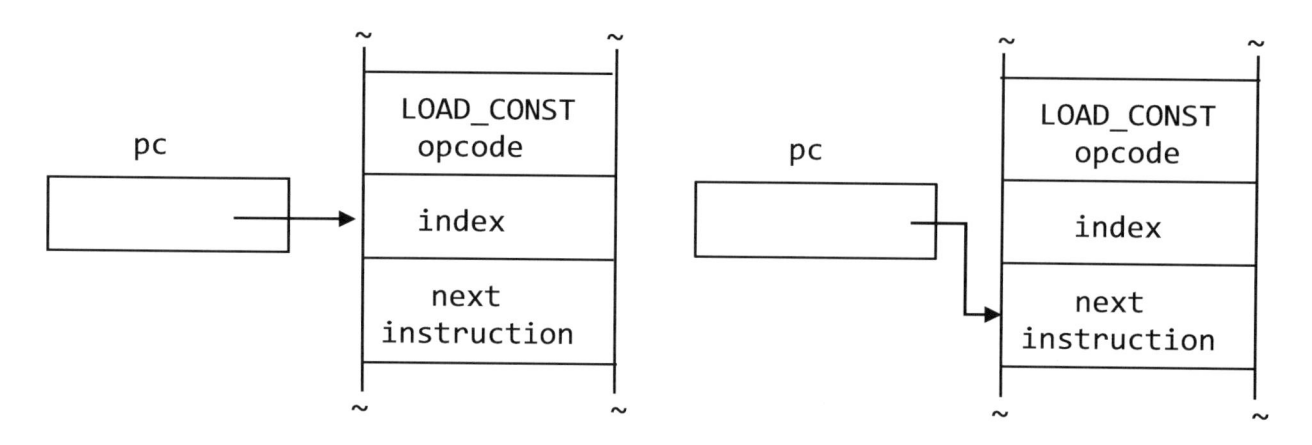

Figure 10.5

The LOAD_CONST instruction is supposed to push the constant in co_consts whose index appears as the second component of the bytecode instruction. Thus, to interpret this instruction, we need the following code from the interpreter above:

```
26          index = co_code[pc]        # get index from inst
27          pc += 1                    # increment pc to next inst
28          value = co_consts[index]   # get value from co_consts
29          stack.append(value)        # push value onto stack
```

The PRINT_ITEM instruction is supposed to pop and display the top of the stack but *not* move the cursor to the next line. The Python statement that does this is

```
        print(stack.pop(), end = '')
```

(two consecutive single quotes)

The second argument in this statement, end = '', has the effect of replacing the newline character normally produced by the print statement with '' (the null string). Thus, this print statement, as required by PRINT_ITEM, does not move the cursor to the next line.

Problems

1. Copy `h1shell.py` to `h1.py`. Then extend `h1.py` so that it functions as described in this chapter. Test your hybrid interpreter by entering

   `python h1.py h1.in`

   The file `h1.in` contains the Python program in Fig. 7.1.

2. The `while` loop in our bytecode interpreter (Fig. 10.4) uses a nested `if` statement that tests opcodes in opcode order. Does the order of testing opcodes matter?

3. Why is `co_names` global but not `co_values`?

4. Does our hybrid compiler necessarily execute more quickly than our pure interpreter?

5. Why is the bytecode instruction `BINARY_ADD` not preceded by bytecode instructions that pop the two operands to be added?

6. Devise a register-oriented (as opposed to stack oriented) intermediate language sufficient to support the source program in `h1.in`. It should consist of a `load`, `store`, `add`, `multiply`, `negate`, `print`, `print_newline`, and `load_constant` instructions, all of which involve a register (an accumulator register). For example, `load` loads the accumulator register from memory, and `print` displays the value in the accumulator register. Implement a hybrid interpreter that uses your new intermediate language. Which is more convenient: stack-oriented or register-oriented?

7. Can `factor()` be modified so two consecutive `UNARY_NEGATIVE` instructions are never generated? Consider

   `a = -(-b)`

8. Copy your `h1.py` interpreter from problem 1 to `p1008.py`. Modify `p1008.py` so that the intermediate language (IL) it generates is postfix notation instead of bytecode. For example, your interpreter should translate the source program below to the IL shown, and then interpret the IL.

Source program	Intermediate language program
`a = 1 + 2*3` `print(a + 10)`	`a 1 2 3 * + =` `a 10 + print`

   Hint: Your tokenizer should distinguish between the name of a variable on the left side of an assignment statement (give it the category LVAL), and the name of a variable in an expression (give it the category RVAL). The postfix interpreter treats an LVAL name and an RVAL name differently. The interpreter pushes the name of an LVAL, but it pushes the value of an RVAL. Test your interpreter by entering

   `python p1008.py h1.in`

11 Raspberry Pi Assembly Language

Introduction

In chapter 10, we constructed a hybrid interpreter—a type of interpreter that has a compiler as one of its components. In this chapter, we start learning how to construct another compiler—one that translates the source program to the Raspberry Pi assembly language.

Machine language is the language of the hardware of the computer. It is the only language that the computer hardware can "understand." Thus, if a program is to be executed by the computer hardware rather than interpreted by an interpreter program, it must be in machine language form. A machine language instruction is a sequence of 0's and 1's. We call each 0 or 1 a *bit*. In the Raspberry Pi, a machine language instruction is 32 bits long.

Assembly language is the symbolic form of machine language. Every assembly language instruction corresponds to one machine language instruction. For example, Fig. 11.1 shows an assembly language instruction and its corresponding machine language instruction.

Assembly language | Machine language

`mov r7, #1` | 11100011101000000111000000000001

Figure 11.1

The first part of an assembly language instruction is a *mnemonic* (for example, `mov` in the instruction in Fig. 11.1). The mnemonic represents the opcode of the machine language instruction. An *opcode* is the sequence of bits in a machine instruction that specifies the operation the instruction is to perform. The program that translates an assembly language program to machine language is called an *assembler*.

Most compilers translate the source program to assembly language, and then, using an internal assembler, translate the assembly language to machine language. Thus, the compiler input is the source program, and the output is a machine language program. However, our compiler will only translate the source program to assembly language. We will then use the Raspberry Pi `as` assembler or the `gcc` C compiler (which includes an assembler) to translate the assembly language program outputted by our compiler to machine language. Alternatively, we can use the `rpi` program (in the software package for this book) to directly interpret the assembly language programs produced by our compiler.

Architecture of the Raspberry Pi (a Simplified View)

The two principal units of the Raspberry Pi computer are the *central processing unit* (CPU) and memory. The CPU is the unit in the computer that performs computations, such as adding and multiplying. In addition to the circuits that perform computations, the CPU has a set of 16 registers called `r0`, `r1`, ..., `r15` (see Fig. 11.2). Registers `r13`, `r14`, and `r15` are also called `sp` (stack pointer), `lr` (link register), and `pc` (program counter), respectively. Each register can hold a four-byte number. A *byte* is 8 bits. Thus, a register can hold a 32-bit number.

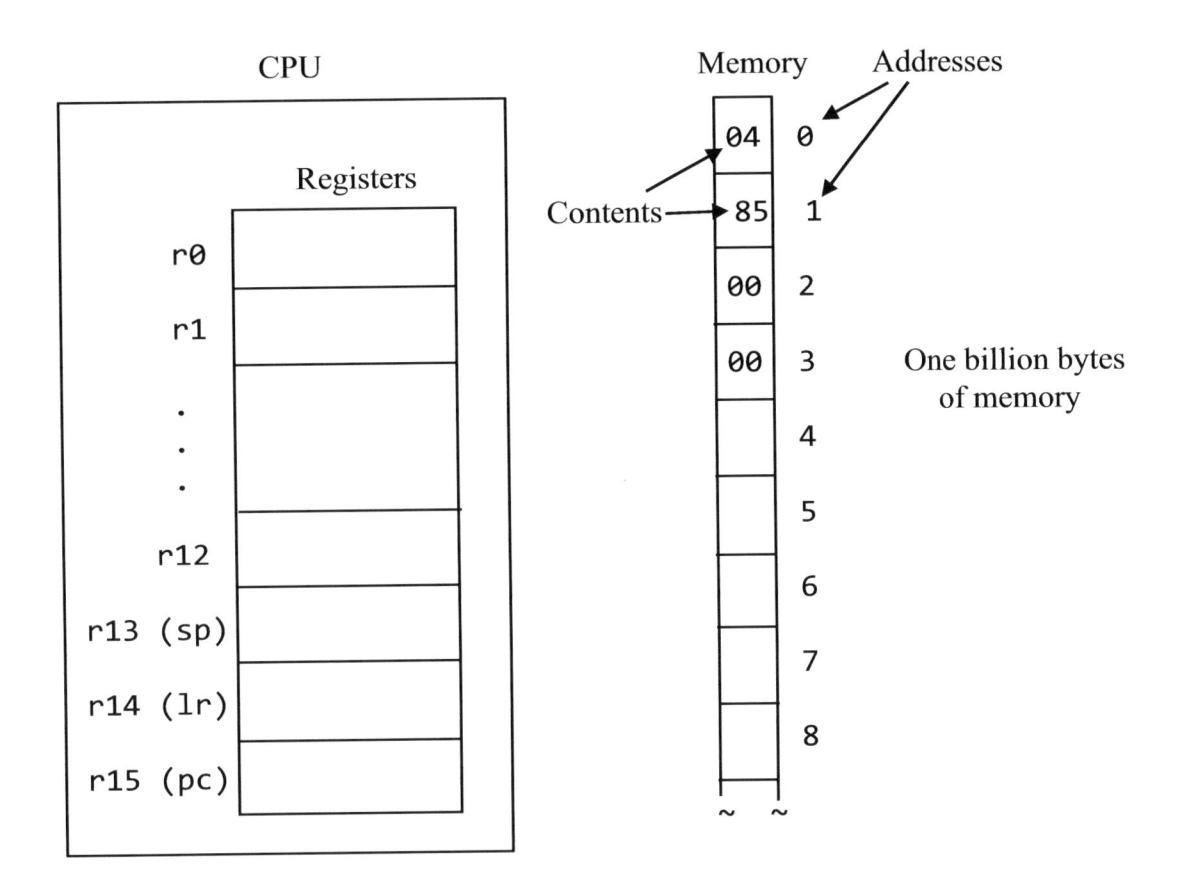

Figure 11.2

When the CPU performs an operation such as addition, it generally gets the operands from registers and places the result in a register. For example, the following assembly language instruction adds the contents of registers `r1` and `r2` and places the sum in register `r0`:

    add r0, r1, r2

The first register specified in an `add` instruction (`r0` in the example above) is the "destination" register. It receives the sum. The second and third registers specified hold the two operands to be added.

Because the computational circuits in the CPU operate on chunks of data that have 32 bits, we call any 32-bit item in the Raspberry Pi computer a *word*. Thus, we can say that each of the 16 registers can hold one word.

The other principal unit of the Raspberry Pi is memory (see Fig. 11.2). The memory size for the Raspberry Pi is may be as large as four gigabytes ("giga" means one billion). Each memory cell can hold one byte. The *address* of a cell is the number that identifies that cell. The *contents* is what is within the cell. Addresses start from 0 and increase by 1 for each byte of memory. For example, in Fig. 11.2, the address of the cell that contains 85 is 1.

Machine language instructions tell the CPU what to do. Without machine language instructions, the CPU cannot do anything. The CPU gets machine language instructions from memory. Thus, before a program can be executed by the CPU, the program must be in machine language form and in memory.

Machine instructions are four bytes long. Thus, if a machine instruction is at address 8000, it occupies the cells at addresses 8000, 8001, 8002, and 8003. The next instruction starts at address 8004, the next after that at address 8008, and so on.

How Instructions are Executed

Fig. 11.3 shows the three-step loop that the CPU performs as it processes instructions:

1. Fetch the instruction pointed to by the pc register, and then increment the pc register by 4.

2. Decode the instruction (i.e., get the operands).

3. Execute the instruction.

Figure 11.3

In step 1, the CPU fetches from memory the instruction pointed to by the pc register (i.e., the instruction whose address is in the pc register). It then increments the pc register by 4 (because instructions are four bytes long) so it points to the next instruction. Thus, the next time the CPU performs step 1, it fetches the next instruction in memory. In step 2, the CPU gets the operands to be used by the instruction from the registers that contain them. In step 3, the computer executes the instruction it fetched in step 1. This three-step loop causes instructions to be executed in the order in which they are in memory. However, this pattern of instruction execution can be changed. Suppose the execution of an instruction in step 3 causes a new address to be loaded into the pc register. Then in the subsequent step 1, the CPU fetches the instruction at this new address. For example, suppose the pc register contains 8000, and the instruction at this address, when executed, loads 8500 into the pc register. Then the following sequence of events occurs:

1) fetch instruction at 8000, and increment pc to 8004
2) decode instruction
3) execute instruction (which causes pc to be loaded with 8500)

1) fetch instruction at 8500 and increment pc to 8504
2) decode instruction
3) execute instruction

1) fetch instruction at 8504 and increment pc to 8508
2) decode instruction
3) execute instructions

and so on.

The loading of 8500 into the pc register causes the CPU to "*branch*" to location 8500. That is, it causes the CPU to switch from the sequence of instructions it is executing to the new sequence that starts at 8500.

The description of the three-step loop the CPU performs given above is somewhat oversimplified. Here is a more accurate description of what really happens, assuming none of the instructions executed cause a branch. Suppose the CPU is about to execute a sequence of three instructions. Let's call them i_1,

i_2, and i_3. When the CPU is doing step 2 on instruction i_1, it is simultaneously doing step 1 on i_2. When the CPU then is doing step 3 on i_1, it is simultaneously doing step 2 on i_2 and step 1 on i_3.

Think of the computer as a pipeline which has three processing stages (see Fig. 11.4). First in the pipeline is stage 1 that performs the step 1 operation (fetch and increment `pc`). Next is stage 2 that performs the step 2 operation (decode), followed by the stage 3 that performs the step 3 operation (execute). Thus, when i_1 is at stage 3, i_2 is right behind it at stage 2, and i_3 is at stage 1.

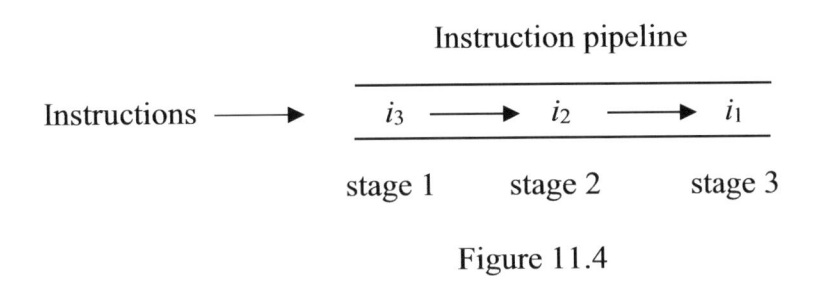

Instruction pipeline

Instructions ⟶ i_3 ⟶ i_2 ⟶ i_1

stage 1   stage 2   stage 3

Figure 11.4

This approach to instruction execution, aptly called *pipelining*, allows the CPU to execute instructions at a faster rate than if it had to complete one instruction before starting the next.

Pipelining has an interesting effect on the `pc` register. Suppose instruction i_1 in the scenario above is at address 8000. When it is executed (i.e., when it is in stage 3 of the pipeline), the `pc` register has already been incremented twice by 4: once when i_1 was in stage 1, and a second time when i_2 was in stage 1. Thus, when i_1 is executed, `pc` contains 8008. Suppose instruction i_1 is

```
bal [pc, #20]
```

When executed, this instruction ("`bal`" stands for "branch always") causes a branch to the address given by the address in the `pc` register plus 20. Because 8008 is in the `pc` register when the `bal` instruction is executed, the branch is to the location 8028 (8008 + 20). Recall from chapter 2 that square brackets are used to specify an optional item. However, in assembly language, square brackets are used to specify an item that represents an address. When the square brackets surround both a register and a constant, as in the `bal` instruction above, the address specified is the contents of the register plus the constant.

The `sp` register (`r13`) is the stack pointer register. It is usually used to hold the address of the item that is on top of the stack. When a value in a register is pushed onto the stack, `sp` is first decremented by 4. Then the value in the register is stored in the new location to which `sp` points (see Fig. 11.5, snapshots 1 and 2). When the top of the stack is popped into a register, the value on top of the stack (i.e., the value to which `sp` points) is first loaded into the register. Then the `sp` register is incremented (see Fig. 11.5, snapshots 3 and 4). The stack instructions on the Raspberry Pi can vary the way the stack operates. For example, on a push, the `sp` register can be incremented rather than decremented. However, we will use the stack instructions that operate as described above.

Pushing the value in a register onto the stack is a convenient way to save that value. To later restore the register with its original value, simply pop the saved value off the stack into the register. In Fig. 11.5, the contents of the registers and memory are shown in hexadecimal (base 16) numbers. Each pair of hex digits represents eight bits and occupies one byte. Thus, when the value 12345678 hex is pushed onto the stack, it occupies four bytes, with 78 in the first, 56 in the second, 34 in the third, and 12 in the fourth (see memory locations 1000 to 1003 in snapshot 2 in Fig. 11.5). This particular order of storing a four-byte word into four one-byte cells of memory—from the rightmost byte to the leftmost byte—is called the *little endian* order because it starts with the "little" end (i.e., the right end which has less weight than the left end).

1) Before a push of the value in `lr`:

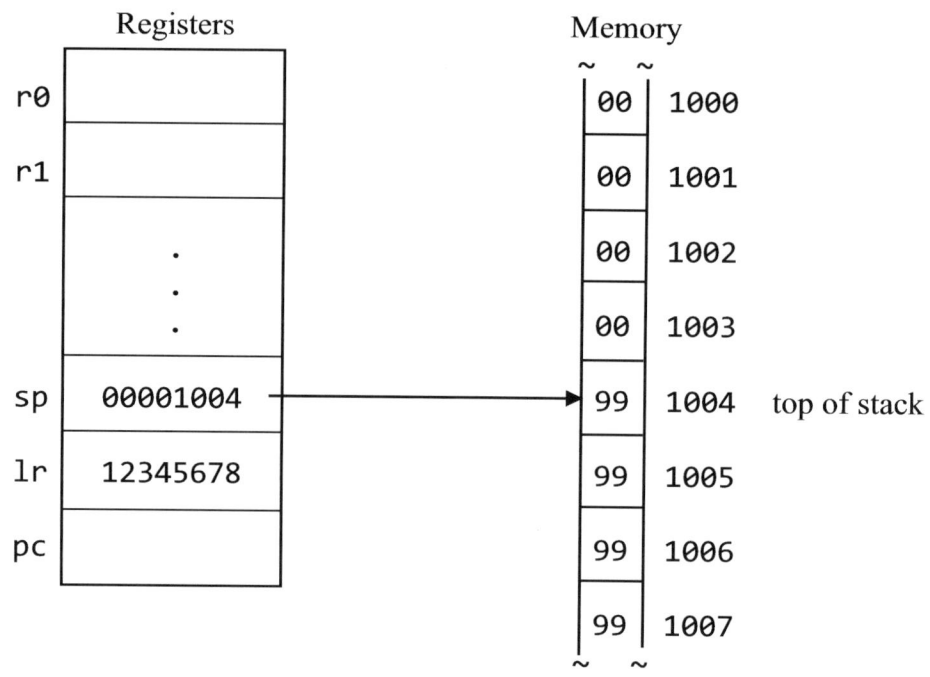

```
         Registers                    Memory
                                    ~     ~
    r0  |              |           | 00 | 1000
                                   
    r1  |              |           | 00 | 1001
                                   
                                   | 00 | 1002
          .
          .                        | 00 | 1003
          .
                                   
    sp  |   00001004   | --------> | 99 | 1004   top of stack
                                   
    lr  |   12345678   |           | 99 | 1005
                                   
    pc  |              |           | 99 | 1006
                                   
                                   | 99 | 1007
                                    ~     ~
```

2) After the push of the value in `lr`:

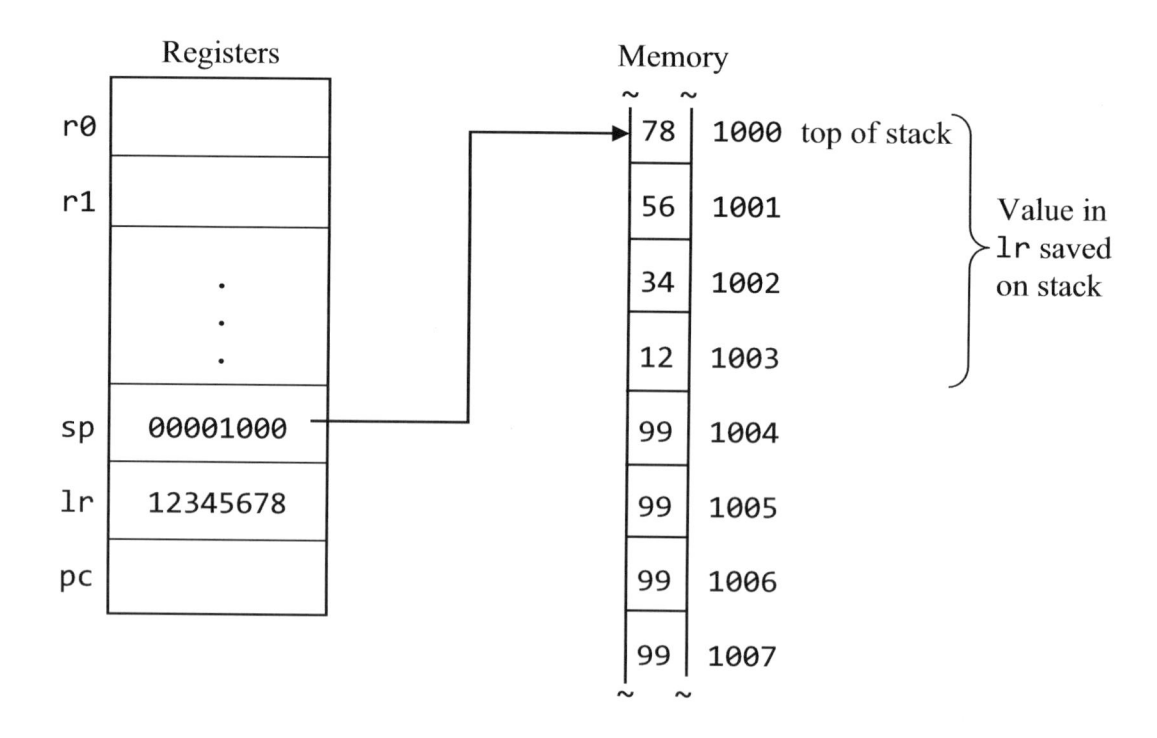

```
         Registers                    Memory
                                    ~     ~
    r0  |              |      ---> | 78 | 1000   top of stack ⎫
                                                              ⎪
    r1  |              |           | 56 | 1001               ⎬ Value in
                                                              ⎪  lr saved
                                   | 34 | 1002               ⎭  on stack
          .
          .                        | 12 | 1003
          .
                                   
    sp  |   00001000   | -----     | 99 | 1004
                                   
    lr  |   12345678   |           | 99 | 1005
                                   
    pc  |              |           | 99 | 1006
                                   
                                   | 99 | 1007
                                    ~     ~
```

Now suppose the value in `lr` is overlaid with 0005555.

3) Before a pop into `lr` register:

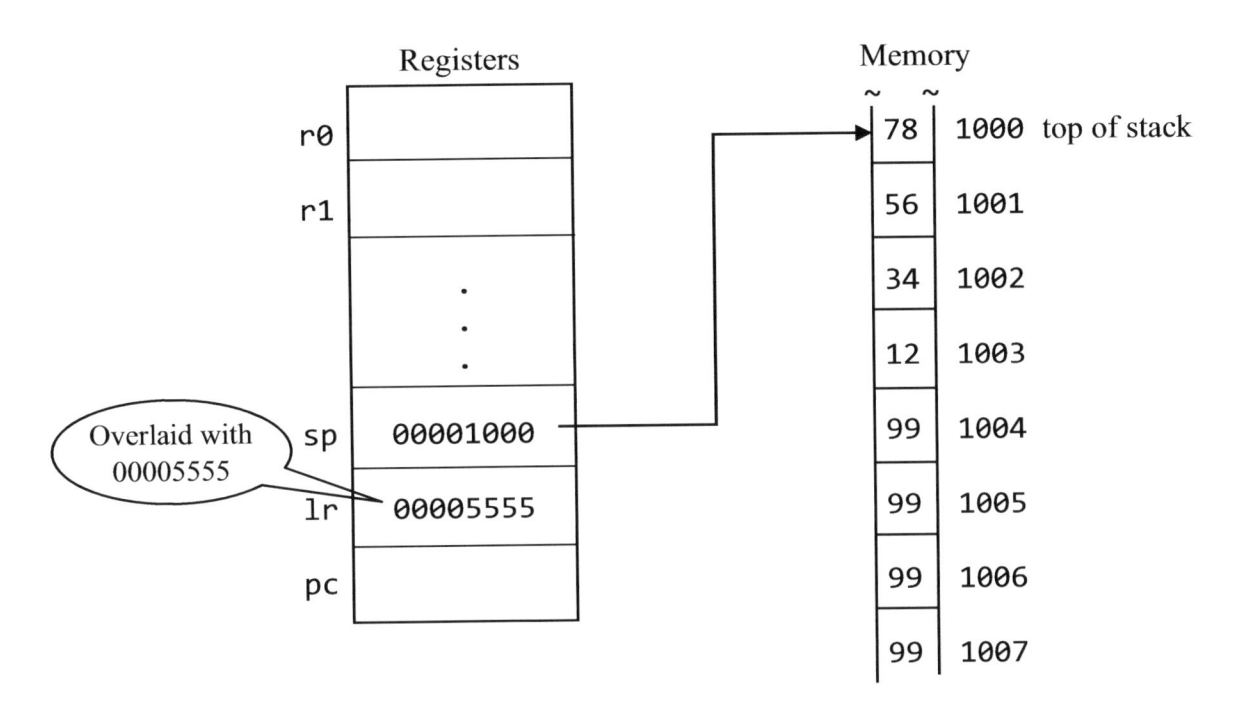

Registers		Memory		
r0		78	1000	top of stack
r1		56	1001	
⋮		34	1002	
		12	1003	
sp	00001000	99	1004	
lr	00005555	99	1005	
pc		99	1006	
		99	1007	

(Overlaid with 00005555 — points to `lr`)

4) After the pop into `lr` (which restores `lr` with its original value).

Registers		Memory		
r0		78	1000	
r1		56	1001	
⋮		34	1002	
		12	1003	
sp	00001004	99	1004	top of stack
lr	12345678	99	1005	
pc		99	1006	
		99	1007	

(Original value restored — points to `lr`)

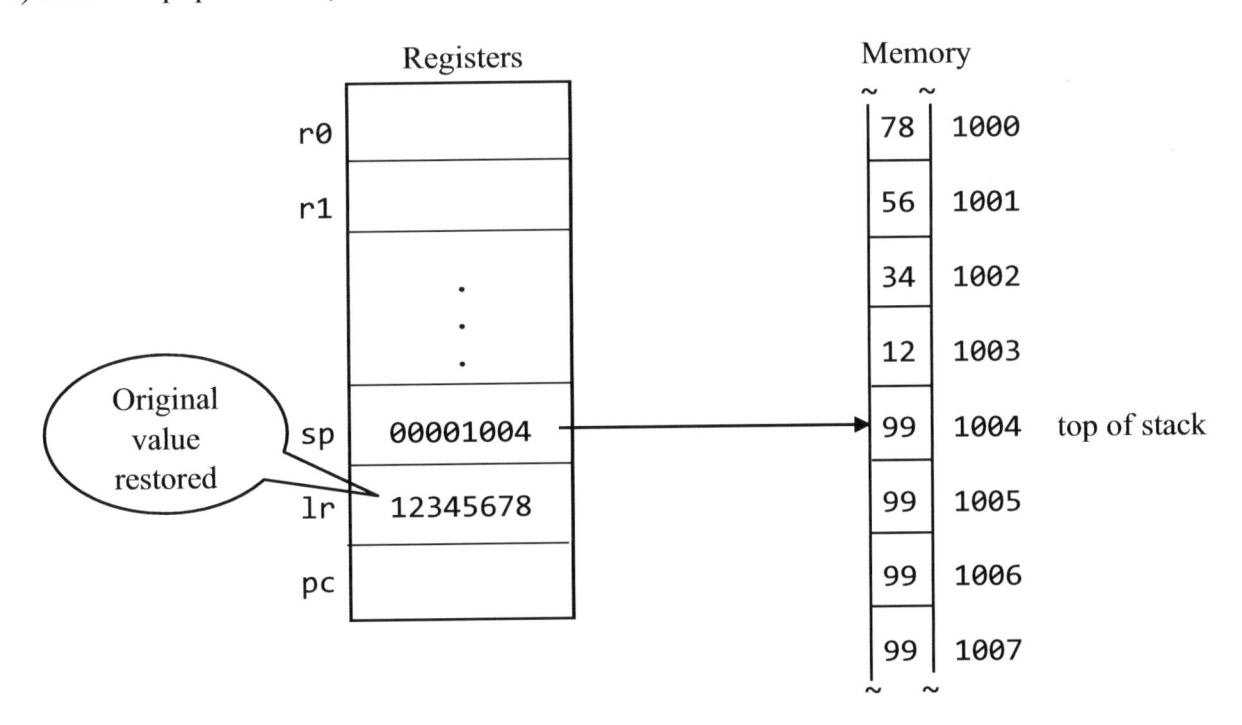

Figure 11.5

Some Simple Assembly Language Programs

Let's start with the simple program in Fig. 11.6. It consists of three instructions: `ldr` (load register), `mov` (move), and `svc` (supervisor call). The line numbers are NOT part of the program.

```
1                               @ ap1.s
2           .text               @ start of read-only segment
3           .global _start
4 _start:
5           ldr r0, x           @ load r0 from x
6           mov r7, #1          @ mov 1 into r7
7           svc 0               @ supervisor call to terminate program
8
9 x:        .word 14            @ the variable x
```

Figure 11.6

".text", ".global", and ".word" are not instructions but assembler *directives*. They direct the assembler to do something. For example, the ".word" directive tells the assembler to insert at that point in the machine language program a word that contains the value specified in the directive. Thus, following the `svc` instruction in Fig. 11.6 is a word that contains the value 14 in binary.

Comments in assembly language start with "@". It is a good practice to comment virtually every line of an assembly language program. Otherwise, it may be very difficult for a reader to figure out what the program does.

On the left side of the program in Fig. 11.6 are two labels, _start and x, each followed by a colon. When a label appears *to the right* of the opcode mnemonic or the directive in an assembly language instruction, the assembler translates it to the address of the word with that label on the left. Think of labels as symbolic addresses that the assembler translates to actual addresses. For example, when the assembler translates the `ldr` instruction on line 5, it translates the label x that appears on line 5 to the address of the word labeled with x (the word on line 9 that contains 14), and incorporates that address in the `ldr` instruction. Thus, when executed, the `ldr` instruction loads r0 with 14, which is in memory when the program is executed. Thus, the effect of an `ldr` instruction is to transfer data from memory to a register.

The `mov` instruction on line 6 moves 1 into r7. The pound sign in "#1" indicates that 1 is *immediate data*. Unlike the `ldr` instruction, the `mov` instruction, when executed, does not transfer data from memory to a register. The 1 specified in the `mov` instruction is in the `mov` instruction itself. Here is the machine language instruction that corresponds to the `mov` instruction in Fig. 11.6:

1110 0011 1010 0000 0111 0000 0000 0001

immediate data equal to 1

When the CPU fetches this instruction, it at the same time gets the data to be moved (because the data is in the instruction). Thus, the data is immediately available to the CPU as soon as the instruction is fetched (hence, the name "immediate data"). When the `mov` instruction is executed, the CPU extracts the 1 from the instruction and puts it into r7. Instructions like the `mov` instruction on line 6 are called *immediate instructions* because the data involved is immediately available to the CPU once the instruction has been fetched. The `ldr` instruction, on the other hand, is not an immediate instruction because after it is fetched, another fetch from memory is needed to get the data to be transferred to the register.

The `svc` instruction causes a branch back to the operating system (OS). What the OS (operating system) does in response to the `svc` instruction depends on what is in `r7`. If `r7` contains 1, the OS simply terminates the program. That is why the `svc` instruction in Fig. 11.6 in combination with the `mov` instruction that precedes it causes the termination of the program.

Before the program in Fig. 11.6 can be executed on a Raspberry Pi computer, it has to be assembled and linked. To assembly it (the program is in the file `ap1.s`) on a Raspberry Pi computer, enter on the command line

```
as ap1.s -o ap1.o
```

This command invokes the `as` assembler. The assembler translates the program in `ap1.s` to a machine language program, which it outputs to the file `ap1.o` (the name that follows the "-o" switch is the output file name). `ap1.o` is called an *object file* or an *object module*. An object file contains machine language instructions, but it is not a complete program. To get a complete program that can be executed, `ap1.o` has to be linked. To do this, enter

```
ld ap1.o -o ap1
```

This command invokes the `ld` linker. The linker then creates an executable program by combining `ap1.o` with any modules it might need, and then outputting the executable program to the file `ap1` (the name that follows the "-o" switch is the output file name). To execute `ap1`, enter

```
ap1   (or ./ap1)
```

To see if the program is working correctly, enter

```
echo $?
```

after executing the program. This command causes the OS to display in decimal what was left in the low-order byte (i.e., the rightmost byte) of `r0`. Thus, for the `ap1` program, which leaves 14 in `r0`, this `echo` command should display 14.

Let's summarize: To execute an assembly language program on the Raspberry Pi computer, it must be assembled by the assembler and then linked by the linker. The assembler inputs the assembly language file and outputs a file called the object file. The linker inputs the object file and outputs an executable file (see Fig. 11.7). By convention on a Raspberry Pi, assembly language file names have the extension ".s", object files names have the extension ".o", and executable file names have no extension. On a Windows system, ".asm", ".obj", and ".exe" are the standard file extensions for assembly, object, and executable files, respectively.

ap1.s assembly language file → `as` assembler → ap1.o object file → `ld` linker → ap1 executable file

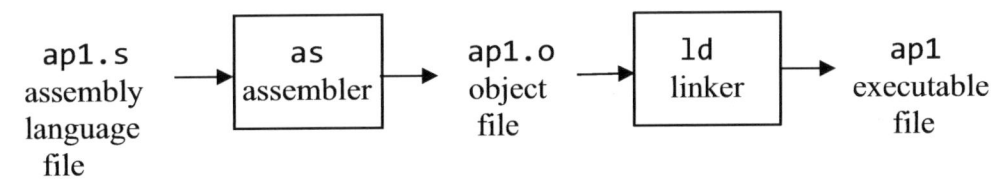

Figure 11.7

If you do not have a Raspberry Pi computer but a Windows, Linux, or OS X computer, you can still run the assembly language programs discussed in this book. You can run them using `rpi`, the Raspberry Pi Assembly Language Interpreter program (included in the software package for this book). To run the assembly language program in `ap1.s` on a Windows system using the `rpi` program (see the file `rpi.txt` for instructions on how to set up and use the `rpi` program), enter

```
rpi ap1.s -r
```

The optional "`-r`" switch causes the `rpi` program to display the final contents of registers `r0` to `r15` when the assembly language program terminates (so you can check if 14 is in `r0`). The `rpi` program is an *interpreter* so it directly executes the assembly language program. Thus, the assembly language program is *not* first assembled and linked. On a non-Windows system, prefix the command above with "`./`".

Because the `_start` label in the program in Fig. 11.6 is on an otherwise blank line, it refers to the `ldr` instruction on the following line. Thus, the assembler treats `_start` as the symbolic address of the `ldr` instruction. The `_start` label specifies the *entry point* for the program. That is, it indicates where in the program execution should start. Because it is on the `ldr` instruction, execution starts with the `ldr` instruction. If instead it were on the `mov` instruction, then execution would start with that instruction. The first instruction in a program does NOT have to be the first instruction executed.

The labels in an assembly language program are generally lost in the translation to machine language. Thus, you might conclude that in the machine language program, the `_start` label cannot indicate where execution should start. In fact it can, but only if the `_start` label appears on a `.global` directive. Such a directive causes the assembler to insert in the machine language file it creates additional information that indicates which machine instruction corresponds to the `_start` label (see Fig. 11.8). This information appears at the beginning of the object file in an area called the *header* (we are simplifying somewhat here, but the basic idea is correct).

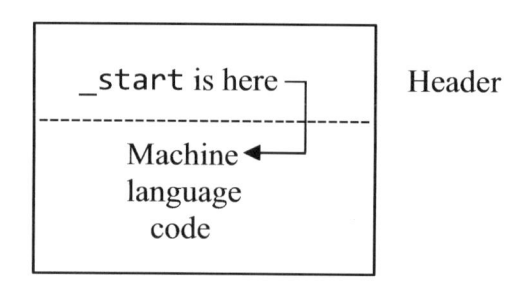

```
┌─────────────────────────┐
│     _start is here ┐    │   Header
│ -------------------│---- │
│       Machine ◄────┘    │
│       language          │
│         code            │
└─────────────────────────┘
```

Figure 11.8

When the linker outputs an executable file, it copies the entry point from the object file it inputs to the header of the executable file it outputs. Thus, when the OS loads an executable file, it can determine from the file's header which instruction should be executed first. Here is what happens when you invoke the `ap1` program by entering `ap1` on the command line:

1. The OS searches for the `ap1` file.
2. The OS loads the `ap1` file into memory, adjusting addresses as necessary
3. The OS determines from the header in the `ap1` file which instruction should be executed first. It branches to that instruction.
4. The `ap1` program executes.
5. The `svc` instruction causes a branch back to the OS.
6. The OS displays the command line prompt, indicating it is ready to accept another command.

A `.text` directive at the beginning of a program segment tells the assembler that what follows should be loaded into read-only memory. A `.data` directive, on the other hand, tells the assembler that what follows should be loaded into read/write memory. Usually, we put a `.text` directive before instructions. A program should never change its own instructions. Thus, it makes sense that instructions should occupy read-only memory. Read-only data (i.e., constants) can also go in a `.text` segment. However, variables whose values can change cannot be in a `.text` segment. The variable x in the program in Fig. 11.6 is not really a variable but a constant (it's not modified). That is why it is okay for x to be in the `.text` segment.

Now consider the program in Fig. 11.9. The `ldr` instruction transfers data from memory to a register. The `str` instruction (store register) does the reverse—it transfers data from a register to memory. The `str` instruction on line 6 in Fig. 11.9 attempts to store the contents of r0 into y. But y is in a `.text` segment (which is, therefore, a read-only segment). A store to read-only memory is illegal.

```
1                                @ ap2.s
2              .text             @ start of read-only segment
3              .global _start
4  _start:
5              ldr r0, x   (illegal)  @ load r0 from x
6              str r0, y         @ store r0 in y (does not work)
7              mov r7, #1        @ move 1 into r7
8              svc 0             @ terminate program
9
10 x:          .word 2           @ the variable x
11 y:          .word 0           @ the variable y
```

Figure 11.9

If you run the program in Fig. 11.9 on a Raspberry Pi, it will terminate on the `str` instruction with the cryptic message

    segmentation error

This message means that your program attempted to do something illegal with some segment of memory, such as store in a read-only segment or access a location that does not belong to your program. For example, you will get a segmentation error if your program attempts to load from a location in the OS.

An easy way to fix the problem in the program in Fig. 11.9 is to change the `.text` directive to `.data`. Then the OS will load the program into read/write memory, in which case the `str` instruction will execute without triggering a segmentation error.

Try executing the program in Fig. 11.9 (it is in the file `ap2.s`) with the `.text` directive, and then with the `.text` directive replaced with a `.data` directive.

User and Supervisor Modes

Programs typically contain multiple functions. One function gets control first. It calls other functions, which in turn call other functions. The program in Fig. 11.10 contains two functions: the _start function and the f function.

```
 1                                  @ ap3.s
 2              .text               @ start of read-only segment
 3              .global _start
 4                                  @                           address (decimal)
 5  f:          mov r0, #3          @ mov 3 into r0             8000
 6              mov pc, lr          @ return to caller          8004
 7
 8  _start:     bl  f               @ call f                    8008
 9              mov r7, #1          @ move 1 into r7            8012
10              svc 0               @ terminate program         8016
```

Figure 11.10

The `_start` function gets control first (because of the label `_start`). It immediately calls the `f` function by executing a `bl` (branch and link) instruction. This instruction loads the `pc` register with the address of `f`, causing a branch to `f`. But it also does something else: It loads the `lr` register with the address of the instruction that follows the `bl` instruction. For example, suppose `f` is at address 8000 decimal. Then the `bl` instruction is at address 8008, and the `mov` instruction that follows it is at 8012. When the `bl` instruction is executed, it loads `pc` with 8000 and `lr` with 8012. Because the `pc` now has the address of the `f` function (8000), the CPU starts executing that function. When the `mov` instruction at the end of the `f` function is executed, it moves the contents of `lr` (which is 8012) into the `pc`, causing a branch to address 8012. Thus, the `mov` instruction on line 6 causes a return to the calling function—specifically to the instruction following the `bl` instruction (to the `mov` instruction on line 9).

This program has an interesting inconsistency. `f` returns to its caller by moving the contents of `lr` to the `pc` register. But `_start` returns to its caller (the operating system) by executing an `svc` instruction. Why this inconsistency? The reason has to do with the operating modes of the CPU. When the CPU is in the *user mode*, the executing program has restricted privileges. For example, it cannot execute some instructions or access every area of memory. The purpose of these restrictions is to make it impossible for the executing program to harm the OS or other programs in the system. The CPU is always in the user mode when a user program (like `ap3`) is executing. If it were not, it would be possible for a user program to crash the system, for example, by overlaying the OS with some garbage data. When the OS is executing, on the other hand, the CPU is always in a *supervisor mode*. Thus, it does not have the restrictions that a user program has. To do its job, the OS has to be able to execute any instruction and access any area of memory. Thus, it has to be in a supervisor mode when it executes.

We now can understand the inconsistency in the program in Fig. 11.10. When the `f` function returns to its caller, we do not want to change from user mode to supervisor mode (because the caller is a part of the user program). But when the `_start` function returns to its caller (the OS), we must have a change from user mode to supervisor mode. Otherwise, the OS cannot do its job. A `mov` instruction that moves a new address into the `pc` register (like the `mov` instruction at the end of the `f` function) causes only a branch, NOT a change of mode. Thus, such an instruction cannot be used to return to the OS. But the `svc` at the end of the `_start` function not only causes a branch but also a change to the supervisor mode.

How an Address Fits into a Machine Instruction

An address is a 32-bit number. How then does an address fit inside an instruction? An instruction is only 32 bits. An address would take up all 32 bits. For example, consider the `ldr` instruction on line 5 in the program in Fig. 11.6:

>   ldr r0, x

Some of the bits in the corresponding machine language instruction are used to represent the opcode for `ldr`. Some are used to represent the `r0` register. Thus, there are fewer than the 32 bits available for an address. This `ldr` instruction, in fact, does *not* hold a complete address. Instead it holds a 12-bit offset. The `ldr` instruction above is translated to machine language as if it were written this way:

>   ldr r0, [pc, #4]

`[pc, #4]` specifies an address: the address given by the contents of the `pc` register plus 4. The constant `#4` is called the *offset* or *displacement*. It is this offset, as 12-bit number, that is in the machine language instruction. The offset can be either positive, negative, or zero. Thus, the `ldr` instruction can load from locations following it or preceding it depending on the sign of the offset.

When the preceding `ldr` instruction is executed, it uses the current address in the `pc` and the offset to determine the actual address. Recall that when an instruction is executed, the `pc` has already been incremented twice because of the pipelining of instructions. Suppose, for example, that the `ldr` instruction is at the address 8000. Then when it is executed, the `pc` contains 8008. Thus, the computed address is 8008 + 4 = 8012. The program in Fig. 11.6 with the `ldr` instruction rewritten with an explicit offset is given in Fig. 11.11.

```
1                                       @ ap4.s
2               .text                   @ start of read-only segment
3               .global _start
4 _start:                               @ address
5               ldr r0, [pc, #4]        @ 8000
6               mov r7, #1              @ 8004
7               svc 0                   @ 8008
8
9 x:            .word 14                @ 8012
```

Figure 11.11

The `ldr` instruction on line 5 in Fig. 11.11 loads `r0` from the address given by the contents of the `pc` register (8008) plus 4 = 8012. Thus, it loads from the location corresponding to x, just like

>   ldr r0, x

The two instructions are the same (i.e., they translate to the same machine language instruction). Which one is better to use when writing the program? If we use `[pc, #4]` to specify the address, we have to determine the correct offset. But if we use just the label x, the assembler determines the correct offset for us. So, the label approach is clearly better, although it hides how the address it computed.

Because the offset field is 12 bits and can be either added to or subtracted from the address in the `pc` register, it can range from −4095 to +4095. This range should be sufficient for most `ldr` and `str` instructions we use in a program. But it is not unlimited. For example, we cannot use a `ldr` instruction to load a word from a location that is 10,000 bytes from the `ldr` instruction.

The type of addressing illustrated by the `ldr` instruction in Fig. 11.6 and Fig. 11.11 is called *pc-relative addressing* (because the actual address is relative to the address in the `pc` register).

Using the .text and .data Directives

Generally, when we write an assembly language program, we put the instructions and constants in a `.text` (i.e., read-only) segment, and the variables in a `.data` (i.e., read/write) segment. We do this in the program in Fig. 11.12.

```
 1                                  @ ap5.s
 2              .text               @ start of read only segment  ⎫
 3              .global _start                                    ⎪
 4  _start:                                                       ⎪
 5              ldr r0, x   (illegal) @ does not work             ⎬ .text segment
 6              mov r7, #1                                        ⎪
 7              svc 0                                             ⎭
 8
 9              .data                @ start of read/write segment ⎫
10  x:          .word 5              @ the variable x             ⎬ .data segment
                                                                   ⎭
```

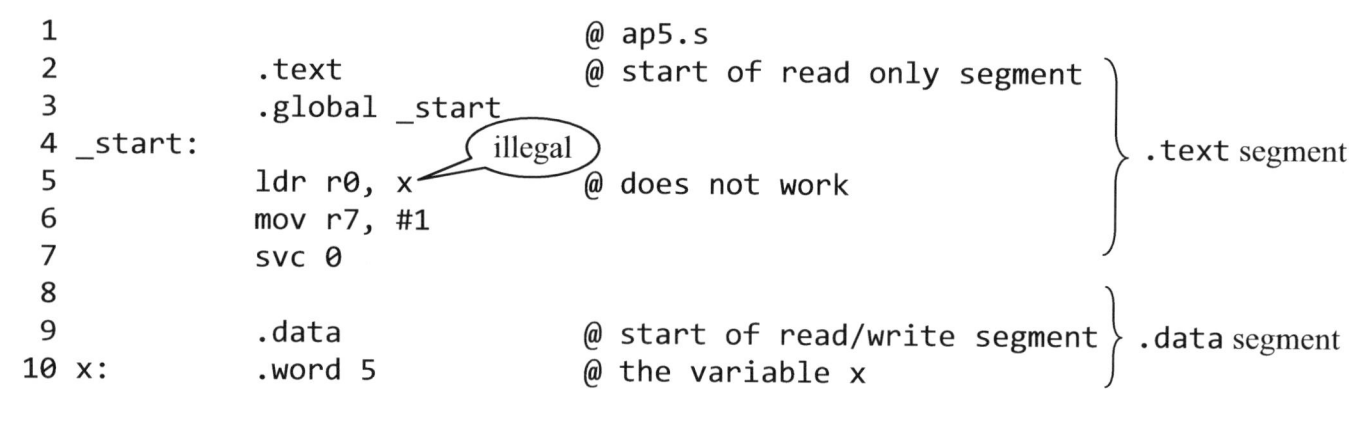

Figure 11.12

This program, however, does not assemble successfully. Here is the reason why. When the OS loads a program into memory, it usually places the `.data` segment right after the `.text` segment (or right before if the `.data` segment is first). However, it is not required to do this. It might put the `.data` segment in some location that is far removed from the `.text` segment. In that case, the `ldr` instruction would not work because x then would be out of the range of the pc-relative addressing used by the `ldr` instruction.

One solution to this problem is to make the entire program a `.data` segment (i.e., change `.text` to `.data`, and remove the second `.data` directive). If, however, we want to have both a `.text` segment and a `.data` segment, we can modify the program to get the program in Fig. 11.13. For the `.word` directive on line 9 in Fig. 11.13,

```
 9  ax:         .word x              @ x is a symbolic address
```

the assembler inserts into the machine language program the address of x. This makes sense: On the right of this `.word` directive is the label x. A label is a symbolic address. So, the assembler inserts the actual address of x into the machine language program at that location. When the executable form of this program is loaded into memory, the location corresponding to line 9 will have the full 32-bit address of x.

```
1                                       @ ap6.s
2               .text                   @ start of read only segment
3               .global _start
4  _start:
5               ldr r0, ax              @ load address of x
6               ldr r0, [r0]            @ load r0 from address in r0
7               mov r7, #1
8               svc 0
9  ax:          .word x                 @ label x is a symbolic address
10
11              .data                   @ start of read/write segment
12 x:           .word 67                @ the variable x
```

Figure 11.13

Thus, the first `ldr` instruction,

```
5               ldr r0, ax              @ load address of x
```

loads `r0` with the 32-bit address of `x`. In the second `ldr` instruction,

```
6               ldr r0, [r0]            @ load r0 from x
```

the square brackets around `r0` indicate that the load should be from the memory location whose address is in `r0`. Because `r0` has the address of `x` as a result of the first `ldr` instruction, the second `ldr` instruction loads `x` (i.e., it loads 67) into `r0`, overlaying the address that is there. The first `ldr` instruction works because `ax` is within the range of the `pc`-relative addressing used by that instruction. The second `ldr` also works because `r0` has the complete 32-bit address of `x`. So, no matter where `x` is in memory, `[r0]` provides its address.

A shorthand way of writing the program in Fig. 11.13 is given in Fig. 11.14.

```
1                                       @ ap7.s
2               .text                   @ read only segment
3               .global _start
4  _start:
5               ldr r0, =x              @ load address of x
6               ldr r0, [r0]            @ load r0 from x
7               mov r7, #1
8               svc 0
9                                       @ literal pool is here
10
11              .data                   @ read/write segment
12 x:           .word 67                @ the variable x
```

Figure 11.14

Note that in the version in Fig. 11.14, the first `ldr` is now written as

```
5           ldr r0, =x          @ load address of x
```

and the first `.word` directive in the original version (on line 9) has been eliminated. The "=x" operand causes the assembler to create a word at the bottom of the `.text` segment that contains the address of x. Moreover, the `ldr` instruction uses pc-relative addressing to access that word. That is, the assembler places in the `ldr` instruction an offset so that it accesses the word at the bottom of the `.text` segment that has the address of x. Thus, the machine code you get is the *same* as the machine code for the program in Fig. 11.13. With this approach, however, you do not have to bother including the `.word` directive at the bottom of the `.text` segment. The assembler puts it there for you automatically. The area at the end of the `.text` segment where the assembler automatically creates words is called the *literal pool*.

Linking Separately Assembled Modules

Consider the two files in Fig. 11.15. The two files, `m1.s` and `m2.s`, together make up one program.

```
                m1.s
         .global _start
_start:
         bl   f
         mov  r7, #1
         svc  0
```

```
                m2.s
         .global f
x:       .word 7
f:       ldr r0, x
         mov pc, lr
```

Figure 11.15

To create an executable program, we have to assemble each file (*note*: the `rpi` program does not support linking). We do this with

```
as m1.s -o m1.o
as m2.s -o m2.o
```

We get two object files `m1.o` and `m2.o`. To get an executable program, we have to link these two object files. We do this with

```
ld m2.o m1.o -o m
```

This command links `m2.o` and `m1.o` in that order and creates the executable file m (see Fig. 11.16). Thus, in the executable file, the code corresponding to `m2.o` precedes the code corresponding to `m1.o`. It would also be legal to link the modules in `m1.o, m2.o` order.

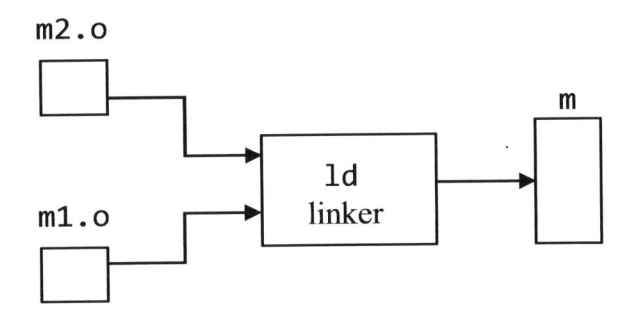

Figure 11.16

When the assembler is assembling `m1.s`, it does *not* know where the label `f` is (because it is in a separate file). Thus, it only partially assembles the `bl` instruction in `m1.s`. One of the jobs of the linker is to fix this `bl` instruction so that when it is executed it branches to the location corresponding to `f`. To do this fix-up, the linker needs to know where `f` is. But how does the linker know where `f` is? The machine code in `m2.o` does not have any labels. But in fact its header has the label `f`. It has this label because of the `.global` directive in `m2.s`. This directive tells the assembler to insert into the header of the `m2.o` object module the label `f` along with the location to which it corresponds (see Fig. 11.17). The linker at link time uses this information to determine where `f` is so that it can make the necessary adjustment to the `bl` instruction in the code for `m1.o`.

The part of an object and executable module that holds label information is called the header (the portions above the dotted lines in Fig. 11.17).

Object and Executable File Format (simplified)

global labels along with locations they correspond to are in the headers

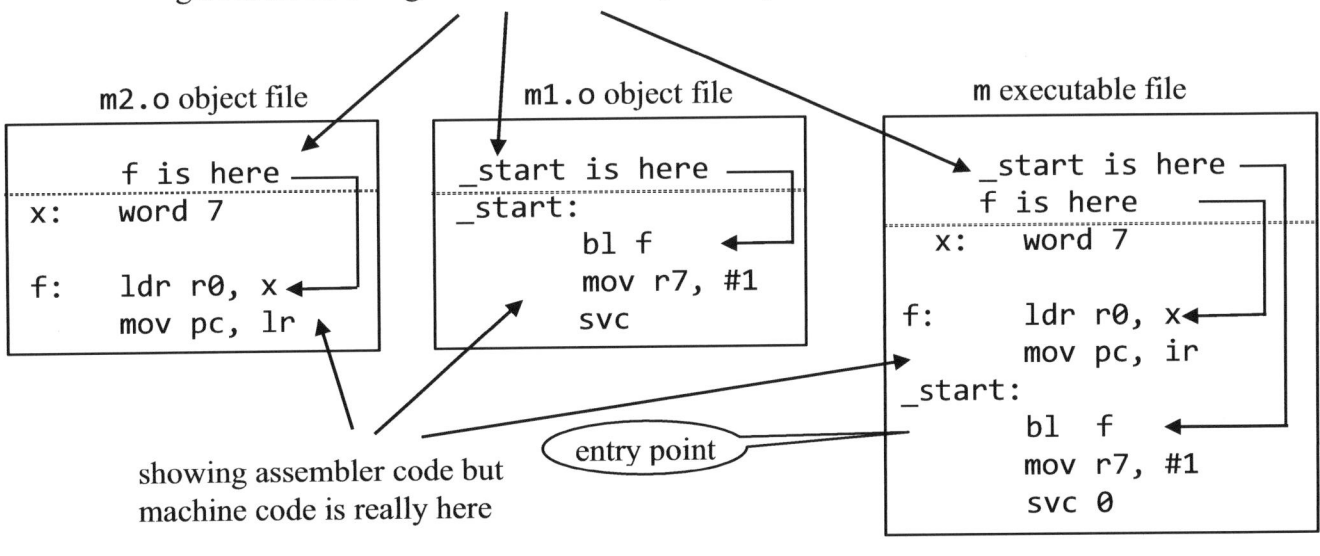

```
m2.o object file              m1.o object file              m executable file

      f is here                  _start is here               _start is here
x:    word 7                   _start:                          f is here
                                   bl f                   x:    word 7
f:    ldr r0, x                    mov r7, #1
      mov pc, lr                   svc                    f:    ldr r0, x
                                                                mov pc, lr
                                                          _start:
                                                                bl f
      showing assembler code but      entry point               mov r7, #1
      machine code is really here                               svc 0
```

Fig. 11.17

In a Raspbian system (the principal operating system for the Raspberry Pi), header information appears both at the beginning and at the end of an object module. The specific format used for both object and executable files is called the *Executable and Linkable Format* (ELF). ELF is somewhat complicated so our description here of its structure and its use by the linker and the operating system is somewhat simplified.

The linker includes the header information it gets from the object modules it links in the header of the executable file it creates. Thus, the executable file m that results from the linking of m2.o and m1.o has a header that shows the locations in the executable file corresponding to the labels _start and f (see the m executable file in Fig. 11.17).

Problems

1. *Note*: A solution to this problem is in the file p1101model.s. Write and run an assembly language program that adds 1, 2, and 3, and leaves the sum in r0. Use add instructions that specify three registers such as

    ```
    add r0, r1, r2      @ add r1 and r2, put sum in r0
    ```

2. Write and run an assembly language program that consists of three functions: _start that loads r0 with 1, f that adds 1 to r0, and g that adds 2 to r0 and terminates the program. _start should call f, and f should call g.

3. Using .word directives, create a list that contains 22, 5, 2, 7, and 1. Your program should add the numbers in this list, and leave the sum in r0. Make your entire program a .data segment.

4. *Note*: A solution to this problem is in the file p1104model.s. Same as problem 3 but use a .text segment for the instructions and a .data segment for the list of numbers. Use the approach in Fig. 11.13.

5. Same as problem 4 except use the approach in Fig. 11.14.

6. The .space directive reserves the specified number of bytes. For example, the .space directive in the following sequence inserts 1000 bytes between the ldr instruction and x:

    ```
            ldr x
            .space 1000
    x:      .word   2
    ```

    If the ldr instruction works here, that means the range of the ldr instruction in the forward direction is at least 1000 bytes. Use the space directive in this way to experimentally determine the range of pc-relative addressing in both the forward and backward directions.

7. What is the default, if any, if neither the .text nor the .data directive is used? Justify your answer.

8. Assemble and link the m1.s and m2.s modules as we did in this chapter. Examine the object and executable files with a hex editor. Try to find the header information. *Note*: Linking is not supported by the rpi program.

9. Why does the following program fail:

```
                            @ p1109.s
            .text
            .global _start
_start:
            ldr  r0,  =a        @ get address of a
            ldr  r0,  [r0]      @ load a
            mov  r7,  #1        @ terminate program
            svc  0
            .space  20000       @ reserve space for 20,000 bytes
            .data
a:          .word   17
```

10. If you have a Raspberry Pi, assemble the program in Fig. 11.6 without the .global directive. Link and run. What happens? If you do not have a Raspberry Pi, execute the program in Fig.11.6 without the global directive using the rpi interpreter. What happens?

11. Move one line in the program in problem 9 so the program does not fail.

12. What happens to the instructions that are already in the pipeline when a branch occurs?

13. What is the advantage of pc-relative addressing?

14. One of the characteristics of the little endian approach is that is makes it difficult to read numbers in a memory display. Why?

15. How much can a pipeline speed up the execution rate of instructions? Assume a pipeline with three stages each requiring x units of time. Why is the optimal speed-up generally not attained with such a pipeline?

16. Suppose two programs are identical except in one the variable x appears in a .global directive and in the other x does not. How do the corresponding executable files differ?

12 Calling C Functions from Assembler Code

Introduction

The C standard library (also known as `libc`) contains many useful functions, such as `printf` (formatted output to the standard output device), `scanf` (formatted input from the standard input device), `strcpy` (string copy), `strcat` (string concatenation), and `malloc` (memory allocation). It would be difficult and time consuming to write these functions in assembly language. But we do not have to. We can simply call any C library function we need from our assembly language program. Then at link time, the linker combines the object modules for these C library functions with the object file for our assembly language program.

What exactly is the C standard library? It is a file that contains the object module (i.e., the code in machine language form) of every standard library function (see Fig. 12.1).

C Standard Library (`libc`)

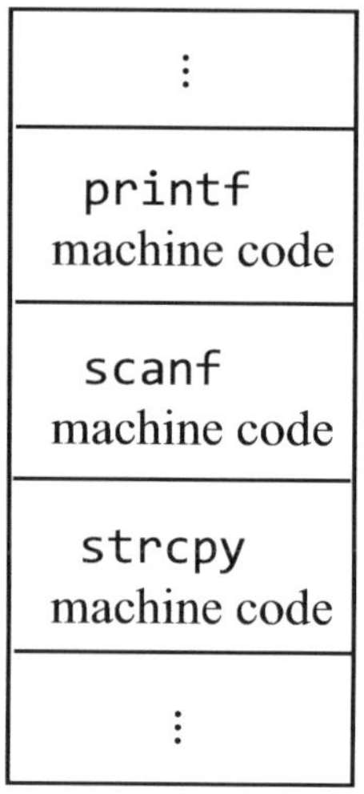

```
⋮
printf
machine code
─────────────
scanf
machine code
─────────────
strcpy
machine code
⋮
```

Figure 12.1

Converting to and from Binary

Everything in computer memory is in binary. For example, the string `'A12'` is stored in memory as a sequence of three binary codes. The code for the character `'A'` is 01000001, the code for the character `'1'` is 00110001, and the code for the character `'2'` is 00110010. Thus, the string `'A12'` is stored in memory as

    01000001 00110001 00110010

The code for each character in `'A12'` is an 8-bit number. The 8-bit code that is used on most computers to represent the characters available on a standard keyboard is the *American Standard Code for Information Interchange* (ASCII). Incidentally, ASCII is now part of an extended coding system called

Unicode that has an encoding for every character in every language in the world.

It is important to understand that the string '12' and the number 12 are represented quite differently inside the computer. The string '12' is represented with the ASCII code for '1' followed by the ASCII code for '2':

00110001 00110010

In contrast, the number 12 is represented by the 32-bit binary number whose value is 12 in decimal:

00000000000000000000000000001100

Suppose the value of a variable x is 12. Thus, the value of x is the 32-bit number shown above. To display this number in decimal on the display screen, it must first be converted to a sequence of ASCII codes that represents its value in decimal. Specifically, the 32-bit binary representation of the value of x has to be converted to the ASCII codes 00110001 and 00110010 for '1' and '2', respectively. These codes then have to be sent to the display monitor. We have to perform the reverse conversion when reading a decimal number from the keyboard into a variable x. For example, suppose on the keyboard you enter the number 12 (i.e., you hit the 1-key, the 2-key, and then the Enter key). This number goes into memory as a sequence of ASCII codes. These codes have to be converted to the 32-bit binary number shown above. The resulting 32-bit number is then stored in the variable x.

Structure of a C program in Executable Form

So far, we have used the svc instruction to terminate our assembly language programs. When an svc instruction is executed, the number in r7 indicates what the operating system should do in response to the svc. If 1 is in r7, the operating system terminates the program. This svc mechanism is referred to as a *syscall* (i.e., system call). There is a large selection of system calls available. Syscall 1 (i.e., executing svc when r7 contains 1) terminates a program. Syscall 5 opens a file. Syscall 79 sets the time of day. There are almost 200 different syscalls. Unfortunately, none of them perform the data conversions that we described above (binary to ASCII decimal and ASCII decimal to binary). How then do we perform these data conversions in an assembly language program? One approach is to write functions in assembly language that perform them and include these functions in our programs. But a much easier approach is to call the functions in the C library that will do the conversions for us.

Consider the C program in Fig. 12.2.

```
1 // display.c
2 #include <stdio.h>
3 int x = 1;
4 int main(void)
5 {
6     printf("x = %d\n", x);
7     return 0;        // return 0 return code
8 }
```

Figure 12.2

When the `printf` function is called, it displays the first argument, `"x = %d\n"`, which is always a string. However, before it does this, it replaces the *conversion code*, `%d`, with the value, converted to ASCII decimal, of the second argument. Thus, we see on the screen

```
x = 1
```

`%d` is called a conversion code because it specifies a particular conversion (the `d` in `%d` indicates conversion to decimal).

`printf` displays its first argument after replacing its conversion codes. Thus, if we use

```
printf("%d\n", x)
```

instead of

```
printf("x = %d\n", x)
```

then the value of `x` is displayed without the `"x = "` prefix. If we also omit `\n` in the first argument, then the cursor on the monitor does not move to the beginning of the next line after displaying the value of `x`.

If you have studied the C programming language, you probably have learned that the `main` function gets control first. This assertion is not quite correct. To execute a C program, it has to be translated to machine code. Then this machine code has to be linked. The link step combines the machine code produced by the compiler with an object module called *start-up code*, in addition to the object module of any function in the C standard library that the program calls.

The `gcc` compiler not only will compile a C program to produce an object file, but also will link the object file to produce an executable program. For example, suppose the C program in Fig. 12.2 is in a file `display.c`. To compile and link `display.c`, enter

```
gcc display.c -o display
```

`gcc` will then output the executable program to the `display` file. Fig. 12.3 shows the structure of the executable program in `display`.

display

| header |
| start-up code |
| machine code for `main` |
| machine code for `printf` |

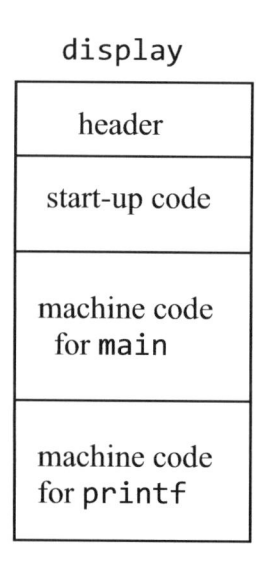

Figure 12.3

When `display` is invoked, the operating system gives control to start-up code. Start-up code performs some initial "housekeeping", then calls `main`. When `main` finishes, it returns to start-up code. Start-up code then performs some final housekeeping and returns to the operating system. Because `main` does not directly return to the operating system, but to start-up code, it does not return to its caller with an `svc` instruction. Instead, it simply branches back to start-up code by putting the return address in the `pc` register The `push {lr}` instruction at the start of `main` (see Fig. 12.4) pushes the return address (which is in `lr`) onto the stack. The `pop {pc}` instruction at the end of `main` pops the return address off the stack into the `pc` register, causing a branch back to start-up code.

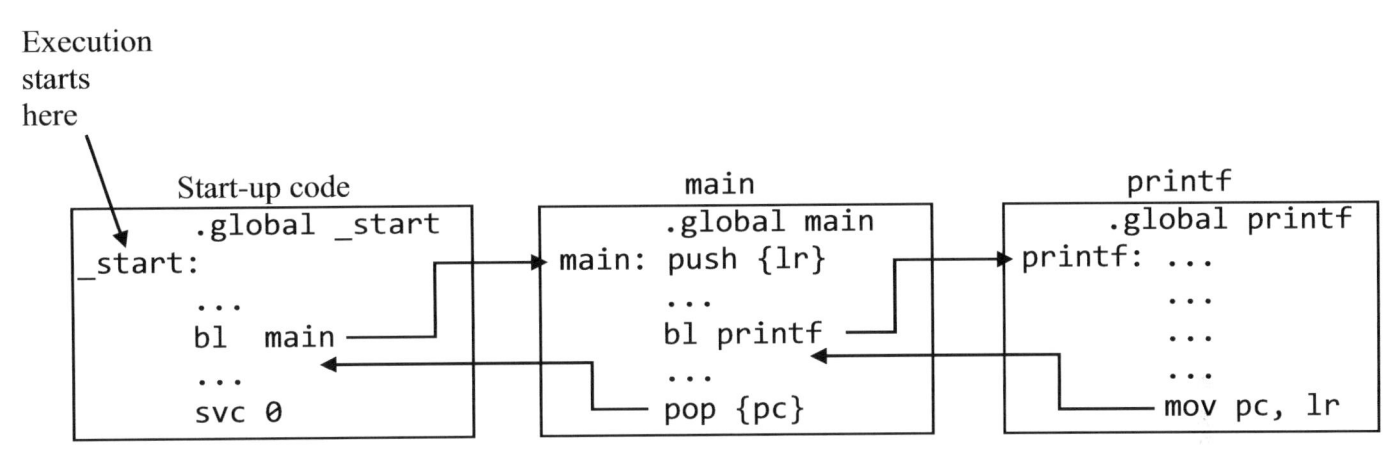

Execution starts here

```
        Start-up code                          main                            printf
        .global _start                    .global main                     .global printf
_start:                            main:  push {lr}                printf: ...
        ...                               ...                              ...
        bl   main                         bl printf                        ...
        ...                               ...                              ...
        svc  0                            pop {pc}                         mov pc, lr
```

Showing assembler code but machine code really is in these modules.

Figure 12.4

Start-up code must be part of any program that calls a C library function. Thus, if an assembly language program calls any C library function, *it must be set up so that it can be linked with start-up code*. In particular, it must have a `main` function (because start-up code calls `main`), and the label `main` must be global. It should NOT have a `_start` label (start-up code is the module that gets control from the operating system so the `_start` label is in start-up code). Moreover, when `main` finishes, it should return to its caller—start-up code—not to the operating system. Thus, it does not use an `svc` instruction. Instead, it returns to start-up code by putting the return address in the `pc` register.

To execute an assembly language program that calls a C library function, it must first be assembled, then linked with start-up code and any C library functions it calls.

Calling printf from an Assembly Language Program

To call `printf` from an assembly language program, we need to use the following assembler directive to create the first argument—the *format string*—to be passed to `printf`:

```
.fmt0:    .asciz   "x = %d\n"    @ null-terminated ASCII string
```

The `.asciz` directive tells the assembler to insert in the machine code the specified string and terminate it with the *null character* (a byte whose eight bits are all zeros). The null character indicates where the string ends. The string specified by the `.asciz` directive must be enclosed in double—not single—quotes. The label `.fmt0` on the directive is an arbitrarily chosen label.

Another directive similar to `.asciz` is `.ascii`. Like `.asciz`, it inserts a string into the machine code, but it does not terminate it with the null character. For example, the following two directives both insert the string "hello" into the machine code. However, the first string consists of the letters of "hello" followed by the null character. The second string consists only of the letters of "hello".

```
.asciz "hello"     @ null character at the end
.ascii "hello"     @ no null character at the end
```

Any string you pass to a C function must be null terminated. Thus, always use `.asciz`, not `.ascii`, to create the format string passed to `printf`.

Start-up code calls `main` by executing the following instruction:

```
bl   main
```

This instruction causes a branch to `main` (see Fig. 12.4), but it also puts the return address (i.e., the address of the instruction in start-up code that follows the `bl` instruction) into the `lr`. Thus, to branch back to start-up code, `main` puts this return address into the `pc` register. When `main` calls `printf`, it also executes a `bl` instruction:

```
bl   printf
```

This `bl` instruction puts a new return address into `lr` (the address of the instruction that follows this `bl` instruction), overlaying the return address in `lr` from start-up code. Thus, `main` must save `lr` before calling `printf`. Otherwise, it loses the return address it needs to return to start-up code. The easiest way to save `lr` is to push its contents onto the stack using

```
push {lr}          @ save lr
```

Then after the call of `printf`, `main` can restore `lr` with a pop instruction:

```
pop {lr}           @ restore lr
```

`main` can then return to start-up code with

```
mov pc, lr         @ move return address in lr into pc
```

Even simpler, we can replace the `pop` and `mov` sequence above with the single instruction

```
pop {pc}           @ pops top of the stack into pc register
```

This instruction pops the top of the stack (which holds the return address from start-up code as a result of the `push {lr}` instruction) into the `pc` register, causing a branch back to start-up code.

Fig. 12.5 shows the assembly language program that calls `printf` to display the value of x. It passes arguments to `printf` via registers `r0` and `r1`. The first argument passed to `printf` is the format string. But the string itself is not passed—just its address via `r0`. The `ldr` instruction on line 6 loads `r0` with the address of this string:

```
6            ldr r0, =.fmt0          @ get address of string
```

Recall that "`=.fmt0`" in this instruction causes the assembler to insert in the literal pool a word that

contains the address of `.fmt0`. The `ldr` instruction loads this address.
   `r1` is used to pass the second argument (the value of `x`):

```
7           ldr r1, =x              @ get address of x
8           ldr r1, [r1]            @ get value of x
```

If we had to pass a third argument, we would use `r2`. If there is a fourth, we would use `r3`. If there are more than four arguments, the arguments beyond the fourth have to be passed via the stack. The C functions expect arguments to be passed this way. So, we must do precisely that when we call a C function in its standard library. If a C library routine returns a value, it returns it in `r0`.

When `main` finishes, it returns a 0 return code via `r0` (line 11 in Fig. 12.5) to start-up code. Start-up code in turn returns this return code to the operating system. A 0 return return code indicates a successful completion of the program. A non-zero return code indicates a failure of some sort.

```
1                                   @ display.s
2           .global main            @ printf assumed global
3           .text                   @ start of read-only segment
4  main:    push {lr}               @ save lr by pushing onto stack
5
6           ldr r0, =.fmt0          @ get address of string
7           ldr r1, =x              @ get address of x
8           ldr r1, [r1]            @ get value of x
9           bl printf               @ call printf
10
11          mov r0, #0              @ 0 return code
12          pop {pc}                @ pop saved lr into pc
13          .data                   @ start of read/write segment
14 .fmt0:   .asciz "x = %d\n"       @ null-terminated ASCII string
15 x:       .word 27                @ value to be displayed
```

Figure 12.5

On return from a C library function, registers `r4` through `r12` are guaranteed to have the same values they had before the call. Registers `r0` through `r3` may have (and usually will have) altered values. So be sure to *never assume* that these four registers are unaltered by a C library function call.

To assemble and link the program in Fig. 12.5 (it is in the file `display.s`), enter

   `gcc display.s -o display`

`gcc` is not only a C compiler—it is also an assembler and a linker. Moreover, it has access to the C standard library of functions. To run the executable program, enter

   `display`   (or `./display`)

Alternatively, we can use `rpi`, the Raspberry Pi Assembly Language Interpreter (included in the software package for this book). See `rpi.txt` for instructions on setting up and using `rpi`. To execute the assembly language program in `display.s` on a Windows system using `rpi`, enter

```
rpi display.s
```

The `rpi` program interprets the assembly code in `display.s` along with the assembly code for start-up code, so an assembly step is not required. The advantage of using the `rpi` program is that a Raspberry Pi computer is not needed.

Start-up code calls `main`. So the assembly language program must have a label `main`. The linker needs to know the location of the label `main` in the `main` function. That is why `main` must be declared a global in the `main` function with the `.global` directive. Suppose `main` were not declared global in the `main` function. Then the linking of start-up code and the `main` function would fail. The linker would not know the location to which start-up code should branch. Thus, it could not correctly adjust the `bl` instruction in start-up code that is supposed to branch to `main`.

Be sure not to make the mistake of assembling and linking the `display.s` program in Fig. 12.5 using the `as` assembler and the `ld` linker:

```
as display.s -o display.o      (works okay)
ld display.o -o display        (warning and error message)
```

The assembly of `display.s` works. But the link step fails. It generates a warning message and an error message. The warning message,

```
warning: cannot find entry symbol _start
```

indicates that the linker expects the program to have a `_start` label. But, in fact, it should *not* have a `_start` label because it is supposed to be linked with start-up code. The `_start` label is in start-up code. The linker also generates an error message:

```
undefined reference to 'printf'
```

which indicates that the linker could not find and therefore could not link the `printf` module with the `display.o` module. Unlike `gcc`, the linker does not have automatic access to the C standard library, which contains all the C library functions, including `printf`. *Rule*: Use `gcc` or the `rpi` program for assembly language programs that call C library functions.

Calling scanf from an Assembly Language Program

The C program in Fig. 12.6 reads in a decimal number from the keyboard, converts it to binary, and puts it in the variable `x`. The `scanf` function performs keyboard input. The first argument in the call of `scanf` tells it how to treat the number entered on the keyboard. `"%d"` tells `scanf` to treat the number entered as a decimal number. The second argument is the address of the location where the binary form of the number should be stored. The "&" in `&x` means "the address of". Thus, `&x` is the address of `x`. We have to pass `scanf` an address. Otherwise, it would not know where to put the value it is reading from the keyboard.

```
1 // keyin.c
2 #include <stdio.h>
3 int x;
4 int main(void)
5 {
6     scanf("%d", &x);        // read int from keyboard into x
7     printf("x = %d\n", x);  // display value of x
8     return 0;
9 }
```

Figure 12.6

The assembly language program corresponding to the C program in Fig. 12.6 is in Fig. 12.7. Note that in Fig. 12.7 for the call of `scanf`, we load `r1` with the *address* of x (line 7), but for the call of `printf`, we load `r1` with the *value* of x (lines 11 and 12).

```
1                                   @ keyin.s
2           .global main             @ printf scanf assumed global
3           .text                    @ start of read-only segment
4  main:    push {lr}                @ save lr by pushing onto stack
5
6           ldr r0, =.fmt0           @ get address of string
7           ldr r1, =x               @ get address of x
8           bl scanf                 @ call scanf
9
10          ldr r0, =.fmt1           @ get address of string
11          ldr r1, =x               @ get address of x
12          ldr r1, [r1]             @ get value of x
13          bl printf                @ call printf
14
15          mov r0, #0               @ 0 return code
16          pop {pc}                 @ return address popped into pc
17          .data                    @ start of read/write segment
18 .fmt0:   .asciz "%d"              @ null-terminated ASCII string
19 .fmt1:   .asciz "x = %d\n"        @ null-terminated ASCII string
20 x:       .word 0
```

Figure 12.7

Problems

1. *Note*: A solution to this problem is in the file `p1201model.s`. Write an assembly language program that reads in three integers from the keyboard, adds them, and displays their sum prefixed with the label "sum = ". Your program should call `scanf` three times, once for each integer.

2. Copy `display.s` in Fig. 12.5 to `p1202.s`. Replace the `.asciz` directive in `p1202.s` with an `.ascii` directive. Run the program. What happens?

3. The file `p1203.s` is identical to `display.c` but with the `.global` directive commented out. Assemble and link with

    gcc p1203.s -o p1203

   or execute with the `rpi` program. What happens?

4. The following sequence of instructions forms a loop that executes n times, where n is a variable that contains a positive integer:

    ```
            ldr  r10, =n
            ldr  r10, [r10]      @ r10 is the loop counter
            mov  r11, #1
    loopstart:
            loop body
            subs r10, r10, r11   @ sub r11 from r10, set cond code
            bne  loopstart       @ branch if cond code shows r10 != 0
    ```

   Write an assembly language program that displays your name 10 times.

5. Write an assembly language program that prompts for a positive count, reads in the count, and then displays your name count number of times. Use a loop (see problem 4).

6. Write an assembly language program that reads a positive integer into the variable n and then displays the sum of the integers from 1 to n. Use a loop (see problem 4).

7. Write an assembly language program that reads a positive integer into the variable n and then displays the sum of the squares of 1 to n. Use a loop (see problem 4).

8. Write an assembly language program that reads a positive integer into the variable n and then sums and displays the sum of the first n positive odd integers. Use a loop (see problem 4).

9. Same as problem 5 but use a syscall 4 in place of the call to `printf`. To execute a syscall 4, execute an `svc 0` instruction when r7 contains 4, r0 contains 1 (1 indicates the output device is the standard output device), r1 contains the address of the string, and r2 contains the number of characters to display.

10. Read in a string from the keyboard using a syscall 3. Then display the string 10 times (see problem 4). Use a syscall 4 to display the string. See problem 9 for the required setup for a syscall 4. For a syscall 3, execute an `svc 0` instruction when r7 contains 3, r0 contains 0 (0 indicates the input device is the standard input device), r1 contains the address of the input buffer, and r2 contains the number of characters to read.

13 Constructing a Compiler

Introduction

In this chapter, we construct a compiler whose target language is the Raspberry Pi assembly language. Our objective is to implement the simplest possible compiler that supports the source language without any regard for the efficiency of the assembler code generated. Once we have accomplished that, we can then address the issue of target code efficiency. The source language is the same as the source language for our `p1.py` parser in chapter 7 (see Fig. 7.1 for a source program and Fig. 7.3 for its grammar).

Our compiler will take advantage of the C library functions. Thus, the code it generates is structured to be linked with start-up code. In particular, the code will have a label `main` declared global, and it will return to its caller (startup-code) with a `pop {pc}` instruction rather than with an `svc` instruction.

Using Both .text and .data Segments

The assembly language programs that our compiler generates consists of two segments: a `.text` segment for the instructions, and a `.data` segment for the variables. Thus, our compiler has to generate two instructions to load from or store to a variable in memory. For example, to load `x` into `r0` requires an `ldr` instruction to get the address of `x` from the literal pool in the `.text` segment and then a second `ldr` instruction to get the value of `x` from the `.data` segment:

```
ldr r0, =x      @ get address of x from the literal pool
ldr r0, [r0]    @ load x using the address of x in r0
```

If, on the other hand, our compiler generated an assembly language program as a single `.data` segment, then only one instruction would be needed to load from or store to a variable. For example, `r0` could be loaded from `x` with just

```
ldr r0, x
```

But then `x` would have to be within the range of the `pc`-relative addressing used in the `ldr` instruction to access `x`. Because of this limitation, our compiler uses the more general but less efficient two-instruction approach.

Minimizing Compiler Complexity

Our compiler keeps all variables in memory rather than in registers. Thus, accessing and modifying them requires load and store instructions. Our compiler also generates code that keeps intermediate values in temporary variables. A *temporary variable* is a location in memory used to temporarily hold the value of an expression or a subpart of an expression. Labels on temporary variables are taken from the sequence `.t0`, `.t1`, `.t2`, and so on. This approach produces inefficient code. But it substantially reduces the complexity of the compiler. For example, the assembler code for

```
a = x + y
```

computes the value of x + y and saves the sum in a temporary variable .t0. To complete the assignment, it loads the value in .t0 into a register and stores it in a. Fig. 13.1 show the assembler code.

```
1       ldr r0, =x          @ get address of x         ⎫
2       ldr r0, [r0]        @ get value of x           ⎪
3       ldr r1, =y          @ get address of y         ⎪  Code for
4       ldr r1, [r1]        @ get value of y           ⎬  x + y
5       add r0, r0, r1      @ add x and y              ⎪
6       ldr r1, =.t0        @ get address of .t0       ⎪
7       str r0, [r1]        @ store sum of x and y in .t0 ⎭

8       ldr r0, =.t0        @ get address of .t0       ⎫
9       ldr r0, [r0]        @ get value of .t0         ⎪  Code for
10      ldr r1, =a          @ get address of a         ⎬  a =
11      str r0, [r1]        @ store .t0 in a           ⎭
```

Figure 13.1

To load the value of a variable from memory into a register requires a two-instruction sequence. First, the address of the variable has to be loaded into a register. Then, using this address, the value of the variable is loaded into a register. For example, the ldr instruction on line 1 in Fig. 13.1 loads r0 with the address of the variable x. Then the ldr instruction on line 2 loads r0 with the value at the address in r0.

Storing the contents of a register into memory also requires a two-instruction sequence. For example, the ldr instruction on line 10 in Fig. 13.1 loads the address of a into r1. Then the str instruction on line 11 stores the contents of r0 at the address in r1. Thus, it stores the contents of r0 in a.

The add instruction on line 5 in Fig. 13.1 computes the sum of x and y. The two-instruction sequence on lines 6 and 7 then stores this sum (which is in r0) in a temporary variable .t0, which completes the evaluation of x + y. The two-instruction sequence on lines 8 and 9 loads the value of .t0 (which contains the sum) into r0. The two-instruction sequence on lines 10 and 11 then stores the sum, which is in r0, in a.

There is a glaring inefficiency in the code in Fig. 13.1. Lines 6 to 9 are unnecessary. After the add operation on line 5, r0 holds the sum. Thus, lines 10 and 11 (that store the sum in r0 into a) can be executed immediately after line 5. However, for our compiler to generate this more efficient code, it would have to be more complex. Remember, for our first compiler our objective is to implement the simplest possible compiler that supports the source language without any regard for the efficiency of the assembler code generated.

To illustrate the complexity of producing efficient code, consider the following four assignment statements (see problems 9 and 10):

```
1. a = x + y        # need to load left and right terms
2. a = x*y + z      # need to load only right term (z)
3. a = x + y*z      # need to load only left term (x)
4. a = w*x + y*z    # no loads needed
```

In the first assignment statement, the compiler has to generate code to load *both* x and y before it generates the `add` instruction. But in the second assignment statement, it only needs to generate code to load z. The code that computes the left term (x*y) leaves the product in a register. Thus, only an instruction to load z is needed (in addition to the code that performs the multiplication) before the `add` instruction. Similarly, in the third assignment statement, only a load of x is needed. Finally, in the last assignment statement, no loads are needed. The two multiplication operations leave their products in registers. Thus, the compiler in this case can immediately generate the `add` instruction. For the compiler to detect and correctly handle all these cases would, of course, substantially increase its complexity.

A program with the code shown in Fig. 13.1 will have `.word` directives for all the variables—not only for the source program variables, but also for the temporary variables:

```
w:          .word 0
x:          .word 0
y:          .word 0
.t0:        .word 0
```

Our compiler starts all the labels it generates with a period. It is illegal for the names of variables in the source program to have any periods. Thus, this convention ensures that a compiler-generated label never matches (and therefore conflicts with) the name of a variable in the source program.

The code our compile produces is grossly inefficient. But this shortcoming can be fixed by incorporating an optimizer in the compiler. The basic goal of an optimizer is to keep variables in registers. Then the overhead of loads and stores is largely eliminated. The Raspberry Pi has a large number of general-purpose registers, so this approach—using registers for variables—can dramatically improve the efficiency of the code generated.

Structure of the Compiler

The front end of our compiler is the `p1.py` parser from problem 1 in chapter 7. In our hybrid interpreter, the instructions that generate the bytecode are embedded in the parser. However, in our compiler, the parser and the code generator are separate. To make our compiler code more readable, let's start the names of the functions in the code generator with "`cg_`".

Let's review the `expr()` function in Fig. 13.2 from the `p1.py` parser.

```
1  def expr():
2      term()
3      while token.category == PLUS:
4          advance()
5          term()
```

Figure 13.2

Suppose it parses the expression x + y + z. Then the first call of `term()` on line 2 parses x, and the second call on line 5 parses y. After parsing y, the compiler should generate code to load x, add y, and store the result in a temporary variable (the next one available in the sequence `.t0`, `.t1`, `.t2`, ...). To generate this code, the `expr()` function has to know what the left and right terms are. The best way to provide this information to `expr()` is via the return mechanism: `term()` can simply return to `expr()` the symbol table index that represents the term it has parsed. Thus, when `term()` parses x, it returns the index of x in the symbol table. Similarly, when the second call of term() parses y, term() returns the index of y in the symbol table. Having these two indices, expr() can then generate the code to load x, add y, and store the result. Fig. 13.3 shows expr() modified to generate the load, add, and store instructions.

```
1  def expr():
2      leftindex   = term()              # get index of left term
3      while token.category == PLUS:
4          advance()
5          rightindex = term()           # get index of right term
6          leftindex  = cg_add(leftindex, rightindex)
7      return leftindex
```

Figure 13.3

After the two calls of term(), expr() has in leftindex and rightindex the indices of the two terms. Thus, for the expression x + y + z, leftindex is the index of x, and rightindex is the index of y. expr() then calls the code generator function cg_add(), passing it leftindex and rightindex. cg_add() generates the appropriate load-add-store sequence, returning the index of the temporary variable used in the store instruction, which is then assigned to leftindex. The third call of term() (on line 5 in Fig. 13.3) which parses z returns the index of z, which is assigned to rightindex. When cg_add() is called a second time, leftindex is the index of the temporary variable, and rightindex is the index of z. Thus, this call of cg_add() generates code to load from the temporary variable, add z, and store the result in the next temporary variable. Corresponding to x + y + z, we get the code in Fig. 13.4.

```
1              @ from first call of cg_add
2              ldr r0, =x           @ get address of x
3              ldr r0, [r0]         @ get x
4              ldr r1, =y           @ get address of y
5              ldr r1, [r1]         @ get y
6              add r0, r0, r1       @ add x and y
7              ldr r1, =.t0         @ get address of .t0
8              str r0, [r1]         @ store sum in .t0
9
10             @ from second call of cg_add
11             ldr r0, =.t0         @ get address of .t0
12             ldr r0, [r0]         @ get .t0
13             ldr r1, =z           @ get address of z
14             ldr r1, [r1]         @ get z
15             add r0, r0, r1       @ add .t0 and z
16             ldr r1, =.t1         @ get address of .t1
17             str r0, [r1]         @ store sum in .t1
```

Figure 13.4

When `expr()` finishes, `leftindex` has the index of the item in the symbol table that represents the value of the entire expression. On line 7 in Fig. 13.3, it returns this index to its caller.

The code for `cg_add()` is given in Fig. 13.5. Lines 2, 4, and 8 of `cg_add()` reference a variable named `symbol`. This variable is one of the two lists that make up the symbol table for the compiler. The symbol table consists of two parallel lists—`symbol` and `value`—initialized in the global section of the compiler with

```
symbol = []
value = []
```

The `symbol` list contains the names of the variables and the names of the constants. The `value` list contains their corresponding values in string form. For example, suppose when `cg_add()` is called, `leftindex` is the index of the variable `x` in the `symbol` list. Then the instruction on line 2 in Fig. 13.5 generates the following instruction:

```
    ldr r0, =x
```

```
1   def cg_add(leftindex, rightindex):
2       outfile.write('            ldr r0, =' + symbol[leftindex] + '\n')
3       outfile.write('            ldr r0, [r0]\n')
4       outfile.write('            ldr r1, =' + symbol[rightindex] + '\n')
5       outfile.write('            ldr r1, [r1]\n')
6       outfile.write('            add r0, r0, r1\n')
7       tempindex = cg_gettemp()  # get index of next temp variable
8       outfile.write('            ldr r1, =' + symbol[tempindex] + '\n')
9       outfile.write('            str r0, [r1]\n')
10      return tempindex
```

Figure 13.5

The code for `enter()`, the function that enters a symbol and its corresponding value into the `symbol`/`value` symbol table, is in Fig. 13.6.

```
1   def enter(s, v):
2       if s in symbol:              # is s already in the table?
3           return symbol.index(s)   # return index of s
4       # otherwise, append s and v and then return index
5       index = len(symbol)          # get index of next available slot
6       symbol.append(s)             # append symbol
7       value.append(v)              # append value
8       return index                 # return index
```

Figure 13.6

In our pure interpreter, we use a Python dictionary—not two parallel lists—to implement the symbol table. Why are we using parallel lists in our compiler? It is because our compiler returns and passes variables and constants via their indices into the symbol table. For example, if the first call of term() in Fig. 13.3 parses the variable x, it returns the symbol table index of x. Thus, in our compiler, we need a data structure for the symbol table whose elements are accessible via an integer index. Python dictionaries are accessible via keys—not integer indices. So, we cannot use a dictionary for the symbol table (for additional considerations, see problem 8). Another difference between the symbol table in our pure interpreter and our compiler is the type of the values stored. In our pure interpreter, the values stored in the symbol table are numbers, not strings. But in our compiler the values stored are strings, not numbers. Our pure interpreter performs calculations as it parses. Thus, it needs numbers. Our compiler, on the other hand, outputs assembler instructions, which are strings of text. Thus, it needs values in string form.

The term() function (see Fig. 13.7) returns the index of the entry in the symbol table that represents the value of the term it parses. The modifications to term() that are required are very similar to the modifications we made above to the expr() function, with two exceptions:

1. term() calls cg_mul instead of cg_add().
2. term() initializes the global variable sign to 1 before each call of factor(). We will explain the purpose of the sign variable shortly.

cg_mul() is the code generator function called by term() that generates a load-multiply-store sequence of assembly language instructions. The only difference between cg_add() and cg_mul() is that the former generates an add r0, r0, r1 instruction, and the latter generates a mul r0, r0, r1 instruction. On computers with older architectures, the first and second registers specified in a mul instruction must be different. On the Raspberry Pi, where the first and second registers can be the same, the as assembler nevertheless enforces this restriction (unless the directive .arch armv6 is in the program). But fortunately, the programs we use—gcc and rpi—to assemble and link or execute assembly language programs do not enforce this restriction. So we can safely ignore it—we do not have to include the .arch armv6 directive in the assembly language programs our compilers generate.

```
1  def term():
2      global sign
3      sign = 1          # initialize sign
4      leftindex = factor()
5      while token.category == TIMES:
6          advance()
7          sign = 1       # initialize sign
8          rightindex = factor()
9          leftindex = cg_mul(leftindex, rightindex)
10     return leftindex
```

Figure 13.7

The cg_gettemp() function (see Fig. 13.8) constructs the name of the next temporary variable by concatenating ".t" with the number in tempcount. cg_gettemp() then enters this name along with a value of '0' into the symbol table by calling the enter() function. The enter() function enters the name/value pair it is passed into the symbol table and returns its index to the caller of cg_gettemp(). cg_gettemp() is called by cg_add() and cg_mul().

```
1 def cg_gettemp():
2     global tempcount
3     temp = '.t' + str(tempcount)  # construct name
4     tempcount += 1                # increment seq number
5     return enter(temp, '0')       # return index of temp
```

Figure 13.8

The `factor()` function uses `sign` to keep track of whether there are an even or odd number of unary minuses. When `factor()` parses a factor that starts with one or more unary minuses, `factor()` flips the sign of `sign` for each unary minus it parses (see Fig. 13.9). Because `term()` initializes `sign` to 1 before it calls `factor()`, an even number of unary minuses leaves 1 in `sign`; an odd number of unary minuses leaves -1 in `sign`. Each pair of unary minuses cancel each other out. Thus, if the number of unary minuses is even (in which case the final value of `sign` is 1), they all cancel each other out. If the number is odd (in which case the final value of `sign` is -1), one unary minus remains in effect.

When `factor()` parses a variable name (lines 17 to 22), it enters the name into the symbol table. If `sign` is -1 (which indicates a unary minus is in effect), `factor()` calls `cg_neg()` (see Fig. 13.10), passing it the index of the variable (line 20 in Fig. 13.9). `cg_neg()` generates code that loads the value of the variable, negates the variable's value (as required by the unary minus), stores the result in a temporary variable, and returns the index of the temporary. `factor()` then advances past the variable name and returns an index—the index of the temporary variable (if `sign` is -1) or the index of the variable (if `sign` is 1). `factor()` also calls `cg_neg()` on line 28 if `savesign` is -1 (which indicates an odd number of unary minuses preceded a parenthesized expression, whose value, therefore, needs to be negated).

```
 1 def factor():
 2     global sign
 3     if token.category == PLUS:
 4         advance()
 5         return factor()
 6     elif token.category == MINUS:
 7         sign = -sign                        # change sign for every unary minus
 8         advance()
 9         return factor()
10     elif token.category == UNSIGNEDINT:
11         if sign == 1:     # is number negative or non-negative?
12             index = enter('.i' + token.lexeme, token.lexeme)
13         else:
14             index = enter('.i_' + token.lexeme, '-' + token.lexeme)
15         advance()
16         return index
17     elif token.category == NAME:
18         index = enter(token.lexeme, '0')
19         if sign == -1:                      # -1 indicate unary minus
20             index = cg_neg(index)           # generate negation code
21         advance()
22         return index
```

```
23        elif token.category == LEFTPAREN:
24            advance()
25            savesign = sign      # must save sign because expr()
26            index = expr()       # calls term() which resets sign to 1
27            if savesign == -1:   # so use the saved value of sign
28                index = cg_neg(index)
29            consume(RIGHTPAREN)
30            return index
31        else:
32            raise RuntimeError('Expecting factor')
```

Figure 13.9

The assembly instruction generated by line 4 in Fig. 13.10

```
neg r0, r0
```

gets the value in the second register specified, negates it, and stores it in the first register. Because both registers specified in the `neg` instruction are `r0`, the `neg` instruction simply negates the value in `r0`.

When `factor()` parses an integer (lines 10 to 16 in Fig. 13.9), it creates a label for the integer and then enters the label and the value of the integer in string form into the symbol table. `factor()` creates labels for integer constants according to the following convention: For a non-negative integer constant, the label consists of ".i" followed by the constant. For example, the label for 5 is `.i5`. For negative integer constants, the label consists of ".i_" followed by the absolute value of the constant. For example, the label for -5 is `.i_5`. This convention allows us to determine the value of an integer constant from just its label—we do not have to search for its `.word` directive to see how it is defined. It also allows the compiler to determine from a label if it corresponds to an integer constant—the compiler simply checks if the label starts with ".i".

If `sign` is 1 on line 11 in Fig. 13.9 (which means the integer constant is non-negative), `factor()` enters the constant's label and its value (which is in `token.lexeme`) into the symbol table with

```
12            index   = enter('.i' + token.lexeme, token.lexeme)
```

If `sign` is not 1 (which means the constant is negative), `factor()` enters the constant's label and value with

```
14            index   = enter('.i_' + token.lexeme, '-' + token.lexeme)
```

Note that for this case the label is prefixed with ".i_" rather than ".i". The value of the constant is its lexeme prefixed with a minus sign. `token.lexeme` is the integer without the preceding unary plusses or minuses, if any. Thus, to represent the value of a negative constant, `factor()` concatenates a minus to `token.lexeme`. For example, suppose the factor is ---7. Then `sign` is -1. So `factor()` enters the label `.i_7` and the value `'-7'` in string form into the symbol table. Then when the `cg_epilog()` function is called at the end of the compile, it outputs the following `.word` directive for the constant:

```
.i_7:       .word -7
```

```
1 def cg_neg(index):
2     outfile.write('          ldr r0, =' + symbol[index] + '\n')
3     outfile.write('          ldr r0, [r0]\n')
4     outfile.write('          neg r0, r0\n')
5     tempindex = cg_gettemp()  # tempindex is index of the temp variable
6     outfile.write('          ldr r1, =' + symbol[tempindex] + '\n')
7     outfile.write('          str r0, [r1]\n')
8     return tempindex
```

Figure 13.10

The assembler code that is generated during parsing needs to be preceded by some "prolog" code and followed by some "epilog" code. Accordingly, the parser() function calls the cg_prolog() and cg_epilog() functions:

```
1 def parser():
2     advance()       # advance to first token
3     cg_prolog()     # generates prolog assembler code
4     program()       # starts the compilation
5     cg_epilog()     # generates epilog assembler code
```

The cg_prolog() function outputs .global, and .text directives, and the push that saves the lr:

```
1 def cg_prolog():
2     outfile.write('          .global main\n')
3     outfile.write('          .text\n')
4     outfile.write('main:\n')
5     outfile.write('          push {lr}\n')
6     outfile.write('\n')
```

The cg_epilog() function outputs the pop instruction that causes a branch back to start-up code, a .data directive, and a .word directive for each variable and constant in the program:

```
1 def cg_epilog():
2     outfile.write('\n')
3     outfile.write('          mov r0, #0\n')
4     outfile.write('          pop {pc}\n')
5     outfile.write('          .data\n')
6     outfile.write('.fmt0:    .asciz "%d\\n"\n')
7
8     size = len(symbol)
9     i = 0
10    while i < size:
11        outfile.write('%-10s' % (symbol[i] + ':') + '.word ' +
12                      value[i] + '\n')
13        i += 1
```

The call of write() in cg_epilog on line 11 uses the conversion code '%-10s'. This conversion code is replaced by the label specified by

> (symbol[i] + ':')

The hyphen in the conversion code specifies left justification, and 10 is the field width. Thus, a label followed by colon occupies 10 positions even if its length is less than 10. As a result, the ".word" directive for each variable starts in the same column (column 11). The assembler does not require this column alignment. But it makes the assembly language program more readable.

assignmentstmt() and printstmt()

assignmentstmt() calls cg_assign(), passing it the symbol table indices that represent the left and right sides of the assignment statement (see line 6):

```
1 def assignmentstmt():
2     leftindex  = enter(token.lexeme, '0')
3     advance()
4     consume(ASSIGNOP)
5     rightindex = expr()
6     cg_assign(leftindex, rightindex)
```

cg_assign() generates the load-store sequence for the assignment statement:

```
1 def cg_assign(leftindex, rightindex):
2     outfile.write('          ldr r0,  =' + symbol[rightindex] + '\n')
3     outfile.write('          ldr r0, [r0]\n')
4     outfile.write('          ldr r1,  =' + symbol[leftindex] + '\n')
5     outfile.write('          str r0, [r1]\n')
```

For example, for

> x = y

it generates

```
          ldr    r0, =y        @ get address of y
          ldr    r0, [r0]      @ get value of y
          ldr    r1, =x        @ get address of x
          str    r0, [r1]      @ store value of y in x
```

printstmt() calls cg_print() passing it the symbol table index that represents the argument in the print statement (see line 5):

```
1 def printstmt():
2     advance()
3     consume(LEFTPAREN)
4     index = expr()
5     cg_print(index)
6     consume(RIGHTPAREN)
```

cg_print() generates the loading of registers required by the C library function printf. cg_print() also generates the bl instruction that calls printf:

```
1 def cg_print(index):
2     outfile.write('        ldr r0, =.fmt0\n')
3     outfile.write('        ldr r1, =' + symbol[index] + '\n')
4     outfile.write('        ldr r1, [r1]\n')
5     outfile.write('        bl printf\n')
```

For example, for

    print(x)

cg_print() generates

```
        ldr r0, =.fmt0      @ get address of format string
        ldr r1, =x          @ get address of x
        ldr r1, [r1]        @ get the value of x into r1
        bl printf           @ call the printf function
```

The reference to .fmt0 in the first ldr instruction above requires the cg_epilog() function to generate

    .fmt0:   .asciz   "%d\n"

The cg_epilog() function does this by executing

    outfile.write('.fmt0:   .asciz "%d\\n"\n')

Commenting the Assembler Code

Each line in the source program should appear as a comment on the assembler code for that source line (see Fig. 13.11). In addition, the assembler code file should start with comments indicating the time and date, your name, the name of the compiler file, the input file name, and the output file name. For example, suppose the source program is

```
a = 1
print(a)
```

Then the corresponding assembler code should look like the listing in Fig. 13.11. To comment your output file in this way requires a simple modification to the program() function. Just before each call of the stmt() function from within the program() function, token.line at that point in the parse has the number of the line of source code about to be parsed. Use this line number to retrieve the corresponding line of source code. Then output that line, prefixing it with "@" so it appears in the output file as a comment. To access a line of source code given its line number, execute in main()

    lines = source.splitlines()

where source is the variable that holds the entire source program. This statement creates a list whose components are the individual lines of source code. Because line numbers start at 1 and indices start at 0, the index for a line of source code in `lines` is one less than its line number. Thus, to access the line of source code whose line number is given by `token.line`, use `lines[token.line - 1]`.

Because our compiler outputs an assembly language file with the source code as comments, there is no real need to have additional output for debugging purposes. For this reason, our compiler, unlike our interpreters, does not have the `trace` variable, which if set to `True` in our interpreters, triggers the output of debugging information.

The `c1shell.py` file provided in the software package for this book is the compiler described in this chapter with the code for the code generator removed. It, however, includes the `main()` function, the tokenizer, the parser, and code to output the time and date, your name, the name of the compiler, the input file name, and the output file name.

Sample Output File

```
@ Mon Feb 12 13:09:00 2018                  YOUR NAME HERE
@ Compiler    = c1.py
@ Input file  = testcomments.in
@ Output file = testcomments.s
@-------------------------------------------- Assembler code

            .global main
            .text
main:
            push {lr}

@ a = 1
            ldr r0,  =.i1
            ldr r0,  [r0]
            ldr r1,  =a
            str r0,  [r1]

@ print(a)
            ldr r0,  =.fmt0
            ldr r1,  =a
            ldr r1,  [r1]
            bl printf

            mov r0, #0
            pop {pc}
            .data
.fmt0:      .asciz "%d\n"
a:          .word 0
.i1:        .word 1
```

Information on compile

prolog code

Source code appears as a comment

Source code appears as a comment

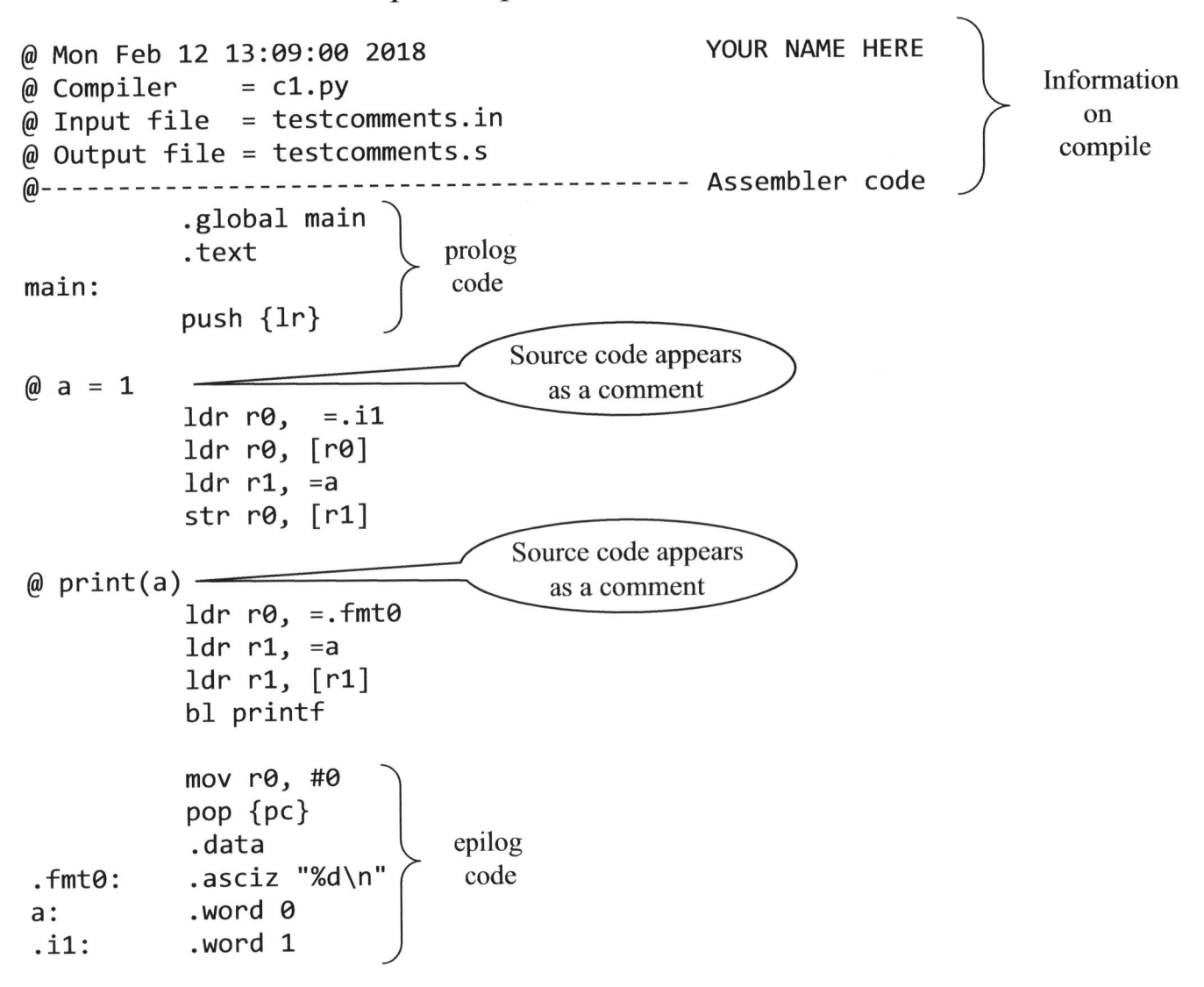

epilog code

Figure 13.11

Problems

1. Copy `c1shell.py` to `c1.py`. Then modify `c1.py` so it compiles as described in this chapter. Test your compiler by entering

       `python c1.py c1.in c1.s`   (produces `c1.s` assembly language file)

   The arguments on this command should be in compiler input file, output file order. The output file (the last argument) should have the extension ".s". Next, use the `rpi` program (see `rpi.txt` for directions on the setup and use of the `rpi` program). Enter

       `rpi c1.s`   (or `./rpi c1.s`)   (executes `c1.s`)

   Alternatively, if you are on a Raspberry Pi, enter

       `gcc c1.s -o c1`   (assembles and links `c1.s`)
       `c1`   (or `./c1`)   (executes `c1`)

2. Does your `c1.py` compiler generate the format string for the `printf` function even if `printf` is never called? If so, modify it so it does not do this.

3. Rewrite by hand the code that your compiler generates for the source program in `c1.in` so that its size is minimal. What is its size relative to the size of the assembler code generated by your compiler?

4. What are the advantages of having instructions and data in separate segments. *Hint*: Consider multiple users on a system running the same program.

5. Copy your `c1.py` compiler from problem 1 to `p1305.py`. Then modify `p1305.py` so that it outputs the assembly language program as a single `.data` segment. Change the code generator functions to take advantage of having both instructions and data in a `.data` segment.

6. Our compiler does not flag the access of a variable whose value is undefined. For example, it does not flag b in the following program:

   `a = b`   `# b has no value`

   How could our compiler detect such errors?

7. Copy your `c1.py` compiler from problem 1 to `p1307.py`. Modify `p1307.py` so that instead of calling `printf`, it calls a function that you write in assembly language. Your function should convert the binary number it is passed to decimal and display it using a syscall. What advantage does this approach have compared to using `printf` in the C standard library?

8. In a compiler, why is it better to pass the symbol table index of a variable rather that the variable itself? *Hint*: Does the name of a variable uniquely specify that variable?

9. Write the most efficient assembler code sequences possible for the following assignment statements (assume the variables initially are all in memory locations, not in registers):

   ```
   a = x + y
   a = x*y + z
   a = x + y*z
   a = w*x + y*z
   ```

   Assume instructions are in a `.text` segment and the variables are in a `.data` segment. How does the code generated by your `c1.py` compiler from problem 1 for these assignment statements compare with the most efficient sequences possible?

10. We discuss compiler optimization techniques in chapter 18. Before you read that chapter, attempt to modify your `c1.py` compiler from problem 1 so that it produces the most efficient sequences possible for the assignment statements in problem 9.

11. Compile the file `p1311a.c` with your `gcc` or `bcc32c` compiler:

    ```
    gcc -S p1311a.c -o p1311a
    ```
    or
    ```
    bcc32c -S p1311a.c
    ```

    Similarly compile `p1311b.c`. The two files are identical except for a sequence of unary minus signs in `p1311a.c` that are not in `p1311b.c`. The unary minus signs all cancel themselves out. Thus, the two programs are equivalent. Because of the `-S` argument, the two commands above output the assembly language equivalents of the input files. Are the two assembly language files the same? Specifically, did the compiler optimize out all the unnecessary unary minuses in `p1311a.c`?

12. Can a temporary variable be used more than once—for example, in one assignment statement and then again in another?

13. Is there an upper limit on the number of temporary variables a program might require?

14. What is the smallest possible assembly language program that can be produced by your `c1.py` compiler?

15. Could unnecessary negations corresponding to unary minuses be eliminated simply by scanning the assembly code generated and eliminating any consecutive pair of negations? Could this technique be used to eliminate other types of inefficiencies? *Hint*: Investigate *peephole optimization*.

14 Constructing a Tokenizer Level 2

Introduction

In this chapter, we upgrade our `t1.py` tokenizer from chapter 6 so it can handle the source program in Fig. 14.1 (also in the file `t2.in`). Incidentally, when the program in Fig. 14.1 is executed, it should display the numbers 1 to 17.

```
1  print(-59 + 20*3)
2  a = 2
3  bb_1 = -(a) + 12
4  print(a*bb_1 + a*3*(-1 + -1 + -1))
5
6  # start of code that tests level 2 features
7  print()                    # print with no args
8  if a <= 2:                 # if, no else
9      if a == 2:             # equal operator
10         if a > 1:          # greater than operator
11             pass           # does nothing
12             print(3)
13 if a != 2:                 # if-else
14     print('err#or')        # this print should be skipped
15 else:                      # else
16     print(4,)              # this print should be executed
17 while a >= 3:              # greater or equal operator
18     print('error')         # this print should be skipped
19 a = ----+--+--5            # multiple unary operators
20 while a < 10:              # while, less than operator
21     print(a)
22     a = +a + .5 + 0.5      # floating-point computation
23 if True:                   # True is a boolean constant
24     pass                   # pass does nothing
25 print('10\n11')            # escape sequence
26 print('1' + '2')           # string concatenation
27 print(-a + 23)             # unary minus operation
28 if a <= 10:                # less than or equal operator
29     print('#14\'\\')       # pound, quote, backslash in string
30 print(15, 16)              # one space between numbers
31 if (None != False):        # None, False, not equal operator
32     print(51/(5 - 2))      # subtraction
```

Figure 14.1

Required Modifications

Most of the features of our new source language require little or no modification of the tokenizer. In the following bulleted list, we place each new feature into one of four categories: no modification required, trivial modification, requiring a little thinking, and requiring serious head scratching:

- No modification required

    subtraction operator

- Trivial modification:

    ```
    pass
    if
    while
    True
    False
    None
    ```
    / (floating-point division)

- Requiring a little thinking

    ```
    ==    (equal)
    !=    (not equal)
    <     (less than)
    <=    (less than or equal)
    >     (greater than)
    >=    (greater than or equal)
    ```
    floating-point constants
    source code comments
    strings delimited by single quotes

- Requiring serious head scratching

    Python indentation

Figure 14.2

Subtraction requires no modification (the original tokenizer already tokenizes the minus sign). The new keywords (`pass`, `if`, `while`, `True`, `False`, and `None`) are handled exactly like the `print` keyword is handled. The code for the one-character tokens is extended so it also handles two-character tokens. Support for the floating-point constants requires only a simple modification of the loop in the tokenizer that processes unsigned integers. Support for comments is easy to add. We simply treat "#" as if it were the newline character. This requires only a minor change to the `getchar()` function. Thus, only the modification to handle Python-type indentation presents us with an interesting challenge.

Adding Support for Two-character Tokens

The dictionary `smalltokens` contains those tokens that are not integers, keywords, or names. Each entry consists of a token lexeme and its category:

```
smalltokens = {'=':ASSIGNOP, '==':EQUAL, '<':LESSTHAN,
               '<=':LESSEQUAL, '>':GREATERTHAN, '>=':GREATEREQUAL,
               '!':ERROR, '!=':NOTEQUAL, '(':LEFTPAREN,
               ')':RIGHTPAREN, '+':PLUS, '-':MINUS, '*':TIMES,
               '\n':NEWLINE, '':EOF, ',':COMMA, ':':COLON, '/':DIV}
```

(Value of "!" is ERROR)

If a token is not an integer, keyword, or name, the tokenizer checks if the current character is in `smalltokens`:

```
1  elif curchar in smalltokens:
2      save = curchar
3      curchar = getchar()   # curchar might be '' (end of source code)
4      twochar = save + curchar         # two chars if curchar != ''
5      if twochar in smalltokens:
6          token.category = smalltokens[twochar]   # get category
7          token.lexeme = twochar                  # get lexeme
8          curchar = getchar()                     # move past end of token
9      else:                                       # one-char token
10         token.category = smalltokens[save]      # get category
11         token.lexeme = save                     # get lexeme
```

If it is, the tokenizer checks if the current character is the start of a two-character token. To do this, it has to get the next character, while saving the current character (see lines 2 and 3 above). It then creates a two-character string, `twochar`, from these two characters (line 4). If `twochar` is in `smalltokens`, the tokenizer gets its category by accessing `smalltokens` (line 6). It also calls `getchar()` again to advance past the two-character token (line 8). If, however, `twochar` is not in `smalltokens`, then the original character in `save` is a one-character token. In that case, the tokenizer uses `save` to access the category of the token (line 10). For this case, the parser is already positioned at the character following the one-character token (because of line 3). Thus, unlike the two-character case, `getchar()` should *not* be called a second time to advance in the source code.

If "!" is the current character and it is not followed by "=", then the code above treats "!" as a one-character token. Thus, lines 9, 10, and 11 are executed. Line 10 gets the value of "!" from `smalltokens` using `save` as the key. Because the value of "!" in `smalltokens` is ERROR, the invalid token, "!", is assigned the ERROR category.

Adding Support for Floating-Point Constants

Support for floating-point constants is added by modifying the loop that handles unsigned integers. Each time `getchar()` is called within the loop that processes digits, test if the character returned is a decimal point, and the category is currently set to UNSIGNEDINT. If so, reset the category to UNSIGNEDFLOAT. Break out of the loop if any non-digit character appears except for the first occurrence of a decimal point.

Adding Support for Comments

Adding support for comments requires a modification of the `getchar()` function. After executing

```
c = source[sourceindex]
sourceindex += 1
```

`getchar()` should check if `c` is `'#'`, and it is not within a string. Note that an occurrence of `'#'` within a string is not the start of a comment. To allow `getchar()` to determine if an occurrence of `'#'` is within a string, `tokenizer()` should set a variable named `instring` to `True` whenever it is processing a string, and to `False` otherwise. Thus, in `getchar()` if `c` is `'#'` and `instring` is `True`, then the `'#'` is not the start of a command. But if `c` is `'#'`, and `instring` is `False`, then the `'#'` is the start of a comment. In that case, `getchar()` should advance in the source code until the variable `c` becomes the newline character at the end of the line. Thus, `'#'` acts like an alias for the newline character if it is not inside a string.

Adding Support for String Data

A string is a sequence of characters not including the newline character that is delimited with single quotes (we are not supporting strings delimited with double quotes). The quote at the start of a string is called the *starting quote*; the quote at the end of the string is called the *terminating quote*. The lexeme corresponding to a string is the string *within* the quotes. In other words, a string token provided to the parser does not include the surrounding quotes.

When the `tokenizer()` function is about to start processing the next token, if the current character is a single quote, then we have the beginning of a string. In that case, the `tokenizer` executes a loop that advances in the source code, building the lexeme with each character it gets from `getchar()`. This process continues until the terminating quote is reached. The code to do this is not as simple as you might think because a string can have embedded escape sequences. For example, the string `'A\'B'`, contains a backslash-quote escape sequence. The backslash that precedes the single quote signals that the quote is an "ordinary" quote, so it is not the quote that signals the end of the string. Thus, to process strings correctly, we have to be able to distinguish ordinary quotes from the terminating quote.

Here is how to handle escape sequences. Within a string, if the current character is the backslash, get the next character. If this character is `'n'`, then insert into the lexeme you are building the newline character (`'\n'`). That is, replace the two-character sequence (backslash-n) with a single newline character. Handle backslash-t (tab) the same way. If the character that follows the backslash is not `'n'` or `'t'`, then discard the backslash and insert only the character that follows the backslash into the lexeme. Thus, if this character is a quote, it is inserted into the lexeme, and processing of the string continues.

Adding Support for Python Indentation

Python uses indentation to specify its code blocks (a *code block* is a group of statements that is treated like a single statement). Each indentation marks the beginning of a new code block. Each *dedentation* (i.e., a change in indentation to the left) marks the end of one or more code blocks. For example, consider the two versions of the same program in Fig. 14.3, one using indentation to specify the code blocks, the other using braces.

           Using indentation   Using braces (illegal in Python)

```
1 if a == 1:
2     print('hello')
3     if b == 2:
4         print('goodbye')
5         if c == 3:
6             print('up')
7 print('down')
8 # end of program
```

```
1  if a == 1:
2  {
3      print('hello')
4      if b == 2:
5      {
6          print('goodbye')
7          if c == 3:
8          {
9              print('up')
10         }
11     }
12 }
13 print('down
```

Figure 14.3

In the indented version, code blocks start on lines 2, 4, and 6. The dedent on line 7 terminates all three code blocks because it starts in a column to the left of the code blocks. In the braces version, three consecutive right braces (on lines 10, 11, and 12) indicate the end of the three code blocks.

In Fig. 14.4, we have a different structure because the dedent on line 7 in the indented version starts in a column that is to the left of the second and third code blocks, but not the first code block. Thus, it terminates only the second and third blocks. In the braces version, the termination of these code blocks is signaled by the two right braces on lines 10 and 11. In the indented version, the end of the program is viewed as a dedent to the extreme left. Thus, it terminates any preceding unterminated code blocks.

So how do we implement Python indentation? The approach we use is to inject brace tokens into the token stream wherever they would have appeared if braces were used instead of indentation to specify the code blocks. For example, if our tokenizer processes the program on the left side of Fig. 14.4, it outputs tokens as if it were the program on the right side (but with line numbers reflecting the indented version).

           Using indentation   Using braces (illegal in Python)

```
1 if a == 1:
2     print('hello')
3     if b == 2:
4         print('goodbye')
5         if c == 3:
6             print('up')
7     print('down')
8 # end of program
```

```
1  if a == 1:
2  {
3      print('hello')
4      if b == 2:
5      {
6          print('goodbye')
7          if c == 3:
8          {
9              print('up')
10         }
11     }
12     print('down')
13 }
```

Figure 14.4

Unfortunately, modifying our tokenizer to handle indentation is not as easy as you would think. Here is the problem. When a dedent occurs, the tokenizer has to know the "indent-to" columns of all the *preceding* indents to know which to terminate. In the indented versions, compare line 7 in Fig. 14.3 with line 7 in 14.4. The former terminates all three code blocks (and, therefore, should cause the output of three right brace tokens), but the latter terminates only two (causing the output of only two right brace tokens).

To handle indentation and dedentation, the tokenizer uses a list named `indentstack` that functions as a stack. `indentstack` is created with

```
indentstack = [1]
```

Thus, initially its only element is 1 (the starting column of the first line of the program). If an indent occurs, say to column 4, then the tokenizer pushes 4 onto `indentstack`. In addition, the tokenizer outputs an `INDENT` token. Each time an indent relative to the preceding line occurs, the tokenizer pushes the "indent-to" column onto the stack and outputs an `INDENT` token. For example, if an indent to 4 is followed by indents to 7 and then to 10, then 1, 4, 7, and 10 would be on `indentstack`, with 10 on the top. In addition, three `INDENT` tokens would be produced. When a dedent occurs, `indentstack` is popped until the top of the stack matches the starting column of the dedented line. For each pop, the tokenizer outputs a `DEDENT` token.

Let's see what happens with the indented program in Fig. 14.4. It has three indents—from 1 to 4, from 4 to 7, and 7 to 10. Thus, when the tokenizer reaches line 6, `indentstack` contains 1, 4, 7, and 10, with 10 on top, and it has outputted three `INDENT` tokens. Next, there is a dedent to column 4 on line 7. So the tokenizer pops values off `indentstack` until the top value is equal to 4. This requires two pops—of 10 and 7. Thus, two `DEDENT` tokens are produced. The stack at this point contains 1 and 4. The program ends on line 8, which is treated as a dedent to column 1 (the tokenizer sets the column number of the `EOF` token to 1). Thus, the tokenizer pops the 4 and outputs one more `DEDENT` token.

What if there are indents to column 1, 4, 7, and 10, and then a dedent to column 5. Then none of the values on the stack equal 5, the dedent-to column. In that case, the tokenizer raises an exception indicating an indentation error.

The code that handles indentation should be inserted into the tokenizer *just before* it appends the variable `token` to `tokenlist`. This location in the tokenizer corresponds to line 123 in Fig. 6.3.

Problems

1. The file `t2.py` contains the tokenizer described in this chapter. Study it carefully. Try it out by entering

   ```
   python t2.py t2.in
   ```

   Convince yourself it works correctly.

2. Does the `t2.py` tokenizer from problem 1 correctly tokenize the following statement:

   ```
   print('good
   bye')
   ```

   Test the tokenizer by entering

   ```
   python t2.py p1402.in
   ```

The tokenizer with `trace` set to `True` will then output a token trace. From the token trace, determine if the tokenizer is correctly tokenizing the program above. How does the Python 3 interpreter respond to this program?

3. Does the `t2.py` tokenizer from problem 1 correctly tokenize the following statement:

   ```
   print('good\
   bye')
   ```

   Test the tokenizer by entering

   ```
   python t2.py p1403.in
   ```

   The tokenizer with `trace` set to True will then output a token trace. From the token trace, determine if the tokenizer is correctly tokenizing the program above. Referring to specific lines of code in `t2.py`, explain how the tokenizer responds to the program above. How does the Python 3 interpreter respond to this program?

4. Where or when should a check be performed on numeric constants to determine if they are within range of their computer representation? In the tokenizer, in the parser, or at run time? Justify your answer.

5. Is there an optimal order in which the tokeninzer should test for the various categories on tokens? If so, what is that order?

6. Where in `t2.py` is the EOF category assigned to to `token.category`?

7. Explain why `getchar()` is called again *after* it returns the null string.

8. How does `t2.py` determine if an indentation or a dedentation occurs?

9. Why is line 205 in `t2.num` necessary?

10. Why is `indentstack` initialized with 1?

11. What are advantages and disadvantages of the indent approach of Python versus the braces approach of C?

12. Why does `getchar()` assign the current character in c to `prechar`?

13. What does `t2.py` do if a string does not have a terminating quote?

14. A name token is required to start with a letter or the underscore character. Could a name token be allowed to start with a digit as long as it contained at least one letter or the underscore character?

15. If you eliminated all spaces other than indentation spaces in a Python program, would it still represent the same program? In other words, is a space ever necessary except for indentation purposes? Are spaces ever necessary in a C program?

15 Constructing a Parser Level 2

Introduction

In chapter 14, we upgraded our tokenizer so that it can handle a substantially richer source language. In this chapter, we similarly upgrade our parser. We start by extending our original grammar (from Fig. 7.3) to get a new grammar (in Fig. 15.1) that defines our extended source language. We then modify our parser to reflect that grammar.

Here is a list of the new language elements that our grammar handles:

- `True`, `False`, and `None`
- floating-point numbers
- strings delimited with single quotes (for example, `'hello'`)
- subtraction
- floating-point division
- relational expressions using ==, !=, <, <=, >, and >=
- `pass` statement
- `if` statement
- `while` statement

Our New Grammar

Fig. 15.1 contains our new grammar. It uses the star, plus, square-bracket, and vertical bar operators, which mean, respectively, zero or more, one or more, zero or one, and "or."

Let's see how our new grammar in Fig. 15.1 differs from our original grammar in Fig. 7.3. We need a new `<stmt>` production that generates a compound statement:

```
<stmt>              → <compoundstmt>
```

A compound statement can be either a `while` statement or an `if` statement:

```
<compoundstmt>      → <whilestmt>
<compoundstmt>      → <ifstmt>
```

The production for the `while` statement is straightforward. The body of a `while` statement is a code block:

```
<whilestmt>         → 'while' <relexpr> ':' <codeblock>
```

New grammar:

```
<program>         → <stmt>* EOF

<stmt>            → <simplestmt> NEWLINE
<stmt>            → <compoundstmt>

<simplestmt>      → <assignmentstmt>
<simplestmt>      → <printstmt>
<simplestmt>      → <passstmt>

<compoundstmt>    → <whilestmt>
<compoundstmt>    → <ifstmt>

<assignmentstmt> → NAME '=' <relexpr>
<printstmt>       → 'print' '(' [<relexpr> (',' <relexpr> )* [',']] ')'
<passstmt>        → 'pass'
<whilestmt>       → 'while' <relexpr> ':' <codeblock>
<ifstmt>          → 'if' <relexpr> ':' <codeblock> ['else' ':' <codeblock>]

<codeblock>       →  NEWLINE INDENT <stmt>+ DEDENT
<relexpr>         → <expr> [ ('<' | '<=' | '==' | '!=' | '>' | '>=') <expr> ]
<expr>            → <term> (('+' | '-') <term>)*
<term>            → <factor> (('*' | '/') <factor>)*

<factor>          → '+' <factor>
<factor>          → '-' <factor>
<factor>          → UNSIGNEDINT
<factor>          → UNSIGNEDFLOAT
<factor>          → NAME
<factor>          → '(' <relexpr> ')'
<factor>          → STRING
<factor>          → 'True'
<factor>          → 'False'
<factor>          → 'None'
```

Figure 15.1

The if statement has an optional else part (as indicated by the square brackets in the production):

```
<ifstmt> → 'if' <relexpr> ':' <codeblock> ['else' ':' <codeblock>]
```
                        check here if else is the current token ⤴

When the `ifstmt()` function in the parser processes an if statement, it parses it through the end of the first code block. If at that point the current token is else, then the parser proceeds to parse the else part of the if statement. Otherwise it returns immediately to its caller. Here is its code:

```
1  def ifstmt():
2      advance()                          # advance past 'if'
3      relexpr()
4      consume(COLON)
3      codeblock()                        # parse code block
4      if token.category == ELSE:         # check if there is an else part
5          advance()                      # advance past "else"
6          consume(COLON)                 # check for and advance past colon
7          codeblock()                    # parse the else code block
```

A code block is an indented sequence of one or more statements preceded by the newline character:

```
<codeblock> → NEWLINE INDENT <stmt>+ DEDENT
```

A relational expression is an expression followed by an optional second part (indicated by the square brackets in the production). The optional part consists of one of six relational operators followed by a second expression. A relational expression can have any of the following seven forms:

```
<expr>
<expr> <   <expr>         <expr> != <expr>
<expr> <=  <expr>         <expr> >  <expr>
<expr> ==  <expr>         <expr> >= <expr>
```

We can capture all seven variations using the "or" and square-bracket operators:

```
<relexpr>         → <expr> [ ('<' | '<=' | '==' | '!=' | '>' | '>=') <expr> ]
```

The part of a relational expression after the initial `<expr>` is optional (as indicated by the square brackets). It consists of one of the six relational operators followed by a second `<expr>`. Here is the code in the parser for the `relexpr()` function:

```
1  def relexpr():
2      expr()
3      if token.category in [LESSTHAN, LESSEQUAL, EQUAL, NOTEQUAL, GREATERTHAN,
4                            GREATEREQUAL]:
5          advance()
6          expr()
```

We also have to modify several productions from the original grammar. We replace `<expr>` with `<relexpr>` in the production for an assignment statement:

```
<assignmentstmt> → NAME '=' <relexpr>
```

Because a `<relexpr>` can be an `<expr>`, this modification expands what is allowed on the right side of an assignment statement.

The `print` statement in our new source language can handle any number of arguments (including zero arguments), each separated from the next by a comma. Each argument is a `<relexpr>`. The production for `<printstmt>` is in Fig. 15.2.

```
<printstmt> → 'print' '(' [ <relexpr> (',' <relexpr> )* [','] ] ')'
```
                                                                    Which comma?

Figure 15.2

This production captures the following forms of the `print` statement:

```
print()              # effect is to go the next line
print(<relexpr>)     # single argument

# comma separates successive <relexpr> arguments
print(<relexpr>, <relexpr>, ..., <relexpr>)

# comma allowed after last <relexpr>
print(<relexpr>, <relexpr>, ..., <relexpr>,)
```

The outer pair of square brackets in the `<printstmt>` production indicates that within parentheses there can be either nothing or

```
<relexpr> (',' <relexpr>)* [',']
```

The square brackets around the right comma indicate that a comma optionally can follow the last argument. The star operator indicates that following an initial `<relexpr>`, there can be additional occurrences of `<relexpr>`, but successive occurrences of `<relexpr>` must be separated by commas.

When the `printstmt()` function is about to parse a comma within the parentheses of a `print` statement, it has to decide which comma it is: Is it the comma that precedes a `<relexpr>`, or is it the comma at the very end of the argument list (see arrows in Fig. 15.2)? The parser makes this determination by advancing in the token stream past the comma and then checking the current token. If it is a right parenthesis, then the comma is the comma at the very end of the argument list. In this case, the `printstmt()` breaks out of the `while` loop associated with the star operator in the production. It then consumes the right parenthesis and returns to `simplestmt()`. If, on the other hand, the comma is not followed by a right parenthesis, `printstmt()` calls `relexpr()` and then proceeds to the exit test at the beginning of the `while` statement corresponding to the star operator in the production. Here is the code for `printstmt()`:

```
1  def printstmt():
2      advance()
3      consume(LEFTPAREN)
4      if token.category != RIGHTPAREN:        # any arguments?
5          relexpr()
6          while token.category == COMMA:
7              advance()
8              if token.category == RIGHTPAREN: # determine which comma
9                  break                        # break if comma at end
10             relexpr()
11     consume(RIGHTPAREN)
```

To include subtraction and division, we modify `expr()` and `term()` as follows:

```
<expr>      → <term> (('+' | '-') <term>)*
<term>      → <factor> (('*' | '/') <factor>)*
```

Here is the `expr()` function extended to handle both addition and subtraction:

```
1  def expr():
2      term()
3      while token.category == PLUS or token.category == MINUS:
4          advance()
5          term()
```

`<factor>` has several new or modified productions:

```
<factor>    → UNSIGNEDFLOAT
<factor>    → '(' <relexpr> ')'
<factor>    → STRING
<factor>    → 'True'
<factor>    → 'False'
<factor>    → 'None'
```

For the UNSIGNEDFLOAT, STRING, 'True', 'False', and 'None' factors, the `factor()` function simply calls `advance()` to advance past the factor. For example,

```
...
elif token.category == UNSIGNEDFLOAT:
    advance()
elif ...
...
```

In the pure interpreter based on this parser that you will write in the next chapter, the parser pushes the factor onto the operand stack before advancing.

Shortcomings of our Grammar

The grammar in Fig. 15.1 can generate strings that are not in the language. For example, because the grammar classifies a string as a factor in an expression, it can generate

```
s = 'hello' / 'bye'
```

Strings are illegal operands for the division operator. So this is an illegal statement. We have the same problem with True, False, and None, because they are also classified as factors. We can minimize the problem by rewriting the grammar so that strings, True, False, and None are not factors. However, for a complete solution we have to perform type checking to ensure operator-operand compatibility (see problem 4 in chapter 16). Context-free grammars have inherent limitations so that, in general, a context-free grammar *cannot* fully capture the rules of the source language. In particular, it cannot ensure operator-operand compatibility. Thus, the compiler or interpreter has to do type checking over and above the syntax checking performed by the parser to ensure the syntactic correctness of the source program. In a language like C, variables have their types specified in the source program. For example, to use a variable `i`, it must first be declared with a specific type. For example,

```
int i;
```

For these languages, type checking is performed by the compiler prior to execution. In dynamically-type languages like Python, variable types are determined at execution time. Thus, type checking is performed during execution.

Problems

1. The file `p2shell.py` contains the tokenizer from chapter 14 and the shell of the parser based on the grammar in Fig. 15.1. Copy `p2shell.py` to `p2.py`. Fill in the missing parts of `p2.py` so that it corresponds to the grammar in Fig. 15.1. Test your completed parser by entering

   ```
   python p2.py p2.in
   ```

   Also run your parser on the input files `p1501a.in`, `p1501b.in`, `p1501c.in`, `p1501d.in`, and `p1501e.in`. These input files all have syntax errors your parser should detect.

2. The following single statement, *indented three columns*, is not a legal Python 3 program:

   ```
      print('hello')    # indented three columns
   ```

   Does your `p2.py` parser from problem 1 generate an error message for this program?

3. Your `p2.py` parser from problem 1 parses every line of the source program from top to bottom. However, the pure interpreter `i2.py` that uses this parser (discussed in the next chapter) does not necessarily parse every line of the source program. Why not?

4. Would it be better if `relexpr()` treated the six cases (LESSTHAN, LESSEQUAL, etc.) individually? Why or why not?

5. Modify the grammar in Fig. 15.1 so that `<simplestatement>` and `<compoundstatement>` are eliminated. Use `<stmt>` for all the statements. Is the new grammar as easily parsed as the original?

6. We typically translate `<stmt>+` to parser code the same way we translate `<stmt><stmt>*`. Alternatively, can we translate it this way `<stmt>*<stmt>`?

7. Extend the grammar in Fig. 15.1 so that it supports the Boolean operators `and`, `or`, and `not`.

8. Rewrite the the grammar in Fig. 15.1 so that `<expr>` and `<term>` are defined recursively. Write the corresponding parser functions. *Hint*: Define `<expr>` with two productions. One is `<expr> -> <term> <tlist>`

16 Constructing a Pure Interpreter Level 2

Introduction

In this chapter, we complete the upgrade of our pure interpreter. Specifically, we extend the parser from chapter 15 so that it executes the source code in addition to parsing it. To execute the code it parses, it has to handle a new situation: branches in the source code. For example, consider the `while` loop. It repeatedly executes its body (a code block) while its exit-test relational expression is true (see Fig. 16.1). When the parser reaches the bottom of the body of a `while` loop, it has to unconditionally branch back to the beginning of the `while` loop—specifically to the exit test (i.e., to the code that evaluates the exit-test expression) that precedes the body of the `while` loop. We call this type of branch—in the direction of the beginning of the program—a *backward branch*. When the exit-test relational expression is false, the parser must exit the `while` loop. That is, it must branch over the body of the `while` loop to the statement that follows it. We call this type of branch—in the direction of the end of the program—a *forward branch*.

```
Unconditional          while relational_expression :        exit-test relational
backward                   statement                        expression
branch                     statement
                           ⋮                                Forward branch if
                           statement                        relational_expression
                                                            is false


                       statement following the while statement
```

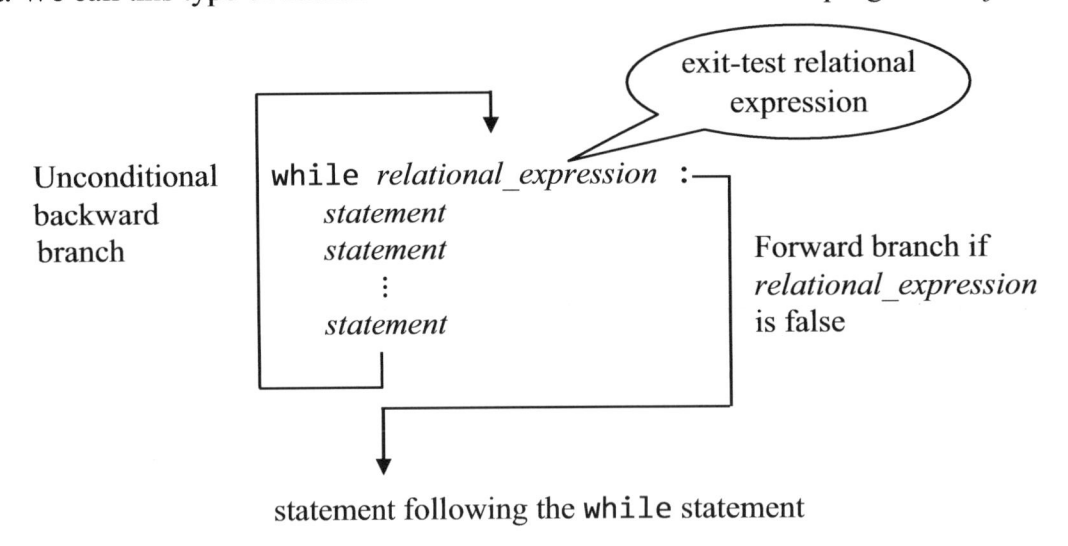

Figure 16.1

Backward branches are easier to handle than forward branches. When the parser has to perform a backward branch, it has already seen the branch-to location, and, therefore, knows its address (i.e., its index in `tokenlist`). But this is not the case for a forward branch. In a forward branch, the parser has to search forward for the location to which to branch.

Determining the Branch-to Address in a Backward Branch

The `whilestmt()` function uses a `while` loop to parse and execute a `while` loop in the source code that the interpreter is interpreting. We refer to the former `while` loop as the "parser `while` loop" (see line 5 in Fig. 16.2) and the latter as the "source code `while` loop."

When the `whilestmt()` function is about to parse the exit-test relational expression in a source code `while` loop, `tokenindex` is the index of the first token in the exit-test relational expression in the source code while loop. This is the location in the token stream to which the parser should branch after it parses and executes the body of the source code while loop. The parser saves this branch-to address with

```
4       savetokenindex = tokenindex         # save address of exit-test expr
```

The parser while loop parses and evaluates the exit-test relational expression (by calling relexpr() on line 6 in Fig. 16.2). If the expression is true, the parser then parses and executes the body of the source code while loop (by calling codeblock() on line 9). The parser then resets its position in the token stream by assigning tokenindex the previously saved tokenindex with

```
10              tokenindex = savetokenindex # backward branch to rel expr
```

and then updating token with

```
11              token = tokenlist[tokenindex]
```

The parser while loop then repeats. In this way, the parser while loop repeatedly parses and executes the source code while loop. When the exit-test expression ultimately evaluates to false, the break statement on line 13 is executed, which causes a break out the parser while loop. The parser at that point is positioned at the beginning of the code block that is the body of the source code while loop. Thus, after breaking out of the parser while loop on line 13, the parser must then do a forward branch over this code block (the code for the forward branch is given in Fig. 16.3).

```
 1 def whilestmt():
 2     global tokenindex, token
 3     advance()                               # advance past while keyword
 4     savetokenindex = tokenindex             # save address of exit-test expr
 5     while True:                             # parser while loop
 6         relexpr()                           # pushes value of exit-test expr
 7         consume(COLON)
 8         if operandstack.pop():              # is exit-test relexpr true?
 9             codeblock()                     # execute loop body
10             tokenindex = savetokenindex     # backward branch rel expr
11             token = tokenlist[tokenindex]
12         else:
13             break                           # must now do forward branch
14 # continued in Fig. 16.3
```

Figure 16.2

Implementing a Forward Branch

Immediately after the parser has parsed the exit-test relational expression in a while loop, the top of the stack has the true/false value of this expression. If this value is false, the parser must branch to the statement that follows the while loop. But the parser at this point does not necessarily know where the end of the while loop is in the token stream. It does know where the loop ends if it has parsed and executed the loop's body at least once. But the exit-test relational expression might initially be false in which case the parser has to branch over the body of the loop without ever having parsed it.

So how does the parser do the forward branch required by a `while` loop? It cannot parse the body of the `while` loop to determine where it ends. That would also execute the loop body after the exit-test relational expression has gone false. Instead, the parser advances over the body of the `while` loop until it advances past the dedent that terminates the code block that makes up the body of the `while` loop. To do this, the parser advances in the token stream until it advances past a DEDENT token whose column is to the left of the INDENT token that starts the body of the `while` loop. This DEDENT token marks the end of the `while` loop. Fig. 16.3 shows the code that does this (this code follows the code in Fig 16.2).

```
14    consume(NEWLINE)              # continued from Fig. 16.2
15    indentcol = token.column      # save column of INDENT token
16    consume(INDENT)
17    while True:
18        # check if dedent is to left of indent column
19        if token.category == DEDENT and token.column < indentcol:
20            advance()             # advance past dedent token
21            break                 # now past the end of while loop
22        advance()                 # still in body of while loop so advance
```

Figure 16.3

The forward branches in an `if` statement are handled in the same way as the forward branch in a `while` statement. An `if-else` statement has two forward branches: a branch on false to the start of the `else` code block, and an unconditional branch over the `else` code block (see Fig. 16.4). An `if` statement without an `else` has only one forward branch: a branch on false to the statement that follows the `if` statement (see Fig. 16.5).

Branching in an `if-else` statement:

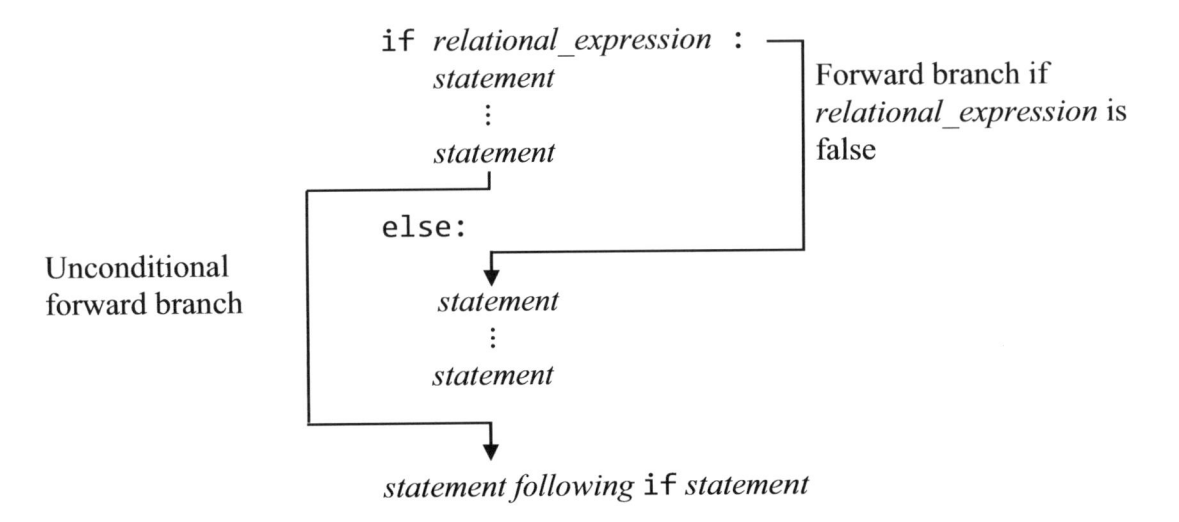

Figure 16.4

Branching in an `if` statement without an `else`:

if relational_expression :
    statement
       ⋮
    statement

Forward branch if *relational_expression* is false

statement following `if` *statement*

Figure 16.5

Here is the structure of the `ifstmt()` function:

```
1  def ifstmt():
2      advance()
3      relexpr()
4      consume(COLON)
5      saveval = operandstack.pop() # save it for line 14
6      if saveval:
7          codeblock()           # do codeblock() if saveval true
8      else:                     # do forward branch if saveval false
9          # code from Fig. 16.3
10         ...
11     if token.category == ELSE:
12         advance()
13         consume(COLON)
14         if not saveval:
15             codeblock()
16         else:                 # do another forward branch
17             # code from Fig. 16.3
18             ...               # missing instructions
```

Executing a Relational Expression

The production for a relational expression is

<relexpr> → <expr> [('<' | '<=' | '==' | '!=' | '>' | '>=') <expr>]

We handle the optional part specified by the square-bracket with a nested `if` statement. Fig. 16.6 shows the code for the `relexpr()` function (with a few instructions omitted). The call of `expr()` on line 2 pushes the value of the expression it parses onto the stack. If this expression is the entire relational expression, then its value is the true/false value of the relational expression. In other words, the parser in this case does not push `True` or `False` onto the stack. It simply leaves the value of the expression on the stack. If, on the other hand, a relational operator follows the expression, then after the second expression is parsed and evaluated (by line 7), the values of the two expressions are popped off the stack (lines 8 and 9) and compared using the relational operator corresponding to the category in `savecat`.

```
 1 def relexpr():
 2     expr()
 3     if token.category in [LESSTHAN, LESSEQUAL, EQUAL, NOTEQUAL,
 4                           GREATERTHAN, GREATEREQUAL]:
 5         savecat = token.category
 6         advance()
 7         expr()
 8         right = operandstack.pop()
 9         left = operandstack.pop()
10         if savecat == LESSTHAN:
11             operandstack.append(left < right)   # push True or False
12         elif savecat == LESSEQUAL:
13             operandstack.append(left <= right)  # push True or False
12         ...                                     # missing instructions
```

Figure 16.6

Problems

1. Copy your `p2.py` interpreter from problem 1 in chapter 15 to `i2.py`. Then modify `i2.py` as described in this chapter (it should handle the program in `i2.in`, the source program in Fig. 14.1). Do not include type checking (see problem 4). *Hint*: To get the proper display of the values of the arguments in a `print` statement, you may want to use in your `printstmt()` function

    `print(operandstack.pop(), end = '')`   (two consecutive single quotes)

   to pop and display the top of the stack, and *not* advance to the next line. Use

    `print(' ', end = '')`   (two consecutive single quotes)

   to display one blank, and not advance to the next line. Use

    `print()`

   to advance to the next line. Test your interpreter by entering

    `python i2.py i2.in`

   Also test your interpreter by entering

    `python i2.py p1601.in`

   Does your `i2.py` interpreter detect the error in `p1601.in`? Does the error message point to the error in the source program or to some location in your `i2.py` interpreter? See problem 4.

2. Would it be better if the tokenizer assigned to all the relational operators the category RELOP, in which case the lexeme field in the token object would be used to determine the specific operator?

3. What is the purpose of the test `token.column < indentcol` on line 19 of Fig. 16.3?

4. Include type checking in your `i2.py` interpreter from problem 1 to ensure that the operands of an arithmetic or relational operator are compatible. Test your modified interpreter by running it on each of the following statements, all of which have incompatible operands:

   ```
   a = 1 + '2'
   a = '1' * '2'
   a = True - '2'
   a = None / '2'
   a = 1 < '2'
   ```

   Your interpreter—not the Python 3 interpreter—should detect the error and raise a `RuntimeError` exception. *Hint*: Use the `type()` function in Python 3 to determine the types of the operands. For example, `type(i)`, `type(x)`, and `type(s)` return `int`, `float`, and `str`, respectively, if `i` is an integer, `x` is a float, and `s` is a string.

5. In C, the body of a `while` loop can be a single statement (as well as a code block delimited by braces). For example, this is a legal `while` statement in C:

   ```
   while (x < 10)
       x++;
   ```

   Why is this particular feature of C a problem for pure interpreters? *Hint*: Consider forward branches.

6. Use both your `i2.py` interpreter from problem 1 and the Python 3 interpreter to execute the following program:

   ```
   # p1606.in
   if 3:
       print('3 is true')
   if 3 == True:
       print('3 == True is true')
   ```

   Any differences? If so, modify your `i2.py` interpreter so it behaves like the Python 3 interpreter.

7. Use both your `i2.py` interpreter from problem 1 and the Python 3 interpreter to execute the following program. Are there any differences? If so, modify your `i2.py` interpreter.

   ```
   # p1607.in
   print(30 > 20 > 10)
   print(10 > 20 > 30)
   print(-30 < -20 < -10)
   ```

17 Constructing a Hybrid Interpreter Level 2

Introduction

In this chapter, we do the same upgrade to our hybrid interpreter that we did to our pure interpreter. Specifically, we upgrade it so that it supports the grammar in Fig. 15.1. To handle the branching associated with the `while` and `if` statements, we need some additional bytecode instructions, as well as some bytecode instructions for subtraction and division.

Some More Bytecode Instructions

Fig. 17.1 shows all the bytecode instructions we need for our upgraded hybrid interpreter.

```
UNARY_NEGATIVE      = 11     # hex 0B
BINARY_MULTIPLY     = 20     # hex 14
BINARY_DIVIDE       = 21     # hex 15
BINARY_ADD          = 23     # hex 17
BINARY_SUBTRACT     = 24     # hex 18
PRINT_ITEM          = 71     # hex 47
PRINT_NEWLINE       = 72     # hex 48
STORE_NAME          = 90     # hex 5A
LOAD_CONST          = 100    # hex 64
LOAD_NAME           = 101    # hex 65
COMPARE_OP          = 106    # hex 6A
JUMP_FORWARD        = 110    # hex 6E
POP_JUMP_IF_FALSE   = 111    # hex 6F
JUMP_ABSOLUTE       = 113    # hex 71
```

Figure 17.1

The `BINARY_DIVIDE` and `BINARY_SUBTRACT` work like the other binary arithmetic instructions: They pop the top two values from the stack, divide or subtract, and then push the result back onto the stack. The operands in a binary operation are pushed in left-to-right order. Thus, the top of the stack has the right operand, and just below it on the stack is the left operand. Which operand is left and which is right does not matter in addition or multiplication, but it does matter in subtraction and division.

`COMPARE_OP` consist of an opcode followed by a code that indicates the type of compare to perform. For example, in the `COMPARE_OP` instruction, 106 0, the 106 is the `COMPARE_OP` opcode, and 0 indicates that a "less than" compare should be performed. When executed, this instruction pops the top two values off the stack, compares them, and pushes `True` or `False`, depending of the result of the compare. Thus, if the left operand (the second value popped off the stack) is less than the right operand (the first value popped off the stack), then `COMPARE_OP` pushes `True` onto the stack. Otherwise it pushes `False`.

Our interpreter supports six compare operations: less than, less than or equal, equal, not equal, greater than, and greater than or equal. Their codes are 0, 1, 2, 3, 4, and 5, respectively (these are the same codes that the Python interpreter uses). Rather than using the integer codes themselves in our interpreter, we give a name to each code, and use their names instead. Fig. 17.2 shows the COMPARE_OP codes and their names.

```
LT = 0    # <  code
LE = 1    # <= code
EQ = 2    # == code
NE = 3    # != code
GT = 4    # >  code
GE = 5    # >= code
```

Figure 17.2

Our description of the COMPARE_OP instruction is a slight simplification of the actual COMPARE_OP bytecode instruction in the Python interpreter. But it does capture its essential features. Here is the code for the relexpr() function (with a few instructions omitted):

```
 1 def relexpr():
 2     expr()
 3     savecat = token.category
 4     if savecat in [LESSTHAN, LESSEQUAL, EQUAL, NOTEQUAL,
 5                    GREATERTHAN, GREATEREQUAL]:
 6         advance()
 7         expr()
 8         co_code.append(COMPARE_OP)
 9         if savecat == LESSTHAN:
10             co_code.append(LT)
11         elif savecat == LESSEQUAL:
12             co_code.append(LE)
13         ...                                    # missing instructions
```

JUMP_FORWARD is a branching instruction (in programming languages, "jump" and "branch" have the same meaning). It consists of its opcode followed by a relative address. The branch-to address is given by this relative address plus the value in pc (recall that pc is the variable that holds the address of the bytecode instruction to be executed next). For example, consider the following segment of bytecode instructions in co_code:

index	co_code	mnemonic
50	110	JUMP_FORWARD
51	5	relative address
52	100	LOAD_CONSTANT
53	2	constant
54	100	LOAD_CONSTANT
55	3	constant
56	23	BINARY_ADD
57	71	PRINT_ITEM

A `JUMP_FORWARD` instruction is at index 50 in `co_code`. Its opcode 110 is followed by the relative address 5. When the `JUMP_FORWARD` instruction is executed, the `pc` has already been incremented to point to the next instruction. Thus, `pc` is equal to 52 when the computation of the branch-to address is performed. Thus, the branch-to address is

$$\text{Value in pc (52)} + \text{Relative address in JUMP\_FORWARD instruction (5)} = 57$$

The branch-to address is 57. The `JUMP_FORWARD` instruction branches to the `PRINT_ITEM` instruction at index 57.

The name of the `POP_JUMP_IF_FALSE` instruction tells us what it does. It pops the value off the top of the stack. If this value is false, the instruction causes a branch. Unlike the `JUMP_FORWARD` instruction, the branch-to address is not a `pc`-relative address, but an absolute address (i.e., the actual index of the instruction to which to branch). For example, the `POP_JUMP_IF_FALSE` instruction, 111 86, causes a branch to index 86 in `co_code` if the value popped off the stack is false. If the popped value is true, then execution proceeds to the instruction that follows the `POP_JUMP_IF_FALSE` instruction. `JUMP_ABSOLUTE` is an unconditional branching instruction. Like `POP_JUMP_IF_FALSE`, the address it specifies is an absolute address. For example, the `JUMP_ABSOLUTE` instruction, 113 100, causes a branch to the instruction in `co_code` at index 100.

Compiling Backward Branches to Bytecode

Compiling the backward branch in a `while` statement is easy. Just before the exit-test relational expression that follows the keyword `while` is parsed, the length of `co_code` gives the index in `co_code` of the bytecode for the exit-test relational expression. This is the branch-to address for the backward branch. We need to save this address before parsing the exit-test relational expression. We do this with

```
backaddress = len(co_code) # save address of relexpr bytecode
relexpr()                  # parse exit-test expression
```

Then at the bottom of the `while` statement (i.e., after parsing the code block that makes up the body of the `while` statement), we use

```
co_code.append(JUMP_ABSOLUTE)
co_code.append(backaddress)
```

to generate the `JUMP_ABSOLUTE` instruction that, when executed, branches back to the bytecode that evaluates the exit-test relational expression.

Compiling Forward Branches to Bytecode

Both the `while` and `if` statements require forward branches. Forward branches are a little tricky to generate. The parser has to generate them before it knows the branch-to address. How is this possible? The parser generates the forward branch instruction using `None` as a "dummy" branch-to address. It also saves the index of this dummy address. When the parser subsequently determines the branch-to address, it replaces the dummy address with the correct address. Here is the Python code we need for the forward branch. We first generate the opcode of the branching instruction:

```
co_code.append(POP_JUMP_IF_FALSE)
```

At this point in the parse, the length of co_code is the index of the address field in the POP_JUMP_IF_FALSE instruction. We save this index with

```
address1 = len(co_code)
```

and then generate the dummy address of the branching instruction with

```
co_code.append(None)
```

Thus, address1 has the index of the dummy address in the POP_JUMP_IF_FALSE instruction. After the parser parses the code block that makes up the body of the while statement, the length of co_code is the index of the statement that follows the while statement. This index is the branch-to address we need for the forward branch. Thus, we replace the dummy address with this index. We do this with

```
co_code[address1] = len(co_code)
```

whilestmt()

In the following code for whilestmt(), line 3 saves the back address needed by the JUMP_ABSOLUTE instruction at the end of the body of the while loop. Lines 10 and 11 output the JUMP_ABSOLUTE instruction using the saved back address. Line 6 and 8 ouput a POP_JUMP_IF_FALSE instruction with None in its second component. Line 12 then replaces the None entry with the correct forward address.

```
1 def whilestmt():
2     advance()
3     backaddress = len(co_code)
4     relexpr()
5     consume(COLON)
6     co_code.append(POP_JUMP_IF_FALSE)
7     forwardaddress = len(co_code)
8     co_code.append(None)
9     codeblock()
10    co_code.append(JUMP_ABSOLUTE)
11    co_code.append(backaddress)
12    co_code[forwardaddress] = len(co_code)
```

ifstmt()

The POP_JUMP_IF_FALSE forward branch for the if statement (i.e., the conditional branch over the if part) is handled in the same way. However, the JUMP_FORWARD forward branch (i.e., the unconditional branch from the end of the if part over the else part if there is an else part) requires a relative address. Here is the code we need:

```
 1  def ifstmt():
 2      advance()
 3      relexpr()
 4      consume(COLON)
 5      co_code.append(POP_JUMP_IF_FALSE)
 6      address1 = len(co_code)
 7      co_code.append(None)
 8      codeblock()                              # if code block
 9      if token.category == ELSE:
10          advance()
11          consume(COLON)
12          co_code.append(JUMP_FORWARD)         # jump over else part
13          address2 = len(co_code)
14          co_code.append(None)
15          startaddress = len(co_code)
16          co_code[address1] = len(co_code)
17          codeblock()                          # else code block
18          co_code[address2] = len(co_code)-startaddress
19      else:
20          co_code[address1] = len(co_code)
```

On line 15, `len(co_code)` is the `co_code` index of the location to which the `pc` points when the `JUMP_FORWARD` instruction is executed. The index is saved in `startaddress`. On line 18, `len(co_code)` is the `co_code` index to which the `JUMP_FORWARD` branches. Thus, the relative address for the `JUMP_FORWARD` is given by the difference on line 18 of `len(co_code)` and `startaddress`. On line 18, this relative address is stored in the second half of the `JUMP_FORWARD` instruction. Line 20 handles the case if the `if` statement has no `else` part.

printstmt()

The `printstmt()` function has to output bytecode that displays a blank between successive relative expressions that appear within the `print` statement's parentheses. Here is the code for `printstmt()` with a description of the instructions to be added that handles the blank:

```
 1  def printstmt():
 2      advance()
 3      consume(LEFTPAREN)
 4      if token.category != RIGHTPAREN:
 5          relexpr()
 6          co_code.append(PRINT_ITEM)
 7          while token.category == COMMA:
 8              advance()
 9              if token.category == RIGHTPAREN:
10                  break
```

```
11                                                  # missing instructions
12          ⇓
13          # output a LOAD_CONST opcode
14          # put ' ' into co_consts if not already there and get its index
15          # output index of ' ' in co_consts
16          # output a PRINT_ITEM opcode
17
18          relexpr()
19          co_code.append(PRINT_ITEM)
20     co_code.append(PRINT_NEWLINE)
21     consume(RIGHTPAREN)
```

factor()

The `factor()` function should handle the factor constants new to our level 2 source language in essentially the same way it handles the `UNSIGNEDINT` factor: It should output bytecode that pushes the the constant onto the stack. For example, here is the code for a `True` factor:

```
1 elif token.category == TRUE:
2     if True in co_consts:
3         index = co_consts.index(True)
4     else:
5         index = len(co_consts)
6         co_consts.append(True)
7     co_code.append(LOAD_CONST)
8     co_code.append(index)
9     advance()
```

It enters `True` into `co_consts` if it not already there (line 6) and gets its index (line 3 or 5). Then it outputs the LOAD_CONST opcode (line 7) followed by the index of the constant (line 8).

interpreter()

The bytecode interpreter in `h1.py` has to be extended to support several additional bytecode instructions required by our upgraded hybrid interpreter: BINARY_DIVIDE, BINARY_SUBTRACT, COMPARE_OP, JUMP_FORWARD, POP_JUMP_IF_FALSE, and JUMP_ABSOLUTE. Here is the interpreter code for the COMPARE_OP instruction (with a few instructions omitted), the JUMP_FORWARD instruction, the POP_JUMP_IF_FALSE instruction, and the JUMP_ABSOLUTE instruction:

```
1 def interpreter():
2     co_values = [None] * len(co_names)
3     stack = []
4     pc = 0
5     while pc < len(co_code):
```

```
 6      opcode = co_code[pc]
 7      pc += 1
 8      if opcode == UNARY_NEGATIVE:
 9          stack[-1] = -stack[-1]
10      elif opcode == BINARY_MULTIPLY:
11          right = stack.pop()
12          left = stack.pop()
13          stack.append(left * right)
14          ...                            # missing instructions
15      elif opcode == COMPARE_OP:
16          op = co_code[pc]               # get type of comparison
17          pc += 1                        # increment pc to next instruction
18          right = stack.pop()            # pop two values off the stack
19          left = stack.pop()
20          if op == LT:                   # check if LT comparison
21              stack.append(left < right) # push True or False
22          elif op == LE:
23              stack.append(left <= right)
24          ...                            # missing instructions
25      elif opcode == JUMP_FORWARD:
26          reladdr = co_code[pc]          # get rel addr from JUMP_FORWARD inst
27          pc += 1                        # increment pc to next instruction
28          pc = pc + reladdr              # load pc with branch-to address
29      elif opcode == POP_JUMP_IF_FALSE:
30          if not stack.pop():            # is top of stack False?
31              pc = co_code[pc]           # absolute branch
32          else:
33              pc += 1                    # go to next instruction
34      elif opcode == JUMP_ABSOLUTE:
35          pc = co_code[pc]
36      else:
37          break
```

The JUMP_FORWARD instruction contains an address relative the beginning of the next instruction. Line 26 assigns this relative address to reladdr. The pc register is incremented on line 27 so it points to the next instruction. The branch-to address is then pc + reladdr, which is assigned to pc on line 28 to effect the branch.

Problems

1. Copy your p2.py parser from problem 1 in chapter 15 to h2.py. Insert the interpreter() function from your h1.py into h2.py. Then modify h2.py so that it can handle the program in h2.in (the source program in Fig. 14.1). Test your interpreter by entering

    python h2.py h2.in

    Note: In Python, print() moves cursor to next line. But print('\n') skips the next line. For the

PRINT_NEWLINE bytecode instruction, you should use `print()` in the bytecode interpreter. For PRINT_ITEM, you should use `print(stack.pop(), end = '')`. The `end` argument suppresses the generation of a newline character (recall PRINT_ITEM does NOT move the cursor to the next line).

2. Run some timing tests on your `i2.py` pure interpreter and your `h2.py` hybrid interpreter. For what type of source program is the pure interpreter faster? For what type is the hybrid interpreter faster?

3. Why does bytecode not use absolute addresses exclusively in its branching instruction? Why not use `pc`-relative addressing exclusively? Why is there no JUMP_BACKWARD instruction?

4. Copy your `h2.py` interpreter from problem 1 to `p1704.py`. Then add code to `p1704.py` that compiles the bytecode to Raspberry Pi assembly language. Write the assembler code to an output file. Is generating assembler code from bytecode a faster or slower process than generating assembler code from the source program? Justify your answer.

5. Copy your `h2.py` interpreter from problem 1 to `p1705.py`. Then modify `p1705.py` so that it creates and interprets postfix rather than bytecode as the intermediate language (see problem 8 in chapter 10). Test your interpreter with `h2.in`.

6. The code in the bytecode interpreter for the JUMP_FORWARD instruction consists of three Python instructions. Replace this three-instruction sequence with a single instruction.

7. After line 35 in the code in this chapter for the `interpreter()` function, should there be a statement that increments `pc` by 1?

8. Can lines 12, 13, and 14 in the code in the chapter for the `ifstmt()` function be repositioned right after line 8?

9. What would be the advantage of using the category number of a relational operator to specify the type of compare in a COMPARE_OP instruction? For example, the encoding for a less than COMPARE_OP bytecode instruction would then be the opcode for COMPARE_OP (106) followed by the category number for "<" (23).

10. Why is compiling a high-level language directly to machine language more difficult than first translating to assembly language and then assembling the assembly language version? *Hint*: Consider forward branches.

11. Copy your `h2.py` from problem 1 to `h1711.py`. Then modify `h1711.py` so that during parsing it checks for syntax errors not caught by the grammar itself. Test your interpreter with

```
print(1 + True)
print(1 + '2')
```

Are both these statements illegal in Python 3? Your `h1711.py` interpreter should handle these statements the same way the Python 3 interpreter handles them.

18 Constructing a Compiler Level 2

Introduction

Our compiler from chapter 13 generates correct but woefully inefficient assembler code. In this chapter, we incorporate into our compiler several optimization techniques that substantially improve the efficiency of the generated code. Optimization techniques can be quite elaborate and computationally complex. However, we will limit ourselves to optimization techniques that are easy to implement.

Temporary Variable Re-use

A value in a temporary variable is never accessed more than once. Thus, once the compiler generates code that accesses the value in a temporary variable, that variable becomes available for re-use. To "free" a temporary variable (i.e., indicate that a temporary variable is available for re-use) is easy: Simply decrement `tempcount` (recall that `tempcount` holds the sequence number for temporary variables). This works because at execution time, the values in temporary variables are accessed in reverse order from which they are created. Thus, whenever a temporary variable should be freed, it is always the most recently created one—that is, the one with the highest sequence number. Decrementing `tempcount` has the effect of freeing the temporary variable with the highest sequence number. For example, suppose `tempcount` is 2 when `gettemp()` is called (see Fig. 13.8). `gettemp()` then creates the temporary variable `.t2` and increments `tempcount` to 3. When the compiler generates assembler code that accesses `.t2`, the temporary variable becomes available for re-use. To free it, the compiler decrements `tempcount` back to 2. Then on its next call, `gettemp()` will again create and return `.t2`, thereby causing the re-use of `.t2`.

Four code generator functions—`cg_assign()`, `cg_print()`, `cg_add()`, and `cg_mul()`—generate code that can access a temporary variable. Each of these functions should test if the item it accesses is a temporary variable. If it is, it should decrement `tempcount` so the temporary variable can be re-used. Here are the required modifications:

In `cg_add()` and `cg_mul()`, insert
```
    if symbol[leftindex].startswith('.t'):
        tempcount -= 1
    if symbol[rightindex].startswith('.t'):
        tempcount -= 1
```

In `cg_assign()`, insert
```
    if symbol[rightindex].startswith('.t'):
        tempcount -= 1
```

In `cg_print()` and `cg_neg()`, insert
```
    if symbol[index].startswith('.t'):
        tempcount -= 1
```

Be sure to insert the code above before any calls of `gettemp()`. Otherwise, you will be using more temps than necessary.

Constant Folding

Consider the statement

x = 2 + 3

Our compiler from chapter 13 translates this statement to assembler instructions that load 2, add 3 and then store the result in x:

```
1  ldr r0, =.i2        @ get address of .i2
2  ldr r0, [r0]        @ load 2
3  ldr r1, =.i3        @ get address of .i3
4  ldr r1, [r1]        @ load 3
5  add r0, r0, r1      @ add 2 and 3
6  ldr r1, =.t0        @ get address of .t0
7  str r0, [r1]        @ store the sum in .t0
8  ldr r0,  =.t0       @ get address of .t0
9  ldr r0, [r0]        @ get the sum in .t0
10 ldr r1, =x          @ get address of x
11 str r0, [r1]        @ store the sum in x
```

Because the operands on the right of the assignment statement are all constants, our compiler can easily do better. The compiler can compute the value of the expression to get 5, and generate the instructions to store 5 in x. In other words, the computation can be done at compile time *by the compiler* rather than at execution time. With this optimization technique in effect, we get the following code for x = 2 + 3:

```
1  ldr r0, =.i5        @ get address of .i5
2  ldr r0, [r0]        @ load 5
3  ldr r1, =x          @ get address of x
4  str r0, [r1]        @ store 5 in x
```

We call this optimization technique *constant folding* because it "folds" multiple constants into a single constant (in the next section, we will see how to produce even more efficient code that accesses constants).

The implementation of constant folding requires a small modification to the cg_add() and cg_mul() functions. When called, these functions should check if both the left and right operands are constants. For example, to determine if the left operand is a constant, they use

    symbol[leftindex].startswith('.i')

leftindex is the parameter passed to cg_add() and cg_mul() that holds the symbol table index of the left operand. Thus, symbol[leftindex] is the left operand. If it starts with ".i", then it is a constant. Thus, if the expression above is true, the left operand is a constant. Otherwise, it is not.

If both operands are constants, then the computation specified is performed by

    result = int(value[leftindex]) + int(value[rightindex])

for addition, or by

    result = int(value[leftindex]) * int(value[rightindex])

for multiplication. The result is then entered into the symbol table with

```
if result >= 0:
    return enter('.i'+ str(result), str(result), False)
else:
    return enter('.i_'+ str(-result), str(result), False)
```

result is a number, so it should be converted to a string before it is entered into the symbol table. Suppose the expression is 2 + 3, in which case the result is 5. Then

```
'.i'+ str(result)
```

produces the string '.i5'. If the expression is -2 + -3, in which case the result is -5, then

```
'.i_'+ str(-result)
```

produces the string '.i_5'.

We have to make one more modification to our compiler. The modifications given above fold constants, but the component constants in the expression still appear at the bottom of the translated program on .word directives. For example, the expression 2 + 3 produces .word directives for 2 and 3 as well as 5 even though .i2 and .i3 are never referenced:

```
.i2:        .word   2
.i3:        .word   3
.i5:        .word   5
```

The generated code includes the instruction that references the constant 5:

```
ldr r0, =.i5         @ get address of .i5
```

So we need the .word directive for 5. But not for 2 or 3. The only constants that need .word directives are the constants that are referenced by some instruction. This observation suggests the following modification that fixes the problem of unnecessary .word directives: We add needword, a third parallel list, to our symbol table. The elements of needword are True/False values. True indicates that the corresponding symbol needs a .word directive; False indicates that the symbol does not need a .word directive. The cg_epilog() function (the function that generates the .word directives) generates a .word directive for a symbol only if its needword value is True.

Our enter() function is extended to support needword (we will further extend enter() when we add support for register allocation):

```
1  def enter(s, v, w):
2      if s in symbol:                 # s already in symbol?
3          return symbol.index(s)      # then return its index
4      # add s, v, w to symbol, value, and needword, respectively
5      index = len(symbol)             # get index of next slot
6      symbol.append(s)                # append s to next slot in symbol
7      value.append(v)                 # append v to next slot in value
8      needword.append(w)              # append w to next slot in needword
9      return index                    # return index of new entry
```

Whenever a constant is entered into the symbol table, its needword value is set to False. For example, the code in factor() for an unsigned integer is

```
elif token.category == UNSIGNEDINT:
   if sign == 1:
      index  = enter('.i' + token.lexeme, token.lexeme, False)
   else:
      index  = enter('.i_' + token.lexeme, '-' + token.lexeme, False)
   advance()
   return index
```

Note that the third argument in the call of enter() is False. Thus, the needword value for an unsigned integer initially is False. Whenever a code generator function generates code that references an item in the symbol table, it should then set the item's corresponding entry in needword to True. For example, if a code generator function executes

```
outfile.write('          ldr r1, =' + symbol[index] + '\n')
```

it should then execute

```
needword[index] = True
```

Putting Constants in the .text Segment

To get our compiler to put constants in the .text segment requires one small modification. The current cg_epilog() function outputs the .data directive and then the .word directives for the constants and variables. We simply modify cg_epilog() so that it first outputs the .word directives for the constants, then the .data directive, and finally the .word directives for the variables. Suppose we want to load r0 with the constant at the label .i3. With this modification, we load r0 with a single instruction,

```
   ldr    r0, .i3           @ load value of .i3
```

rather than with the two-instruction sequence,

```
   ldr    r0, =.i3          @ get address of .i3
   ldr    r0, [r0]          @ load value of .i3
```

Register Allocation

There are 9 registers (r4 to r12) available for register allocation. We will avoid using registers r0 to r3, reserving them for passing arguments. We will also avoid using r13, r14, and r15 because they are the sp, lr, and pc registers, respectively.

Because of the limited number of registers, if there are more variables than registers, the compiler has to decide which variables get to use registers and which are stored in memory—a very difficult task to do well. If a variable is accessed only once, its location—in a register or in memory—has little impact on execution time. However, if a variable is accessed from within a loop that iterates millions of times, then the location of the variable could be a significant factor in execution time.

To do register allocation really well requires complex algorithms. But we will take a very simple approach: first-parsed-first-allocated. That is, registers are allocated to variables in the order the variables are parsed, until no more registers are available. This allocation scheme is far from optimal. But for many programs, it works quite well. Its advantage is that is very easy to implement.

The order in which variables are parsed is the order in which they are entered into the symbol table by the enter() function. Thus, to implement our simple register allocation scheme, we use the enter() function to allocate registers to variables. enter() allocates registers on a first-come-first-served basis until there are no more registers left to allocate. Fig. 18.1 shows the code for our modified enter() function. If the symbol passed to enter() is already in the symbol table, enter() simply returns its index. Otherwise, if the symbol is a variable, and registers are available, then enter() allocates a register for that variable.

```
1  def enter(s, v, w):
2      global nextreg
3      if s in symbol:       # check if s already in symbol
4          return symbol.index(s)
5      # if s is a constant or reg not available, then don't allocate
6      if s.startswith('.i') or nextreg > 12:
7          loc.append(None)
8      else:                 # allocate register
9          loc.append('r' + str(nextreg))
10         nextreg += 1
11
12     # add s, v, and w to symbol, value, and needword, and return index
13     index = len(symbol)  # get index of next slot
14     symbol.append(s)     # append s to next slot in symbol
15     value.append(v)      # append v to next slot in value
16     needword.append(w)   # append w to next slot in needword
17     return index         # return index of new entry
```

Figure 18.1

Registers are allocated in number order from 4 to 12. nextreg is a global variable that holds the number of the next register to be allocated. Thus, if nextreg is greater than 12, then there are no more registers left to allocate.

To support register allocation, the symbol table has a fourth parallel list called loc. To create our new symbol table, we now create four lists:

```
symbol = []        # list of symbols
value = []         # value of corresponding symbol
needword = []      # indicates if .word directive is needed
loc = []           # None or 'r' concatenated with reg number
```

If a symbol is not allocated a register, its corresponding slot in the loc list contains None. If it is allocated a register, its corresponding slot in the loc list contains 'r' concatenated to the register number. For example, if 'x' is in symbol[0] and it is allocated r10, then the string 'r10' is in loc[0] (see Fig.

18.2). If `'x'` is not allocated a register, then `None` is in `loc[0]`.

symbol	value	needword	loc
'x'	'0'	False	'r10'

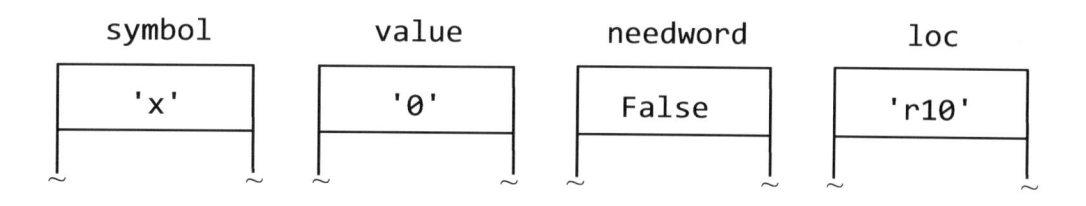

Figure 18.2

Next, we modify the code generator functions so that they generate code depending on the location of a variable, as indicated by its `loc[]` entry. This is where things get complicated. For example, for the assignment statement,

```
x = y
```

if `r10` has been allocated to x, and `r7` to y, the code generator generates the following code:

```
    mov     r10, r7
```

If x and y are not allocated to registers, then the code generator generates

```
    ldr     r0, =x      @ get address of x
    ldr     r0, [r0]    @ get x
    ldr     r1, =y      @ get address of y
    str     r0, [r1]    @ store x in y
```

Implementing register allocation is complicated because of the many variations that are possible for a single statement, each requiring a different sequence of instructions. For example, the variable on the left side of an assignment statement might be in memory or in a register. The right side might be a constant in memory, a variable in memory, or a variable in a register. There are two possibilities for the left side, and three possibilities for the right. Thus, there are a total of 2 × 3 = 6 possibilities, each requiring a different sequence of instructions.

The code to handle all these possibilities is tedious to write, but not hard to figure out. Simply use a nested `if` statement that tests for each one of the possible six cases and generates code accordingly (see the code for `cg_assign()` in Fig. 18.3). `cg_add()` and `cg_mul()` require a similar analysis. They differ from `cg_assign()` in that they return the symbol table index of the temporary variable that represents the result of the operation. The pseudocode for `cg_add()` is in Fig. 18.4.

```
1  def cg_assign(leftindex, rightindex):
2      global tempcount
3
4      if symbol[rightindex].startswith('.t'):
5          tempcount -= 1                          # free temporary variable
6
7      # determine what is on left and right sides
8      if symbol[rightindex].startswith('.i'):
```

```
 9              constonright = True
10          else:
11              constonright = False
12          if loc[rightindex] == None:
13              regonright = False
14          else:
15              regonright = True
16              rightreg = loc[rightindex]
17          if loc[leftindex] == None:
18            regonleft = False
19          else:
20              regonleft = True
21              leftreg = loc[leftindex]
22
23          # handle each case
24          if regonleft and regonright: # case 1: left and right are regs
25              outfile.write('          mov ' + leftreg + ', ' + rightreg + '\n')
26
27          elif regonleft and constonright: # case 2: left reg, right const
28              outfile.write('          ldr ' + leftreg + ', ' +
29                          symbol[rightindex] + '\n')
30              needword[rightindex] = True
31
32          elif regonleft and not constonright: # case 3: left reg, right var
33              outfile.write('          ldr r0, =' + symbol[rightindex] + '\n')
34              outfile.write('          ldr ' + leftreg + ', [r0]\n')
35              needword[rightindex] = True
36
37          elif regonright:              # case 4: left in mem, right reg
38              outfile.write('          ldr r0, =' + symbol[leftindex] + '\n')
39              outfile.write('          str ' + rightreg + ', [r0]\n')
40              needword[leftindex] = True
41
42          elif constonright:            # case 5: left in mem, right const in mem
43              outfile.write('          ldr r0, ' + symbol[rightindex] + '\n')
44              outfile.write('          ldr r1, =' + symbol[leftindex] + '\n')
45              outfile.write('          str r0, [r1]\n')
46              needword[rightindex] = True
47              needword[leftindex] = True
48
49          else:                         # case 6: left in mem, right var in mem
50              outfile.write('          ldr r0, =' + symbol[rightindex] + '\n')
51              outfile.write('          ldr r0, [r0]\n')
52              outfile.write('          ldr r1, =' + symbol[leftindex] + '\n')
53              outfile.write('          str r0, [r1]\n')
54              needword[rightindex] = True
55              needword[leftindex] = True
```

Figure 18.3

```
 1      def cg_add(leftindex, rightindex):
 2          global tempcount
 3
 4          if both left and right operands are constants
 5              fold the two constants together
 6                  enter the folded constant into the symbol table
 7                  return the symbol table index returned by the enter() function
 8
 9          # reuse temps
10          if symbol[leftindex].startswith('.t'):
11              tempcount -= 1
12          if symbol[rightindex].startswith('.t'):
13              tempcount -= 1
14
15          leftreg = 'r0'
16          rightreg = 'r1'
17          destreg = 'r0'
18
19          if left operand is not in a register
20              if left operand is a constant
21                  output instruction to load constant into r0
22              else        ldr to load address of left operand, second ldr to load left operand
23                  output two instructions to load r0 with left operand
24              needword[leftindex] = True;
25          else
26              assign register's name (in the loc array) to leftreg
27
28
29          Repeat statement in preceding box but for right operand (use r1 in place of r0,
30          rightreg in place of leftreg and rightindex in place of leftindex)
31
32          tempindex = cg_gettemp()
33          if symbol[tempindex] is in a register
34              save its name in destreg
35
36          outfile.write('          add '
37                        + destreg + ', ' + leftreg + ', ' + rightreg + '\n')
38
39          if symbol[tempindex] is not in a register
40              outfile.write('          ldr r1, ='
41                            + symbol[tempindex] + '\n')
42              outfile.write('          str r0, [r1]\n')
43              needword[tempindex] = True;
44          return tempindex
```

Figure 18.4

Chapter 18: Constructing a Compiler Level 2

`cg_neg()` and `cg_print()` have only one parameter. Thus, they need to handle only three cases: constant not in a register, variable not in a register, or variable in a register. Fig. 18.5 has the code for `cg_neg()` and the pseudocode for `cg_print()`.

```
1  def cg_neg(index):
2      global tempcount
3
4      if symbol[index].startswith('.t'):
5          tempcount -= 1
6      if loc[index] == None:                              # not in a register?
7          if symbol[index].startswith('.i'):      # constant?
8              outfile.write('          ldr r0, ' + symbol[index] + '\n')
9          else:                                           # variable
10             outfile.write('          ldr r0, =' + symbol[index] + '\n')
11             outfile.write('          ldr r0, [r0]\n')
12         needword[index] = True
13     else:                                               # in a register
14         outfile.write('          mov r0, ' + loc[index] + '\n')
15     outfile.write('          neg r0, r0\n')
16     tempindex = cg_gettemp()
17     if loc[tempindex] == None:                          # temp not in a register?
18         outfile.write('          ldr r1, =' + symbol[tempindex] + '\n')
19         outfile.write('          str r0, [r1]\n')
20         needword[tempindex] = True
21     else:                                               # temp in a register
22         outfile.write('          mov ' + loc[tempindex] + ', r0\n')
23     return tempindex
```

```
1   def cg_print(index):
2       global tempcount, needfmt0
3       needfmt0 = True    # set to True so epilog outputs .fmt0 string
4       outfile.write('          ldr r0, =.fmt0\n')  # setup for printf
5
6       if cg_print() argument corresponding to index is a temp, code to reuse temp
7
8       if cg_print() argument corresponding to index is not in a register
9           if cg_print() argument corresponding to index is a constant
10              output instruction to load constant argument into r1
11          else           ldr to load address of argument, second ldr to load argument
12              output two instructions to load variable/temp argument into r1
13          needword[index] = True
14      else
15          outfile.write('          mov r1, ' + loc[index] + '\n')
16      outfile.write('          bl printf\n')
```

Figure 18.5

`cg_print()` sets needfmt0 to True, indicating that a `printf` format string is needed. The `cg_epilog()` function then should output the format string only if needfmt0 is True:

```
# code in cg_epilog()
if needfmt0:
    outfile.write('.fmt0:       .asciz "%d\\n"\n')
```

Compare the output of our unoptimized compiler (Fig. 18.6) with the output of our optimized version (Fig. 18.7). Quite a difference!

Unoptimized version

```
 1 @ Mon Feb 12 21:03:17 2018                        YOUR NAME HERE
 2 @ Compiler    = c1.py
 3 @ Input file  = c1.in
 4 @ Output file = c1.s
 5 @------------------------------------------ Assembler code
 6             .global main
 7             .text
 8 main:
 9             push {lr}
10
11 @ print(-59 + 20*3)
12             ldr r0, =.i20
13             ldr r0, [r0]
14             ldr r1, =.i3
15             ldr r1, [r1]
16             mul r0, r1, r0
17             ldr r1, =.t0
18             str r0, [r1]
19             ldr r0, =.i_59
20             ldr r0, [r0]
21             ldr r1, =.t0
22             ldr r1, [r1]
23             add r0, r0, r1
24             ldr r1, =.t1
25             str r0, [r1]
26             ldr r0, =.fmt0
27             ldr r1, =.t1
28             ldr r1, [r1]
29             bl printf
30
31 @ a = 2
32             ldr r0, =.i2
33             ldr r0, [r0]
34             ldr r1, =a
35             str r0, [r1]
36
```

```
37  @ bb_1 = -(a) + 12
38          ldr  r0, =a
39          ldr  r0, [r0]
40          neg  r0, r0
41          ldr  r1, =.t2
42          str  r0, [r1]
43          ldr  r0, =.t2
44          ldr  r0, [r0]
45          ldr  r1, =.i12
46          ldr  r1, [r1]
47          add  r0, r0, r1
48          ldr  r1, =.t3
49          str  r0, [r1]
50          ldr  r0, =.t3
51          ldr  r0, [r0]
52          ldr  r1, =bb_1
53          str  r0, [r1]
54
55  @ print(a*bb_1 + a*3*(-1 + -1 + -1))
56          ldr  r0, =a
57          ldr  r0, [r0]
58          ldr  r1, =bb_1
59          ldr  r1, [r1]
60          mul  r0, r1, r0
61          ldr  r1, =.t4
62          str  r0, [r1]
63          ldr  r0, =a
64          ldr  r0, [r0]
65          ldr  r1, =.i3
66          ldr  r1, [r1]
67          mul  r0, r1, r0
68          ldr  r1, =.t5
69          str  r0, [r1]
70          ldr  r0, =.i_1
71          ldr  r0, [r0]
72          ldr  r1, =.i_1
73          ldr  r1, [r1]
74          add  r0, r0, r1
75          ldr  r1, =.t6
76          str  r0, [r1]
77          ldr  r0, =.t6
78          ldr  r0, [r0]
79          ldr  r1, =.i_1
80          ldr  r1, [r1]
81          add  r0, r0, r1
82          ldr  r1, =.t7
83          str  r0, [r1]
84          ldr  r0, =.t5
85          ldr  r0, [r0]
```

```
86              ldr r1, =.t7
87              ldr r1, [r1]
88              mul r0, r1, r0
89              ldr r1, =.t8
90              str r0, [r1]
91              ldr r0, =.t4
92              ldr r0, [r0]
93              ldr r1, =.t8
94              ldr r1, [r1]
95              add r0, r0, r1
96              ldr r1, =.t9
97              str r0, [r1]
98              ldr r0, =.fmt0
99              ldr r1, =.t9
100             ldr r1, [r1]
101             bl printf
102
103             mov r0, #0
104             pop {pc}
105
106             .data
107 .fmt0:      .asciz "%d\n"
108 .i_59:      .word -59
109 .i20:       .word 20
110 .i3:        .word 3
111 .t0:        .word 0
112 .t1:        .word 0
113 a:          .word 0
114 .i2:        .word 2
115 bb_1:       .word 0
116 .t2:        .word 0
117 .i12:       .word 12
118 .t3:        .word 0
119 .t4:        .word 0
120 .t5:        .word 0
121 .i_1:       .word -1
122 .t6:        .word 0
123 .t7:        .word 0
124 .t8:        .word 0
125 .t9:        .word 0
```

Figure 18.6

Optimized version

```
 1 @ Mon Feb 12 21:13:16 2018                    YOUR NAME HERE
 2 @ Compiler    = c2.py
 3 @ Input file  = c2.in
 4 @ Output file = c2.s
 5 @----------------------------------------- Assembler code
 6             .global main
 7             .text
 8 main:
 9             push {lr}
10
11 @ print(-59 + 20*3)
12             ldr r0, =.fmt0
13             ldr r1, .i1              # -59 + 20*3 folded into 1
14             bl printf
15
16 @ a = 2
17             ldr r4, .i2              # a in r4
18
19 @ bb_1 = -(a) + 12
20             mov r0, r4
21             neg r0, r0
22             mov r6, r0               # .t0 in r6
23             ldr r1, .i12
24             add r6, r6, r1
25             mov r5, r6               # bb_1 in r5
26
27 @ print(a*bb_1 + a*3*(-1 + -1 + -1))
28             mul r6, r4, r5
29             ldr r1, .i3
30             mul r7, r4, r1           # .t1 in r7
31             ldr r1, .i_3             # 3*(-1 + -1 + -1) folded into -3
32             mul r7, r7, r1
33             add r6, r6, r7
34             ldr r0, =.fmt0
35             mov r1, r6
36             bl printf
37
38             mov r0, #0
39             pop {pc}
40 .fmt0:      .asciz "%d\n"            # constants in .text segment
41 .i3:        .word 3
42 .i1:        .word 1
43 .i2:        .word 2
44 .i12:       .word 12
45 .i_3:       .word -3
```

Figure 18.7

Problems

1. Copy your `c1.py` compiler from problem 1 in chapter 13 to `c2.py`. Then modify `c2.py` so that includes all the optimization techniques described in this chapter. To check if your compiler is optimizing fully, compare the code it produces with the code in Fig. 18.7. *Hint*: Implement `c2.py` incrementally—that is, one optimization at a time. When one optimization is working correctly, then implement the next optimization.

2. `c2.py` from problem 1 determines the type of a symbol table entry by examining the beginning of the symbol (".i" indicates an integer constant and ".t" indicates a temporary variable). Copy `c2.py` to `p1802.py`. Then modify `p1802.py` so that it determines the type of a symbol table entry from a parallel list in the symbol table. Each element in this list should indicate the type (constant, temporary, or variable) of the corresponding symbol. Which approach to determining the type of a symbol table entry is better? Justify your answer.

3. Do parentheses and order affect the efficiency of the generated code? Compare the code generated by your `c1.py` and `c2.py` compilers for the following programs:

    ```
    Program 1                    Program 2
    x = 1 + 2 + 3 + 4            x = (1 + 2) + (3 + 4)
    y = 1 + 2 + x                y = x + 1 + 2
    z = 1 + (2 + x)              z = x + (1 + 2)
    ```

    Explain any discrepancies between the generated code for the two programs.

4. Why do we assemble and link an assembly language program that calls a C library routine with `gcc` rather than with `as` and `ld`?

5. Does your `c2.py` compiler from problem 1 generate unnecessary `neg` instructions for the following `print` statements:

    ```
    print(-(2))    # code produced should be the same as that for print(-2)
    print(-(-2))   # code produced should be the same as that for print(2)
    print(-(-x))   # code produced should be the same as that for print(x)
    ```

    If so, modify your `c2.py` compiler so that it does not generate any `neg` instructions for these `print` statements. *Hint*: Modify `cg_neg()`.

6. Use your `c2.py` from problem 3 to compile the program below, which is in the file `p1806.in`. Does it put nine variables in registers and the rest in memory?

    ```
    a = 1
     ⋮
    z = 26
    ```

7. If you have nine variables in your source program, they do not necessarily all go into registers. Why not? Assemble a program that shows this.

8. A variable in the `.data` segment is loaded with a two-instruction sequence in the `.text` segment: the first to load the address, the second to load the value using its address. Devise an optimization scheme in which each variable in the `.data` section can be loaded with a single instruction in the `.text` segment. Write an assembler program that illustrates your technique. Test your program on Raspbian (*Note*: the `rpi` program does not support operands that are expressions with + or - so the standard solution to this problem will not work with `rpi`). *Hint*: At the beginning of a program, load a register with the address of the beginning of the `.data` segment.

9. Rewrite the code in Fig. 18.7 so that it is more efficient. What changes to your compiler would be needed to get it to produce this more efficient code?

10. Propose a register allocation scheme that would work better than first-come-first-serve but is still relatively easy to implement.

11. To optimally allocate registers, what would have to be determined about the use of variables and expressions in a program?

12. In some programming language a variable can be referenced with more than one designation. For example, in C the name `x` and `*p` both reference `x` if `p` points to `x`. Does this feature of C cause problems for the register allocation scheme?

13. Would it be better if the `loc` table held the register number rather than the register name. For example, if `r10` is allocated to `x`, then the `loc` entry for `x` would contain the number 10, not the string 'r10'.

14. Is there any advantage if the assembler distinguished variables that have initial values from variables that do not have initial values? In what way could uninitialized variables be treated differently than initialized variables?

15. When a constant is entered into the symbol table, should its `needword` value be set to `True`?

16. Copy `c2.py` from problem 1 to `p1816.py`. Then modify `p1816.py` so that the generated code uses immediate values wherever possible. For example, instead of generating

    ```
    ldr r0, .i5
    ```

    your compiler would generate

    ```
    mov r0, #5
    ```

    The `mov` instruction is a faster instruction than the `ldr` instruction, and it does not require the constant in memory. Immediate values can also be used in `add` instructions. For example,

    ```
    add r0, r0, #17
    ```

    Thus, a constant can be added to a register without first having to load it from memory. Test your program using the source program `c2.in`.

19 Constructing a Pure Interpreter Level 3

Introduction

In this chapter, we upgrade our pure interpreter so that it supports function definitions (but not nested function definitions) and function calls of user-defined functions as well as the Python functions `input()` and `int()`. Adding support for functions also requires us to add support for global and local variables, the `global` and `return` statements, and parameter passing. The grammar for our upgraded source language is in Fig. 19.1.

The previous version of our pure interpreter essentially executes from top to bottom, with possibly some intervening loops. However, with function calls, we have a more complex flow of control. For example, a call of a function at the bottom of a program can invoke a function at top of the program. This new type of flow of control presents us with some new challenges.

New Symbol Tables

We need two symbol tables, one for local variables and one for global variables. Each symbol table is a dictionary. The local symbol table is initialized in the global section of the interpreter with

```
localsymbol = {}
```

The global symbol table is initialized with

```
globalsymbol = {}
```

To determine which symbol table to use for a given variable, the parser needs to know which variables are global and which are local. For this purpose, it uses `globalsdeclared` and `infunction`. `globalsdeclared` is a list declared in the global section of the interpreter which is initialized to the empty list whenever a function is called:

```
globalsdeclared = []
```

Every variable that is declared global in that function is appended to this list. For example, if within a function there is the statement

```
global f
```

then `'f'` is appended to `globalsdeclared`.

```
<program>         → <stmt>* EOF

<stmt>            → <simplestmt> NEWLINE
<stmt>            → <compoundstmt>

<simplestmt>      → <assignmentstmt>
<simplestmt>      → <printstmt>
<simplestmt>      → <passstmt>
<simplestmt>      → <globalstatment>
<simplestmt>      → <returnstmt>
<simplestmt>      → <functioncall>

<compoundstmt>    → <whilestmt>
<compoundstmt>    → <ifstmt>
<compoundstmt>    → <defstmt>

<assignmentstmt> → NAME '=' <relexpr>
<printstmt>       →'print' '(' [<relexpr> (',' <relexpr> )* [',']] ')'
<passstmt>        → 'pass'
<globalstmt>      → 'global' NAME (',' NAME)*
<returnstmt>      → 'return' [<relexpr>]
<whilestmt>       → 'while' <relexpr> ':' <codeblock>
<ifstmt>          → 'if' <relexpr> ':' <codeblock> ['else' ':' <codeblock>]
<defstmt>         → 'def' NAME '(' [NAME (',' NAME)*] ')' ':' <codeblock>

<codeblock>       →   NEWLINE INDENT <stmt>+ DEDENT
<relexpr>         → <expr> [ ('<' | '<=' | '==' | '!=' | '>' | '>=') <expr> ]
<expr>            → <term> (('+' | '-' ) <term>)*
<term>            → <factor> (('*' | '/') <factor>)*

<factor>          → '+' <factor>
<factor>          → '-' <factor>
<factor>          → UNSIGNEDINT
<factor>          → UNSIGNEDFLOAT
<factor>          → NAME
<factor>          → '(' <relexpr> ')'
<factor>          → STRING
<factor>          → 'True'
<factor>          → 'False'
<factor>          → 'None'
<factor>          → 'input' '(' STRING ')'
<factor>          → 'int' '(' <relexpr> ')'
<factor>          → <functioncall>
<functioncall>    → NAME '(' [<relexpr> [',' <relexpr>]*] ')'
```

Figure 19.1

infunction is a counter that keeps track of the function call depth. If execution is not inside any function, infunction is 0. On each function call, infunction is incremented by 1; on each return, infunction is decremented by 1. For example, in the program in Fig. 19.2, infunction is 0 before f() is called. Inside f() before g() is called, infunction is 1. Inside g(), infunction is 2. When g() returns to f(), infunction is decremented. So infunction reverts back to 1. Similarly, when f() returns, infunction reverts back to 0.

```
1  def g():
2      global y    # infunction = 2 here
3      y = 1
4  def f():
5      z = 2       # infunction = 1 here
6      g()
7      z = 3       # infunction = 1 here
8
9  x = 1           # infunction = 0 here
10 f()
11 x = 2           # infunction = 0 here
```

Figure 19.2

Execution of the program in Fig. 19.2 starts at line 9. The parser has to enter x and its value into the symbol table. But which symbol table? When line 9 is executed, infunction is 0, indicating execution is not in any function. Because a variable not inside any function is necessarily a global variable, x must be a global variable. So the parser enters x and the value 1 into the global symbol table (i.e., the globalsymbol dictionary). When line 5 is executed, infunction is 1. Moreover, z in not in the globalsdeclared list, and, therefore, z is a local variable. Thus, the parser enters z and the value 2 into the local symbol table (i.e., the localsymbol dictionary). When line 3 is executed, y is in the globalsdeclared list. So the parser enters y and its value into the global symbol table. When line 11 is executed, x is already in one of the symbol tables. Thus, the symbol table that has x is updated with its new value.

Here is the logic that the parser uses to determine the treatment of a variable v, where v is a variable on the *left side* of an assignment statement:

```
if v in globalsdeclared or infunction == 0:
```
   Enter v and its value into the global symbol table, or update its value if it is already there
```
else:
```
   Enter v and its value into the local symbol table, or update its value if it is already there

The parser also uses infunction when it parses a return statement. If at that time infunction is 0, then that return statement is not inside any function. Thus, there is no calling statement to return to. In that case, the parser raises a RuntimeError exception.

When the factor() function parses a variable, it gets the variable's value by calling getvalue(). It pushes the value obtained from getvalue() onto the operand stack. getvalue() first searches the local symbol table for the variable name. If it is not there, it searches the global symbol table:

```
1 def getvalue(s):
2     if s in localsymbol:
3         return localsymbol[s]
4     if s in globalsymbol:
5         return globalsymbol[s]
6     else:
7         raise RuntimeError('No value for ' + s)
```

How a Function Definition is Handled

Consider the following program:

```
1 x = 2
2 def f(z)
3     print(x + z)
4 f(10)
```

The assignment of 2 to x on line 1 is at the outermost level of the program (i.e., it is not within a function). Thus, x is a global variable. When the parser processes line 1, it enters 'x' and its value 2 into the global symbol table. The definition of the function f(), like x, is at the outermost level of the program. Thus, the symbol f is also global. When the parser first reaches line 2, it handles f in the same way it handles x. Specifically, the defstmt() function (which is called by compoundstmt() which is called by stmt()), enters 'f()' and its address (i.e., the index of the token f in the token stream) into the global symbol table (see line 4):

```
1  def defstmt():
2      advance()                    # advance past def
3      if token.lexeme + '()' not in globalsymbol:
4          globalsymbol[token.lexeme + '()'] = tokenindex
5      else:
6          raise RuntimeError('Duplicate function definition')
7      while token.category != INDENT:
8          advance()                # adv up to INDENT at end of function header
9      indentcol = token.column     # save column of INDENT token
10     while True:
11         if token.category == DEDENT and token.column < indentcol:
12             advance()            # advance past DEDENT
13             break
14         advance()
```

Note that the function name (in token.lexeme) and '()' are concatenated on line 4 above. The resulting string is then entered into globalsymbol along with the starting address of the function (which is in tokenindex). The parentheses concatenated to the end of the function name allows function names in the symbol table to be easily distinguished from variable names.

After entering the function name into globalsymbol, defstmt() advances to the INDENT that starts the function body. It saves the column of the INDENT token (line 9), and then advances past the function body (lines 10 to 14).

Saving Return Addresses

Suppose a program calls `f()` which calls `g()` which calls `h()` (see Fig. 19.3). When `h()` is done, it returns to `g()`. Similarly, when `g()` is done, it returns to its caller, `f()`, and when `f()` is done, it returns to its caller. When `f()` is called, the *return address* (i.e., the address `f()` should return to when it is done) has to be saved somewhere. Otherwise, `f()` would not know where to return to. For the same reason, when `f()` calls `g()` and when `g()` calls `h()`, the return addresses have to be saved. In Fig. 19.3, the arrows show the flow of control.

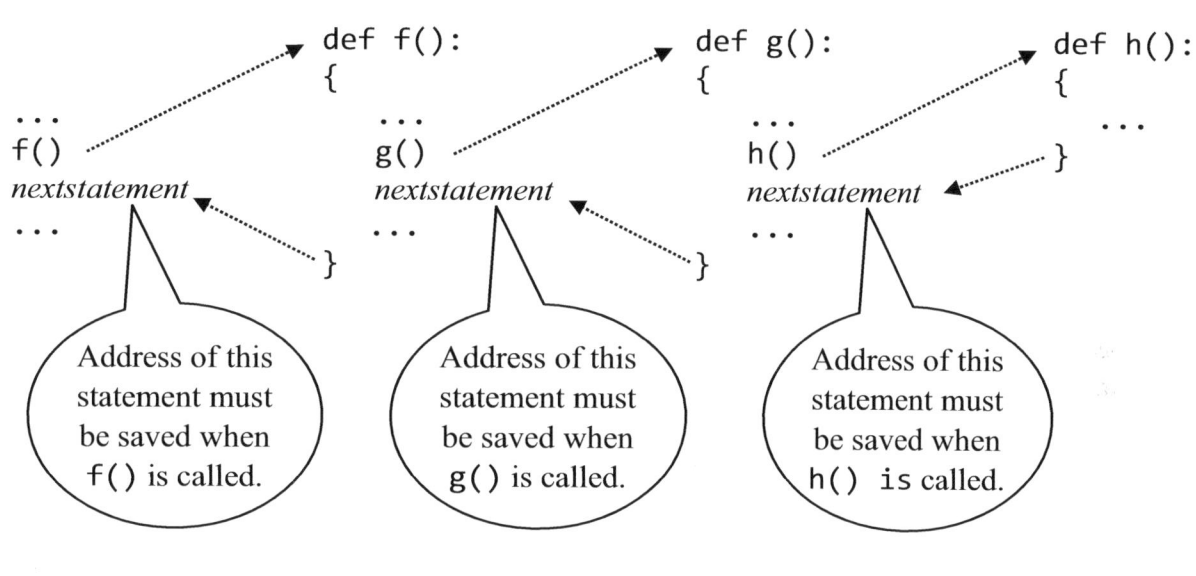

Figure 19.3

The return addresses are needed in reverse order from the order in which they are saved. Thus, the natural data structure to hold return addresses is a stack (recall a stack is a last-in-first-out data structure). We use `returnstack` for this purpose. It is initialized in the global section of the interpreter with

`returnstack = []`

Our interpreter has five stacks: `operandstack` (holds operands), `indentstack` (holds indent-to column numbers), `returnstack` (holds return addresses) and two more—`localsymtabstack` (holds local symbol tables) and `globalsdeclaredstack` (holds `global` declarations)—which we discuss below.

Saving the Local Symbol Table

Local variables and their values are held in the local symbol table. When one function calls another, the local symbol table changes: It no longer holds the local variables of the calling function. Instead, it holds the local variables of the called function. When the called function returns to its caller, the local symbol table reverts back to the way it was before the call. Thus, whenever any function it executing, the local symbol table holds its and only its local variables and their values.

When one function calls another, the local symbol table of the calling function has to be saved. Otherwise, the local symbol table of the calling function could not be restored when the called function returns to the calling function. Suppose `f()` calls `g()`, and `g()` calls `h()`. When `f()` calls `g()`, the local symbol table for `f()` is saved. When `g()` calls `h()`, the local symbol table of `g()` is saved. When `h()` then returns to `g()`, the local symbol table of `g()` is restored. When `g()` returns to `f()`, the local symbol table of `f()` is restored. Note that the symbol tables are restored in the reverse order from the order in which they are saved. So a stack is the natural data structure to use to save local symbol tables. We use `localsymtabstack` for this purpose. It is initialized in the global section of the interpreter with

```
localsymtabstack = []
```

Saving Global Declarations

When a function is executing, a set of `global` declarations is in effect. For example, in Fig. 19.4, when `f()` is executing, the `global` declarations in effect are those from line 5. When `f()` calls `g()`, a new set of `global` declarations goes into effect: namely, the one from line 11. When `g()` returns to `f()`, the `global` declarations for `f()` are restored. When a function calls another function, its `global` declarations must be saved so that they can be restored later when the called function returns to the calling function.

```
1  x = 1                    # x is global here
2  y = 2                    # y is global here
3  z = 3                    # z is global here
4  def f():
5      global x, y
6      x = 10               # x is global here
7      y = z                # y and z are global here
8      g()
9      print(x)             # x is global here
10 def g():
11     global y
12     x = 40               # x is local here
13     y = 50               # y is global here
14     z = 60               # z is local here
15 f()
16 print(x)                 # displays 10
17 print(y)                 # displays 50
18 print(z)                 # displays 3
```

Figure 19.4

The `global` declarations are restored in the reverse order from the order in which they are saved. So a stack is the natural data structure to use to save the `global` declarations. We use `globalsdeclaredstack` for this purpose. It is initialized in the global section of the interpreter with

```
globalsdeclaredstack = []
```

Structure of the functioncall() Function

To support function calls, we add the following productions to our grammar:

```
<simplestmt>    → <functioncall>
<factor>        → <functioncall>
<functioncall>  → NAME '(' [<relexpr> (',' <relexpr>)*] ')'
```

When `functioncall()` is first entered, `token.lexeme` (the lexeme of the current token) is the name of the function to be called. `functioncall()` calls `getvalue()` to get the value (i.e., address) of this function (recall that function names are stored in the symbol table with '()' concatenated to their tail ends so they can be distinguished from variable names):

```
addressoffunc = getvalue(token.lexeme + '()')
```

Next it initializes a local list named `arglist` to the empty list with

```
arglist = []
```

It then advances to the argument list in the function call by calling `advance()` and `consume()` as needed. Once positioned at the argument list, it parses it, appending the *value* of each argument to `arglist`. Finally, it executes the sequence of instructions on lines 3 to 18 in Fig. 19.5.

```
1  def functioncall()
2      ...                                              # missing instructions
3      advance()                                        # adv past right parenthesis
4      returnstack.append(tokenindex)                   # save return address
5      infunction += 1                                  # increment function call depth
6      localsymtabstack.append(localsymbol)             # save local symbol table
7      globalsdeclaredstack.append(globalsdeclared)     # save globalsdeclared
8      tokenindex = addressoffunc                       # reset tokenindex
9      token = tokenlist[tokenindex]                    # get token at this address
10     try:
11         functiondef(arglist)                         # execute called function
12     except Returnsignal:
13         pass
14     localsymbol = localsymtabstack.pop()              # restore local symbol table
15     globalsdeclared = globalsdeclaredstack.pop()      # restore globalsdeclared
16     infunction -= 1                                   # decrement function call depth
17     tokenindex = returnstack.pop()                    # reposition parser at ret addr
18     token = tokenlist[tokenindex]                     # get current token
```

Figure 19.5

The call of `advance()` on line 3 of Fig. 19.5 advances past the right parenthesis at the end of the function call. For example, consider the following statements:

```
                   ┌── parser positioned here (on NEWLINE) after advance() on line 3 of Fig. 19.5
                   ▼
        f()
        y = f() + 5
                ▲
                └── parser positioned here after advance() on line 3 of Fig. 19.5
```

When `functioncall()` is parsing the first call of `f()` shown above, the `advance()` on line 3 in Fig. 19.5 positions the parser on the NEWLINE that follows the right parenthesis. When `functioncall()` is parsing the second call, the `advance()` on line 3 positions the parser on the plus sign that follows the right parenthesis on the call. In both cases, the parser is positioned at the location to which the called function should return when it is done executing. Recall that the variable `tokenindex` is maintained so that it always holds the index of the current position of the parser in the token stream. Thus, after the `advance()` on line 3 in Fig. 19.5, `tokenindex` holds the return address for each function call. Line 4 saves this return address by pushing it onto `returnstack`.

Line 5 in Fig. 19.5 increments the function call depth counter, `infunction`. Recall that on each function call, `infunction` is incremented. On each return, `infunction` is decremented. Because `infunction` is initialized to 0, it equals 0 whenever execution is not within any function, and it is greater than 0 when a function is executing.

Lines 6 and 7 save the local symbol and the `globalsdeclared` tables. The called function creates its own local symbol and globalsdeclared tables. These tables are saved so that on return from the called function, the local symbol and globals declared tables of the calling function can be restored (lines 14 and 15 do the restoring).

Line 8 in Fig. 19.5 assigns to `tokenindex` the address of the function to be called. This assignment changes the position of the parser in the token stream. After the assignment, the parser is positioned at the beginning of the called function. Line 9 then updates `token` with the new current token (recall that `token` is the variable that holds the current token—that is, the token on which the parser is positioned).

On line 11, `functioncall()` calls `functiondef()`, passing it `arglist` (the list of the values of the arguments in the function call in the source program. `functiondef()` is the function that parses and executes functions. Thus, to do a function call, `functioncall()` not only has to reposition the parser in the token stream to the beginning of the called function but also call `functiondef()`.

`functiondef()` can return to `functioncall()` in two ways. It can execute to its end, in which case it returns to line 14 in Fig. 19.5. If, however, the called function executes a `return` statement, then `functiondef()` raises a user-defined `Returnsignal` exception (see the discussion of exceptions in the appendix A). This exception causes an immediate branch to the `except` block on line 12. After the `except` block finishes (the `pass` statement does nothing), the next statement executed is on line 14 in Fig. 19.5. Thus, both types of returns return to line 14. The remaining lines in `functioncall()` complete the call by restoring the local symbol and the globals declared tables of the caller, adjusting `infunction`, and repositioning the parser at the return address in the token stream.

Structure of the functiondef() Function

The parser function that parses and executes a function in the source code is `functiondef()`. When `functiondef()` is called, it starts by initializing `localsymbol` and `globalsdeclared`:

```
localsymbol = {}
globalsdeclared = []
```

Next, `functiondef()` advances to the parameter list by calling `advance()` and `consume()` as needed. Once positioned at the parameter list of the function, it parses it using a loop. After parsing each parameter, it enters into `localsymbol` the parameter name and its value obtained from `arglist`—the list of argument values passed to `functiondef` by `functioncall()` (see line 11 in Fig. 19.5) The value of the first parameter is in `arglist[0]`, the value of the second parameter is in `arglist[1]`, and so on. In addition, `functiondef()` checks if the number of parameters and the number of arguments are the same. It they are not, it raises an exception.

Parameters are all local to the called function. That is why `localsymbol` (the local symbol table) is initialized with them. After consuming the right parenthesis that ends the parameter list, and the colon, `functiondef()` calls `codeblock()`. As the code block (which is the body of the called function) is parsed, it is executed. Any new local variables that are used within the code block are added to the local symbol table.

```
1  def functiondef(arglist):
2      global localsymbol, localvalue, globalsdeclared, token, tokenindex
3      consume(NAME)
4      consume(LEFTPAREN)
5      argindex = 0
6      localsymbol = {}
7      globalsdeclared = []
8      while token.category != RIGHTPAREN:
9                                                    # missing instructions
10
11         # check if token.category is NAME (if not, RuntimeError)
12         # check if argindex < len(arglist) (if not, RuntimeError)
13         # enter parameter name (i.e., token.lexeme) and its value
14         # (i.e., arglist[argindex]) into localsymbol dictionary
15         # increment argindex
16         advance()
17         if token.category == RIGHTPAREN:
18             break
19         consume(COMMA)
20     if len(localsymbol) < len(arglist):
21         raise RuntimeError('More arguments than parameters')
22     consume(RIGHTPAREN)
23     consume(COLON)
24     codeblock()
25     operandstack.append(None)        # always return something
```

Figure 19.6

A function returns a value simply by pushing it onto the operand stack. Then on return, the calling function gets the returned value by popping it off the stack. If the parser reaches the bottom of `functiondef()`, that means that no `return` statement was executed in the body of the called function, and, therefore, no value is returned. But a function is supposed to always return something. For this reason, `functiondef()` pushes `None` onto the operand stack just before returning to its caller:

```
25      operandstack.append(None)       # always return something
```

`functiondef()` then returns to `functioncall()` which immediately returns to its caller, which is `factor()` or `simplestmt()`.

Structure of the returnstmt() Function

On entry, `returnstmt()` checks the value of `infunction`. If `infunction` is 0, then the `return` statement is not inside any function. Thus, there is no calling statement to return to. In that case, `returnstmt()` raises a `RuntimeError` exception.

The `return` statement has two forms:

1. `return <relexpr>`
2. `return`

The first form returns the value of the relative expression (by pushing it onto `operandstack`). The second form by default returns `None`. Thus, the `return` statement always returns something.

After advancing past the `return` keyword, `returnstmt()` checks if the current token is the newline character. If it is, the `return` statement is of the second form above. So `returnstmt()` pushes `None`. If the current token is not the newline character, then the `return` statement is of the first form. So `returnstmt()` calls `relexpr()`. In either case, `returnstmt()` raises a `Returnsignal` exception to trigger a return to `functioncall()` (to line 13 in Fig. 19.5).

What happens to the value returned? If the function call is a factor in an expression, then the returned value is used as the value of that factor. For example, in the assignment statement

```
y = 2*f()
```

the value returned is multiplied by 2 and then assigned to `y`. But what if the function call is a standalone statement, such as

```
f()
```

This type of function call gets executed by `simplestmt()` calling `functioncall()` calling `functiondef()`. Here is the call of `functioncall()` that is in `simplestmt()`:

```
functioncall()
operandstack().pop()        # pop and discard value returned
```

Note that after the call, the value returned is popped off `operandstack` and discarded.

Problems

1. Copy your `i2.py` interpreter from problem 1 in chapter 16 to `i3.py`. Then modify `i3.py` so that it corresponds to the grammar in Fig. 19.1. Start by extending the tokenizer so that it recognizes the keywords `def`, `return`, `global`, `input`, and `int`. Test your interpreter by entering

```
python i3.py i3.in
```

2. Copy your `i3.py` interpreter from problem 1 to `p1902.py`. Modify `p1902.py` so that it handles the `return` statement correctly but does not use the exception mechanism. *Hint*: Have the relevant parser functions return 0 if the caller should continue executing or 1 if the caller should immediately return to its caller.

3. `arglist` in `functioncall()` is a local variable. Could it also be a global variable? Justify your answer.

4. Does the Python 3 interpreter generate an error message for a duplicate definition of a function name? Does your `i3.py` interpreter from problem 1 generate an error message?

5. What problem might occur if function names are stored in the symbol table without '()' concatenated to their tail ends?

6. What is the purpose of line 18 in Fig. 19.5?

7. Why is a return to the calling function triggered by a `return` statement handled differently than a return from a function that does not have a `return` statement?

8. Is line 25 in `functiondef()` in Fig. 19.6 always executed when `functiondef()` is called? Justify your answer.

9. Are the colons syntactically needed in the source language? Copy your `i3.py` interpreter from problem 1 to `p1909.py`. Then modify `p1909.py` so that it does not expect any colons. Test `p1909.py` by entering

    ```
    python p1909.py p1909.in
    ```

10. Run the following program using both the Python 3 interpreter and your `i3.py` interpreter from problem 1. Do you get different results? If so, explain why?

    ```
    x = 5
    def f():
        print(x) # Is this stmt legal?
        x = 10
    f()
    ```

11. Write a hybrid interpreter that uses Python byte code as the intermediate language that supports all the statements in `i3.in`.

12. Python searches the local symbol table and the global symbol table in that order to access a variable. Why not the reverse order? Are there any advantages if Python used the reverse order? How would programs have to be written differently if the reverse order were used?

20 Constructing a Hybrid Interpreter Level 3

Introduction

A hybrid interpreter translates the source program to an intermediate language (IL), and then interprets the IL form of the program. The hybrid interpreters we constructed in chapters 10 and 17 use Python bytecode as the IL. In this chapter, we construct a hybrid interpreter that uses an *abstract syntax tree* (AST) as the IL. An AST of a source program is essentially its parse tree from which all unnecessary nodes have been removed. Thus, an AST can be processed more easily and more quickly than a parse tree.

Postfix is another IL that is sometimes used in interpreters (see problem 8 in chapter 10 and problem 5 in chapter 17). Postfix requires a relatively minor alteration of the source program. Thus, interpreters that use postfix as the IL are more on the pure side of the spectrum than on the hybrid side.

Compilers as well as interpreters often use an AST as the IL. The compilers we constructed in chapters 13 and 18 translate the source program directly to the target language (assembly language). However, most compilers typically first translate the source program to an IL, such as an AST. Next, the compiler performs a variety of operations on the IL, such as semantic checks and optimization. Finally, the compiler translates the modified IL to the target language.

Fig. 20.1 shows a simplified block diagram of both an interpreter and a compiler that use an AST as the IL. The front ends for the interpreter and the compiler are the same: a tokenizer and a parser (which generates the AST). In an interpreter, the AST is interpreted. In a compiler, the AST is translated to the target program.

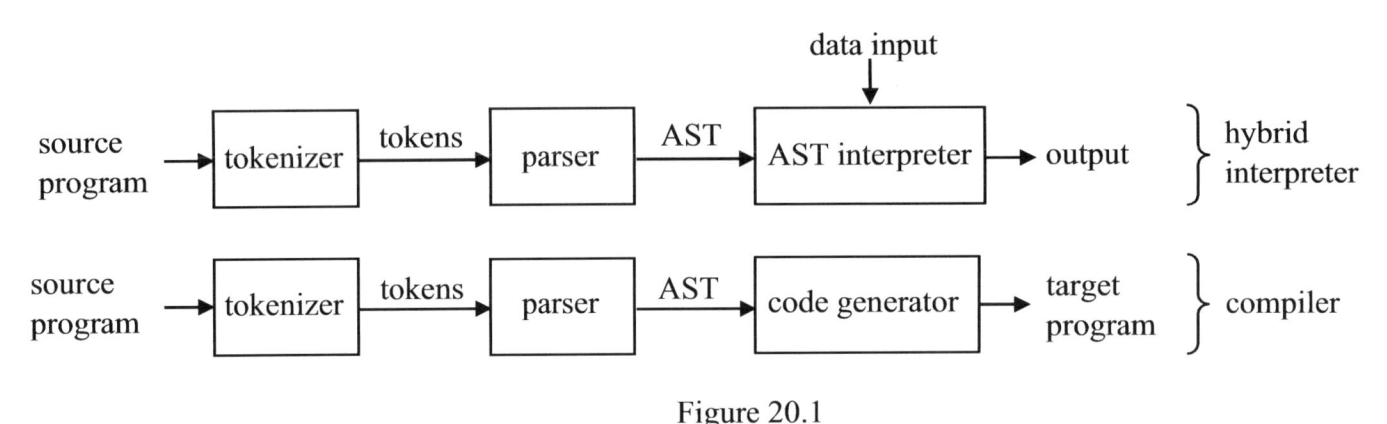

Figure 20.1

The source language for the hybrid interpreter we describe in this chapter is the language defined by the grammar in Fig. 7.3, which is source language supported by our level 1 language processors (`i1.py`, `h1.py`, and `c1.py`).

Parse Trees Versus ASTs

Let's examine the parse tree and the AST in Fig. 20.2 for the following one-line program:

    a = 1 + 2 + 3

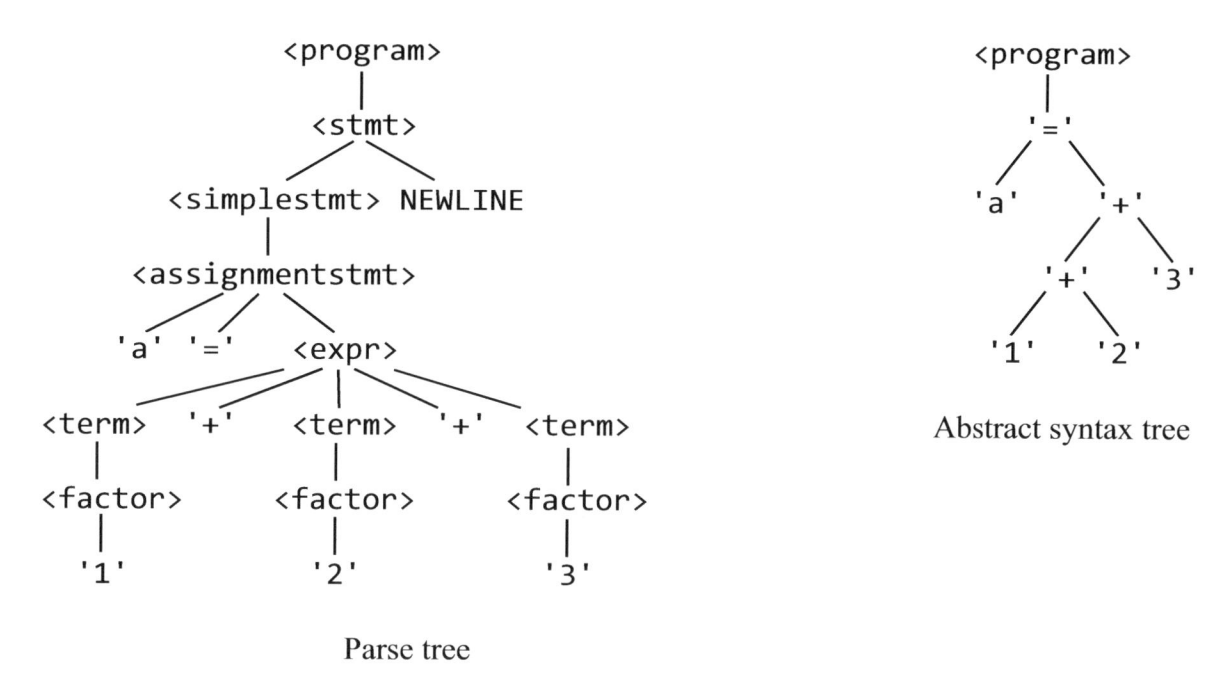

```
                    <program>                          <program>
                       |                                  |
                    <stmt>                               '='
                   /      \                             /   \
            <simplestmt>  NEWLINE                    'a'    '+'
                 |                                          /  \
           <assignmentstmt>                               '+'   '3'
             / |    \                                    / \
           'a' '='  <expr>                             '1' '2'
                  / | | | \
            <term> '+' <term> '+' <term>            Abstract syntax tree
              |        |        |
           <factor> <factor> <factor>
              |        |        |
             '1'      '2'      '3'

                    Parse tree
```

Figure 20.2

Note that the AST does not have any nonterminal symbols, except for the start symbol (<program>) in the root node. It also does not have the NEWLINE terminal symbol. The NEWLINE terminal symbol is not needed in the AST because the structure of the tree defines the end of each statement (each subtree of the <program> node corresponds to one statement). Parentheses in the source code that show the order of operation are also not needed—the tree structure of the AST shows the order of operation. You can see that an AST is a highly simplified version of the parse tree of source program, yet it retains all the essential structural features of the source program.

Representing an AST

We represent each node in an AST with a Node object that has three fields: type, left, and right (see Fig. 20.3). Some nodes in an AST have two "children" (i.e., nodes below a given node to which the given node points); some nodes have only one "child." In the former case, the left and right fields point to the two children. In the latter case, the left field points to the only child (the right field is not used). For all nodes the type field indicates the type of the node (PROGRAM, ASSIGNOP, PRINT, PLUS, TIMES, NEGATE, INTEGER, or NAME). Some nodes have an unlimited number of children. For example, a PROGRAM node has one child for each statement in the source program. In such a node, its left field is a Python list whose elements are the children of the node.

```
1  class Node:
2      def __init__(self, type, left, right):
3          self.type = type      # type of the node
4          self.left = left      # pointer to left child
5          self.right = right    # pointer to right child (if any)
```

Figure 20.3

Constructing an AST

We construct an AST from the bottom up—specifically, starting from the `factor()` function. For an integer or a name token, `factor()` creates a node for that token. For example, `factor()` executes the following code for an unsigned integer:

```
23      if token.category == UNSIGNEDINT:
24          node = Node(INTEGER, sign*int(token.lexeme), None)
25          advance()
26          return node
```

It creates an object from the `Node` class and initializes it with the type `INTEGER` and the value adjusted by `sign` of the unsigned integer (we want its numeric value—not a string—because the interpreter is going to perform computations with it). The pointer (i.e., reference) to this node (which is assigned to the variable `node`) is then returned to the caller of `factor()`. `factor()` takes a similar action for a variable name. It creates an object from the `Node` class and initializes it with the type `NAME` and the lexeme of the token. If `sign` is -1, it also creates a `NEGATE` node which points to the `NAME` node. It then returns a pointer to the `NAME` node (if `sign` is 1) or the `NEGATE` node (if `sign` is -1):

```
27      elif token.category == NAME:
28          node = Node(NAME, token.lexeme, None)
29          advance()
30          if sign == -1:
31              node = Node(NEGATE, node, None)
32          return node
```

Fig. 20.4 shows the nodes that are created for the terminal symbols 1 and x.

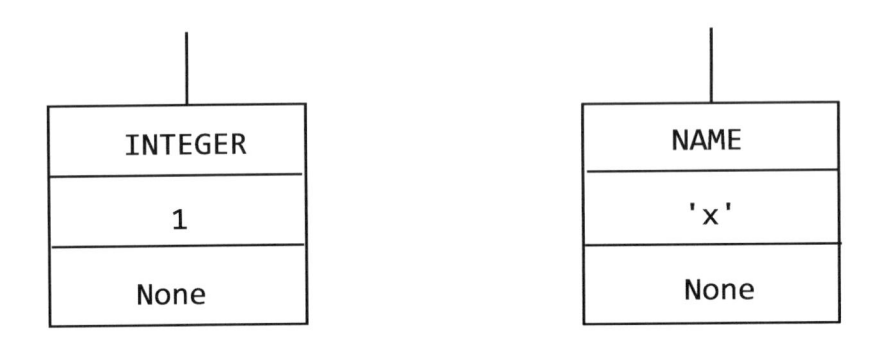

INTEGER
1
None

NAME
'x'
None

Figure 20.4

Whenever `term()` calls `factor()`, it gets back from `factor()` a pointer to the node that represents the factor just parsed. Let's see what happens when `term()` parses the first term in the expression `1*2*x + 3` (the first term is `1*2*x`; the second term is `3`):

```
1  def term():
2      global sign
3      sign = 1
4      left = factor()      # get reference to left factor
5      while token.category == TIMES:
6          advance()
7          sign = 1
8          right = factor()  # get reference to right factor
9          # create Node with TIMES, left, and right
10         node = Node(TIMES, left, right)
11         left = node       # node becomes left factor
12     return left
13
14 def factor():
15     global sign
16     if token.category == PLUS:
17         advance()
18         return factor()
19     elif token.category == MINUS:
20         sign = -sign
21         advance()
22         return factor()
23     if token.category == UNSIGNEDINT:
24         node =  Node(INTEGER, sign*int(token.lexeme), None)
25         advance()
26         return node
27     elif token.category == NAME:
28         node = Node(NAME, token.lexeme, None)
29         advance()
30         if sign == -1:
31             node = Node(NEGATE, node, None)
32         return node
33     elif token.category == LEFTPAREN:
34         advance()
35         savesign = sign     # must save sign because expr()
36         node = expr()       # calls term() which resets sign to 1
37         if savesign == -1:  # so use the saved value of sign
38             node = Node(NEGATE, node, None)
39         consume(RIGHTPAREN)
40         return node
41     else:
42         raise RuntimeError('Expecting factor')
```

Figure 20.5

Chapter 20: Constructing a Hybrid Interpreter Level 3

- On line 4 in Fig. 20.5, `term()` calls `factor()`. `factor()` returns a pointer to a node containing 1. The pointer to this node is assigned to a local variable `left`.
- On line 6, `term()` advances past the asterisk between the 1 and 2 in `1*2*x + 3`.
- On line 8, `term()` calls `factor()`, which returns a pointer to a node containing 2. The pointer to this node is assigned to a local variable `right`.
- On line 10, `term()` creates an object from the `Node` class, and initializes it with `TIMES`, `left`, and `right`. After this node is initialized, `left` on line 11 is assigned the pointer to this node.

Fig. 20.6 shows the resulting structure.

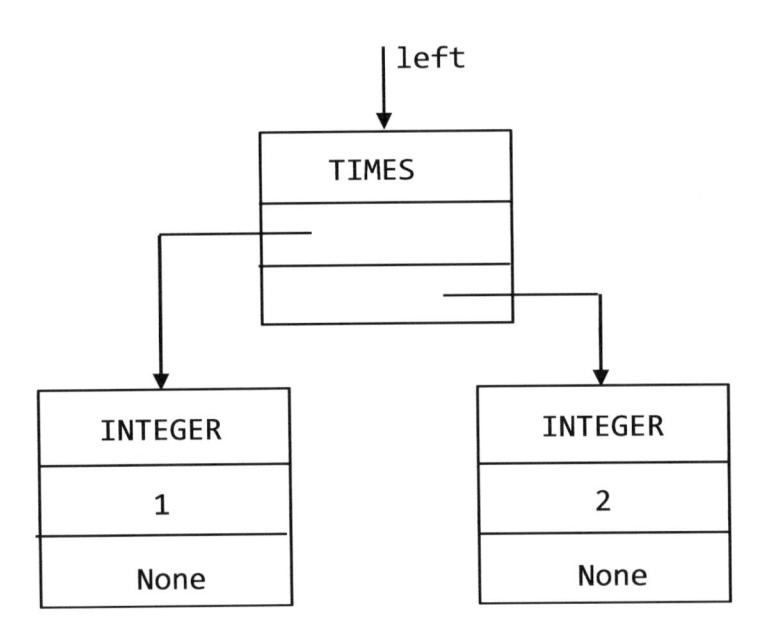

Figure 20.6

At this point we are back at the top of the `while` loop (line 5 in Fig. 20.5). `term()` just parsed the 2 in `1*2*x + 3` by calling `factor()`. So the current token is the asterisk between 2 and x, in which case the category of the current token is `TIMES`. Thus, the `while` loop on line 5 continues to execute.

- On line 6, `term()` advances past the asterisk between the 2 and x in `1*2*x + 3`.
- On line 8, `term()` calls `factor()`. `factor()` returns a pointer to a node containing x. The pointer to this node is assigned to `right`.
- On line 10, `term()` creates an object from the `Node` class, and initializes it with `TIMES`, `left`, and `right`. After this node is initialized, `left` is assigned the pointer to this node on line 11.

We now have a tree structure that represents the term `1*2*x` (see Fig. 20.7). We are again back at the top of the `while` loop. But this time the current token is the plus sign in `1*2*x + 3`. Thus, the `while` loop ends. On line 12, `term()` returns `left` to its caller. `left` contains the pointer to the abstract tree structure in Fig. 20.7 corresponding to the term `1*2*x`.

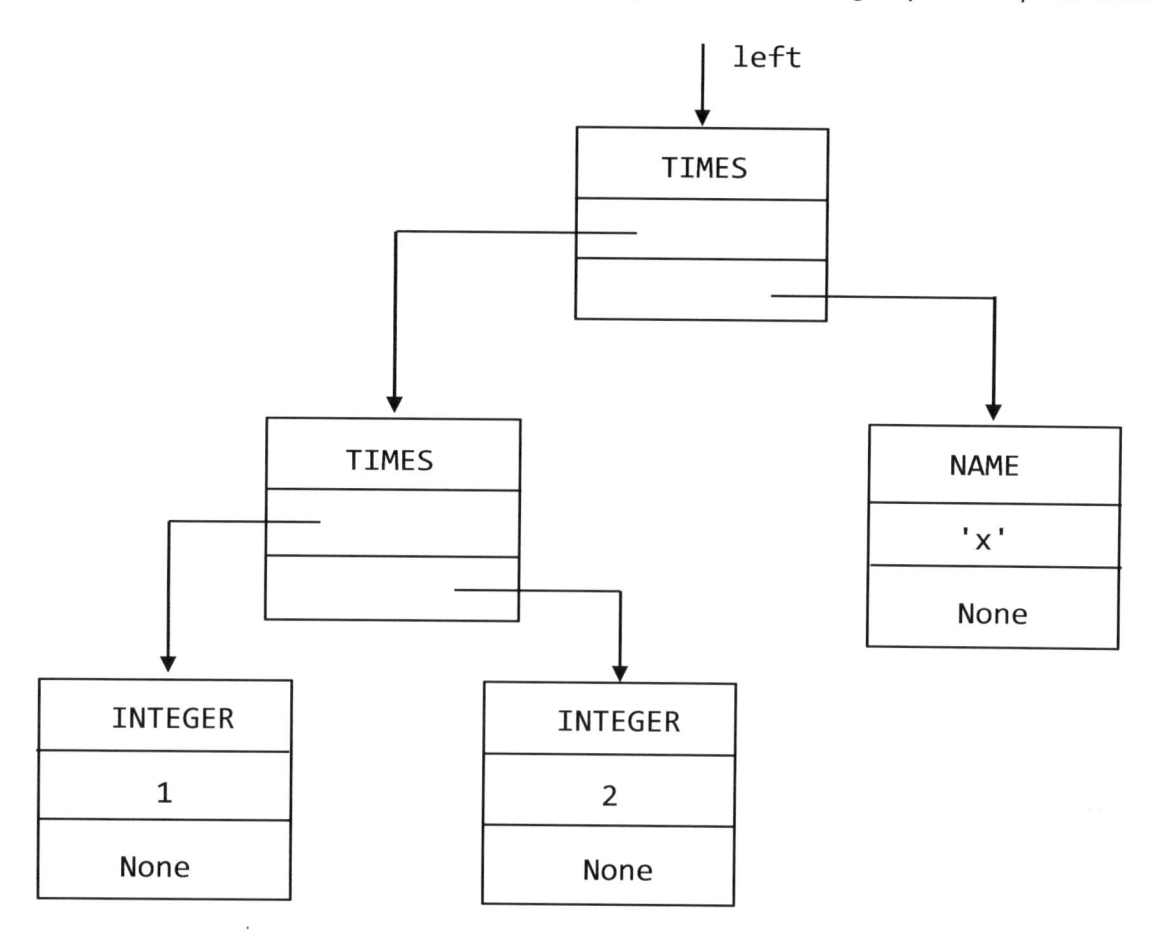

```
                    │ left
                    ▼
                ┌─────────┐
                │  TIMES  │
                ├─────────┤
           ┌────│         │────┐
           │    └─────────┘    │
           ▼                   ▼
       ┌─────────┐         ┌─────────┐
       │  TIMES  │         │  NAME   │
       ├─────────┤         ├─────────┤
    ┌──│         │──┐      │   'x'   │
    │  └─────────┘  │      ├─────────┤
    ▼               ▼      │  None   │
┌─────────┐   ┌─────────┐  └─────────┘
│ INTEGER │   │ INTEGER │
├─────────┤   ├─────────┤
│    1    │   │    2    │
├─────────┤   ├─────────┤
│  None   │   │  None   │
└─────────┘   └─────────┘
```

Figure 20.7

The `expr()` function works just like the `term()` function, except it calls `term()` instead of `factor()`, does not initialize `sign`, and it creates nodes whose type is PLUS instead of TIMES. `expr()` returns to its caller a pointer to the abstract tree structure that corresponds to the expression it parses.

`assignmentstmt()` calls `expr()` to get the abstract tree structure for the right side of the assignment statement (see line 32 of Fig. 20.8). It constructs a node whose type is ASSIGNOP. Its `right` field points to the AST created by the call of `expr()`. Its `left` field is assigned the lexeme corresponding to the variable on the left side of the assignment statement. `printstmt()` is similar to `assignmentstmt()`. It constructs a node whose type is PRINT. Its `left` field points to the AST created by the call to `expr()`.

We know from the grammar for the source language (see Fig. 7.3), `program()` calls `stmt()` which calls `simplestmt()` which calls the function that parses the current statement and creates its AST. For example, suppose `simplestmt()` calls `assignmentstmt()`. `assignmentstmt()` parses the current statement (an assignment statement) and creates its AST. It then returns the AST to `simplestmt()` which returns it to `stmt()` which returns it to `program()`. Each time `program()` receives an AST, it appends it to `stmtlist` (see line 10 in Fig. 20.8). When all the statements have been parsed, `program()` constructs a node whose type is PROGRAM and whose `left` field is the list of the ASTs corresponding to the statements in the source program (see line 13 in Fig. 20.8). This PROGRAM node is the root of the AST for the entire program.

```
 1 def parser():
 2     if trace:
 3         print('---------------------------------------- Program output')
 4     advance()              # advance so token holds first token
 5     return program()       # call start symbol function
 6
 7 def program():
 8     stmtlist = []
 9     while token.category in [NAME, PRINT]:
10         stmtlist.append(stmt())
11     if token.category != EOF:
12         raise RuntimeError('Expecting EOF')
13     return Node(PROGRAM, stmtlist, None)
14
15 def stmt():
16     ast = simplestmt()
17     consume(NEWLINE)
18     return ast
19
20 def simplestmt():
21     if token.category == NAME:
22         return assignmentstmt()
23     elif token.category == PRINT:
24         return printstmt()
25     else:
26         raise RuntimeError('Expecting statement')
27
28 def assignmentstmt():
29     lexeme = token.lexeme    # save token.lexeme
30     advance()
31     consume(ASSIGNOP)
32     node = Node(ASSIGNOP, lexeme, expr())
33     return node
```

Figure 20.8

On line 13 in Fig. 20.8, `program()` returns to `parser()` a pointer to the AST for the program. `parser()` in turn returns the pointer to the AST to `main` where `main` assigns it to the variable `ast`. `main` then calls the AST interpreter, passing it `ast` (the pointer to the AST for the program):

```
# code in main function
try:
    tokenizer()           # tokenize source code in source
    ast = parser()        # parse and create AST
    ...  ⇐============== # missing except block that displays error msg
    interpreter(ast)      # call interpreter passing it the AST
```

Fig. 20.9 shows the structure passed to the bytecode interpreter.

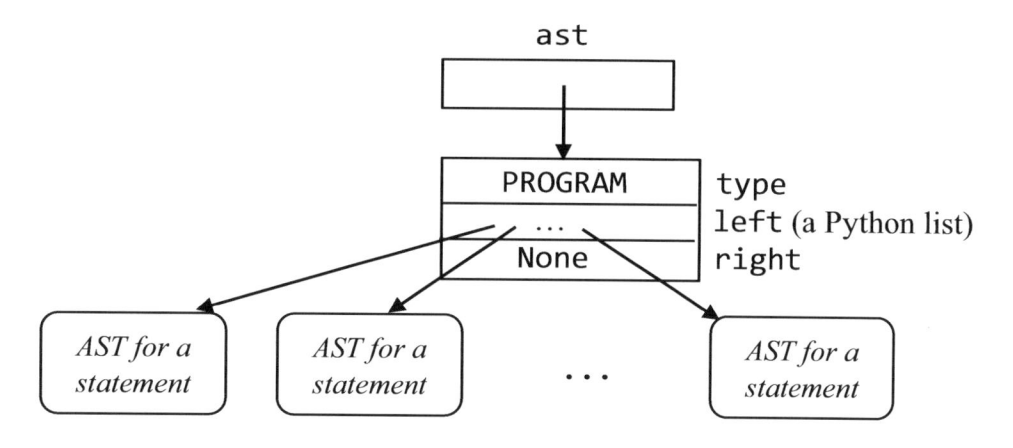

```
                        ast
                     ┌──────┐
                     └──┬───┘
                        ▼
                ┌──────────────┐  type
                │   PROGRAM    │  left (a Python list)
                │     ...      │  right
                │    None      │
                └──────────────┘
     ┌──────┬──────┴──────┬──────────────┐
     ▼      ▼             ▼              ▼
  AST for  AST for       ...          AST for
    a        a                           a
statement statement                  statement
```

Figure 20.9

You can see from the foregoing discussion that it not hard to construct an AST. Once you have the parser, it takes only minor adjustments to get it to construct the AST.

In an AST, every statement is represented by a node. For example, as we discussed above, the assignment statement is represented by a node whose `left` and `right` fields represent the left and right sides of the assignment statement. What about a code block and a `while` statement? Like `program()`, `codeblock()` creates a list of statements, and uses a single node to represent it. A `while` statement consists of two parts: the exit-test expression and a code block. It is represented with a node whose type is `WHILE`, whose `left` field points the tree structure corresponding to the exit-test expression, and whose `right` field points to the tree structure corresponding to the code block.

Interpreting an AST

If you have had any formal courses on data structures, you probably learned that there are simple algorithms for processing tree structures, and most of them use recursion. So it is no surprise that our AST interpreter uses recursion.

Our interpreter is passed a pointer to the root node of the AST. This pointer points to the node created by the `program()` function. The `left` field of this node is a list whose elements correspond to the statements in the source program. Our AST interpreter goes through this list, taking the appropriate action for each element (see Fig. 20.10).

```
1  def interpreter(ast):
2      for stmt in ast.left:
3          if stmt.type == ASSIGNOP:
4              symtab[stmt.left] = value(stmt.right)
5          elif stmt.type == PRINT:
6              print(value(stmt.left))
7          else:
8              raise RuntimeError('Expecting stmt')
```

Figure 20.10

For example, for an ASSIGNOP node, the interpreter performs the assignment operation specified by the node (see lines 3 and 4 in Fig. 20.10). Specifically, it assigns to the variable on the left side (obtained from the left field in the node that represents the assignment statement) the value of the right side (obtained from the right field). symtab is a dictionary that holds the name-value pairs for each variable in the source program. Thus, line 4 in Fig. 20.10 assigns to the variable given by stmt.left the value corresponding to stmt.right (obtained by a call of the value() function—see Fig. 20.11).

The value of an AST structure is determined from the bottom up. For example, to compute the value corresponding to the AST structure in Fig. 20.7, we start from the bottom. We first compute 1*2 to get 2. We then use the computed value (2) in the next higher level in the tree, where we compute 2*x, where the value of x is obtained from the symtab dictionary. This value is the value of the AST structure. To perform this bottom-up evaluation, we use a depth-first recursive algorithm. The idea behind this algorithm is simple. To process a tree, you perform the following steps on the root of the tree:

1. Evaluate the left subtree.

2. Evaluate the right subtree

3. Using the values of the left and right subtrees, compute the value of the root node of the tree according to the operation specified by the root node of the tree.

For example, suppose the root node has the type PLUS, and the value of the left subtree is 2 and the value of the right subtree is 3. Then the value of the root node is 2 + 3 = 5. But how do you evaluate the left and right subtrees? Simple: you do a traversal on those subtrees (and their subtrees, and so on). When this procedure finally reaches the nodes at the bottom of the tree (these nodes contain values or variable names), it obtains their values and then moves up the tree performing computation in a bottom-up order.

This traversal algorithm sounds complicated. On one level, it is. But the code that implements it is really simple (see Fig. 20.11). When value() is called, if the node it is passed has type INTEGER, then value() simply returns the integer value in that node (see line 3 in Fig. 20.11). Similarly, if the node has type NAME, then value() returns the integer value of the variable obtained from symtab (see line 5 in Fig. 20.11).

```
1  def value(node):
2      if node.type == INTEGER:
3          return node.left
4      elif node.type == NAME:
5          return symtab[node.left]
6      elif node.type == PLUS:
7          return value(node.left) + value(node.right)
8      elif node.type == TIMES:
9          return value(node.left) * value(node.right)
10     elif node.type == NEGATE:
11         return -value(node.left)
12     else:
13         raise RuntimeError('Invalid structure')
```

Figure 20.11

Now for the recursion: If the node has type PLUS, then `value()` makes two recursive calls—one for the left subtree and one for the right subtree (see Fig. 20.12). Each of these calls returns the value of the corresponding subtree. `value()` then computes the value of the PLUS node using these two values. It then passes the computed value up the tree. A TIMES node and a NEGATE node are handled similarly.

```
7        return value(node.left) + value(node.right)
```

- addition is done after the two recursive calls
- recursive call on the left subtree
- recursive call on the right subtree.

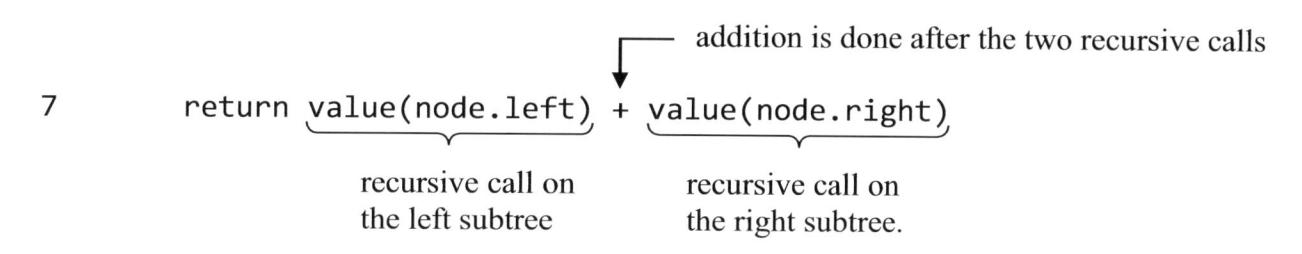

Figure 20.12

Problems

1. Copy the `h1.py` from problem 1 in chapter 10 to `h3.py`. Then modify and extend `h3.py` so that it creates and then interprets an AST. Your h3 interpreter should support our level 1 source language (see Fig. 7.1 for a source program and Fig. 7.3 for its grammar). *Note*: Each parser function (except `advance()` and `consume()`) in `h3.py` should return (with a `return` statement) the AST for what it parses (for example, see the parser functions in Fig. 20.8). Test your interpreter by entering

    `python h3.py h3.in`

2. Modify `h3.py` from problem 1 so that it displays the AST if `trace` is set to `True`. *Hint*: Use a breadth-first traversal algorithm to display the AST. Test your interpreter with `trace` set to `True` by entering

    `python h3.py h3.in`

3. Modify your `h3.py` interpreter from problem 2 so that it optimizes the AST before it interprets it by performing *constant folding*. For example, replace a PLUS node whose children are both constants with a node that holds the sum of the two constants. Test your interpreter with `trace` set to `True`, which should display the AST both before and after modification) by entering

    `python h3.py h3.in`

4. Copy your `h3.py` interpreter from problem 1 (or problems 2 or 3 if you did those problems) to `h4.py`. Then modify `h4.py` so that it can handle the source program in `h4.in` (identical to the source program in Fig. 14.1). Test your interpreter by entering

    `python h4.py h4.in`

5. Copy `h3.py` from program 1 (or problem 3) to `c4.py`. Then modify `c4.py` so that the AST is passed to a `codegen()` function that outputs the Raspbian Pi assembler code corresponding to the AST it is passed.

21 Constructing a Compiler Level 3

Introduction

In our implementation of our `c1.py` compiler from chapter 13 that translated to Raspberry Pi assembly language, we cheated a little: We generated code as if the source language were not dynamically typed. But our source language—a subset of Python—is dynamically typed. That is, a variable in Python has the type of whatever was last assigned to it. Thus, we need to fix our compiler.

Consider the following Python program:

```
1 s = input('input yes or no: ')
2 if s == 'yes':
3     x = 1              # x and y are integers
4     y = 2
5 else:
6     x = 'hello'        # x and y are strings
7     y = 'bye'
8 a = x + y              # addition or concatenation?
```

The assignment statement on line 8 performs either an addition or a concatenation depending on the types of x and y. If in response to the prompt on line 1, the user enters "yes", then x and y are assigned integers, in which case the assignment statement on line 8 performs an addition. If, on the other hand, the user enters a word other than "yes", then x and y are assigned strings, in which case the assignment statement on line 8 performs a concatenation.

The types of x and y when line 8 is executed depend on what the user enters in response to the prompt. If the compiler compiles line 8 to an addition, an error occurs if the user enters "no" on line 1 (because x and y are strings). If the compiler compiles line 8 to a concatenation, an error occurs if the user enters "yes" on line 1 (because x and y are integers).

So how does the compiler compile line 8? It generates two sequences of assembler code: one that performs an addition and one that performs a concatenation. Preceding these two sequences, the compiler generates assembler code that determines *at run time* the types of x and y and then branches to the sequence (the addition sequence or the concatenation sequence) appropriate for the types of x and y (see Fig. 21.1).

Source code

a = x + y

Assembler code

Instructions to determine the types of x and y
Branch to the concatenation sequence if x and y are strings
Instructions to add
Branch over the concatenation instructions
Instructions to concatenate
Instructions to assign result to a

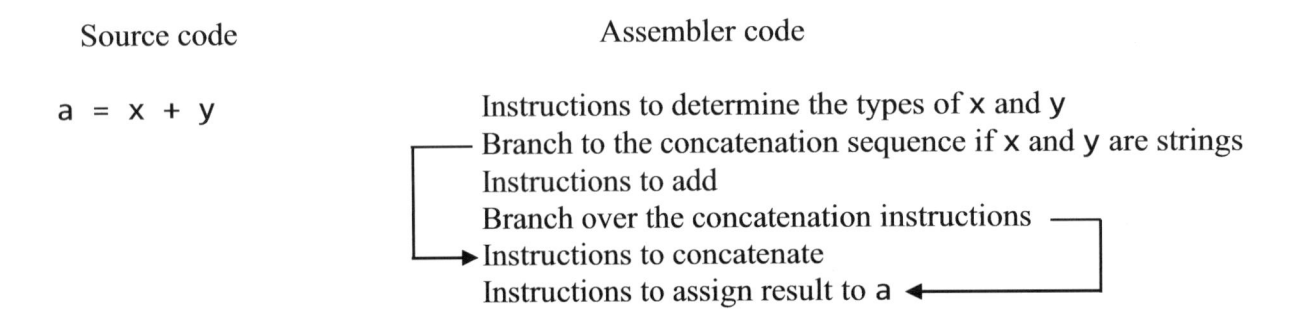

Figure 21.1

The compiler has to generate a lot of extra assembler code for a source program written in a dynamically-typed source language, such as Python. Fortunately, modern computers are so fast that even with the overhead associated with source programs written in a dynamically-typed language, most programs have short run times.

Our `c1.py` compiler from chapter 13 works fine, but it does not generate the assembler code that is needed for a dynamically typed language. We were able to get away with this because the source language for that compiler supports only one type. Thus, the type analysis that normally is necessary could be omitted. In this chapter, we add support for strings. But now we have more than one data type. So our new compiler has to generate the code for run-time type analysis.

The source language for the compiler we discuss in this chapter is the same as the source language for our level 1 language processors (`i1.py`, `h1.py`, and `c1.py`), but with the addition of strings.

Representing Dynamically-Typed Variables

In a dynamically-typed language, a variable does not hold a value. Instead it holds a reference (i.e., a pointer) to an object. The object has two fields (or more if needed), the first of which indicates the current type of the variable. For example, suppose the following instructions are executed:

```
x = 7
y = 'hello'
```

Then the structures in Fig. 21. 2 are created for the variables x and y.

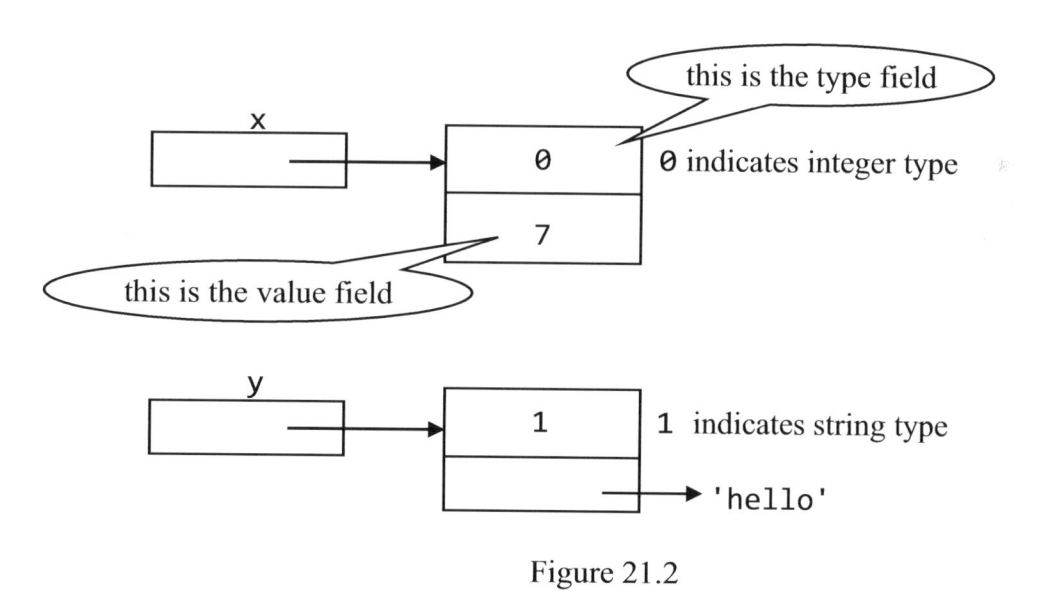

Figure 21.2

x and y each point to an object with two fields. We call the first field the *type field*, and the second field the *value field*. The variable x points to an object that has 0 in its type field, indicating that x currently has the type integer. The value field of x holds 7, the current value of x. The variable y points to an object that has 1 in its type field, indicating that y currently has the type string. Its value field holds a pointer that points to the string `'hello'`. Why is a pointer to the y string in the second field of its object rather than the string itself? The fields in these objects are of fixed length—only one word. Thus, only a very short string could fit into the second field. To accommodate strings of any length, the second field points to the string rather than hold the string itself. A pointer is always one word in length, regardless of what it is

pointing to. Thus, a pointer can always fit into the second field.
What happens if we now execute the following statement:

x = y

We then get the structure in Fig. 21.3.

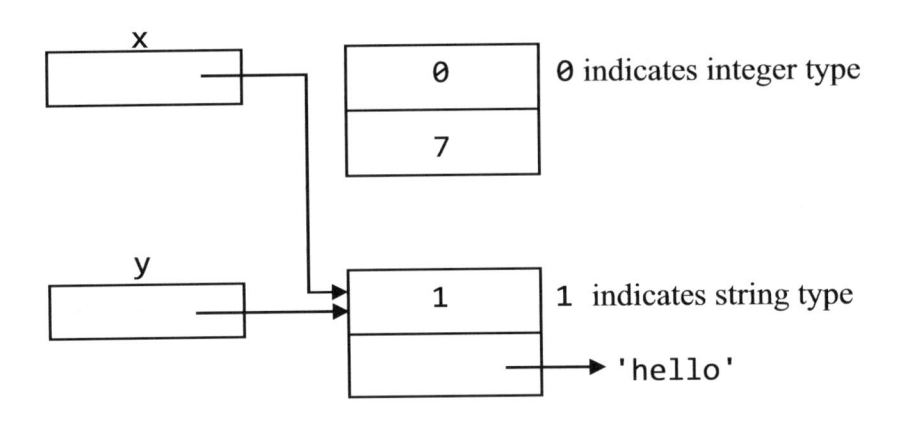

Fig. 21.3

The assignment statement copies the pointer in the y variable into the x variable. Thus, after the assignment, both x and y are pointing to the object corresponding to the string 'hello'. Because an assignment of one variable to another is just a copy operation, the assembler code for it (generated by cg_assign()) is simple (see Fig. 21.4)

```
@ x = y
        ldr  r0,  =y        @ get address of y
        ldr  r0,  [r0]      @ get pointer in y
        ldr  r1,  =x        @ get address of x
        str  r0,  [r1]      @ store pointer in x
```

Figure 21.4

The symbol table for our new compiler is the same as the symbol table for the c1.py compiler discussed in chapter 13. It consists of two parallel lists: symbol and value. As in c1.py, each element of the value list is the value (in string form) of the corresponding symbol in the symbol list. For example, suppose the symbol table contains the variable x, the temporary variable .t0 whose value is '0', the constant '7', and the string .s0 whose value is 'hello'. Then the symbol and value lists are as shown in Fig. 21.5.

symbol
'x'
'.t0'
'.i7'
'.s0'

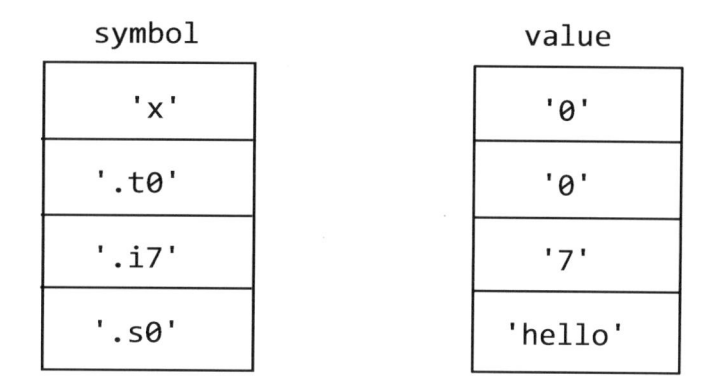

value
'0'
'0'
'7'
'hello'

Figure 21.5

The symbol for a temporary variable is '.t' followed by a sequence number. Similarly, the symbol for a string is '.s' followed by a sequence number. Sequence numbers start from 0. Thus, the first string encountered in the source program is given the name '.s0', the second string is given the name '.s1', and so on. Strings are entered into the symbol table by the factor() function. If on entry into factor(), token.category is STRING, then the following code is executed in factor():

```
if token.lexeme in value:     # check if already in symbol table
    index = value.index(token.lexeme)
else:
    index = enter('.s' + str(strcount), token.lexeme)
    strcount += 1
advance()
return index
```

If the string is not already in the symbol table, factor() calls enter(), passing it the name of the string (constructed by concatenating '.s' with a sequence number), and the string itself (which is in token.lexeme). factor() then increments strcount so that the next string entered gets a name with the next higher sequence number.

When the compiler is run, the main() function calls parser(), which in turn calls advance(), cg_prolog(), program(), and cg_epilog():

```
1 def parser():
2     advance()        # advance to first token
3     cg_prolog()      # generates prolog assembler code
4     program()        # generates assembler code for program
5     cg_epilog()      # generates epilog assembler code
```

cg_epilog() generates the assembler code needed at the bottom of the target program, including the .word directives for each entry in the symbol table. In c1.py, for each entry in the symbol table, cg_epilog() generates one .word directive. In our new compiler, however, each variable and each constant are three-word structures: a pointer and a two-word object. For a string object, there is also an .asciz directive for the string. Fig. 21.6 shows the directives that cg_epilog() generates for the symbol table in Fig. 21.5.

```
x:          .word x + 4         @ pointer to object
            .word 0             @ integer initial type
            .word 0             @ 0 initial value

.t0:        .word .t0 + 4       @ pointer to object
            .word 0             @ not assigned anything yet
            .word 0

.i7:        .word .i7 + 4       @ pointer to object
            .word 0             @ 0 indicates integer type
            .word 7             @ value

.s0:        .word .s0 + 4       @ pointer to object
            .word 1             @ 1 indicates string type
            .word .s0 + 12      @ pointer to its string
            .asciz "hello"      @ string
```

Figure 21.6

Each variable and constant starts with a pointer that points to the object right below it. For example, in

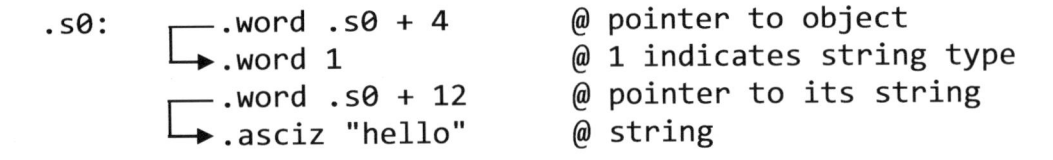

```
.s0:        .word .s0 + 4       @ pointer to object
            .word 1             @ 1 indicates string type
            .word .s0 + 12      @ pointer to its string
            .asciz "hello"      @ string
```

the label .s0 represents the address of the first word of this block. Thus, .s0 + 4 is the address of the second word (remember each word is four bytes). Similarly, .s0 + 12 is the address of the fourth word (which is the word in which the string "hello" starts). The assembler correspondingly translates the first .word directive to the address of the second word, and the third word to the address of the string. Thus, these directives create the following structure:

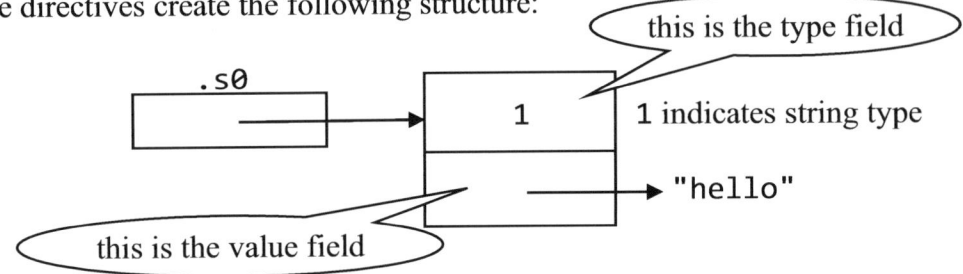

To access the type and value fields, we first get the pointer in .s0 into a register using a two-instruction sequence. For example, the following two-instruction sequence gets the pointer in .s0 into r0:

```
    ldr r0, =.s0        @ get address of .s0 into r0
    ldr r0, [r0]        @ load pointer in .s0 into r0 using address in r0
```

We can then load the type field using the address in r0, and the value field using the address in r0 plus 4.

```
ldr r1, [r0]       @ get type, loads from address in r0
ldr r2, [r0, #4]   @ get value, loads from address in r0 plus 4
```

The directives in Fig. 21.6 reflect the status of the variables and constants before the program starts executing. The variables x and .t0 have not yet been assigned anything so their value fields contain 0.

Fig. 21.7 shows the structure of the loop in cg_epilog() that generates the .word directives that appear at the bottom of the target program. The conversion code, '%-10s', on lines 5 and 12 specifies a string field width of 10. The minus sign in this conversion code indicates the string (symbol[i] + ':') is left justified in this field. For example, if symbol[i] is '.i0'. then lines 11 and 12 output

```
.i0:        .word .i0 + 4
```

```
1    size = len(symbol)
2    i = 0
3    while i < size:
4       if symbol[i].startswith('.s'):     # string?
5          outfile.write('%-10s' % (symbol[i] + ':') + '.word ' +
6                        symbol[i] + ' + 4\n')
7          outfile.write('          .word 1\n')
8          outfile.write('          .word ' + symbol[i] + ' + 12\n')
9          outfile.write('          .asciz "' + value[i] + '"\n')
10      else:                             # integer, variable, or temp
11         outfile.write(
12            '%-10s' % (symbol[i] + ':') + '.word ' + symbol[i] + ' + 4\n')
13         outfile.write('          .word 0\n')
14         outfile.write('          .word ' + value[i] + '\n')
16      i += 1
```

Figure 21.7

Translating Multiplication

For the expression x*y, the assembler code generated has to do the following:

- Get the addresses of the x and y objects from the x and y variables.
- Check if x and y are both integers (strings cannot be multiplied). If they are not, signal an error.
- Get the values of x and y into registers.
- Multiply the value of x and the value of y
- Get a temporary variable
- Store 0 (the type code for integer) into the type field of the object for the temporary variable.
- Store the result of the multiply in the value field of the object for the temporary variable.

The function in our new compiler that generates the multiplication assembler code is cg_mul(). Its first line is

```
def cg_mul(leftindex, rightindex):
```

cg_mul() is essentially a long list of calls to the write() method that outputs the code shown in Fig. 21.8. When term() calls cg_mul(), it passes the symbol table indices of the two items to be multiplied, which are received by the parameters leftindex and rightindex. cg_mul() uses these indices to access the names of the variables. It needs these names for the two instructions that load the address of the variables (lines 1 and 8 in Fig. 21.8). Thus, lines 1 and 8 are dependent on what is passed to cg_mul(). For example, the Python code that produces line 1 in Fig. 21.8 is

```
outfile.write('            ldr r0, =' + symbol[leftindex] + '\n')
```

where leftindex is the the parameter in cg_mul() that receives the index of the left operand (x in this example) in the multiplication. Similarly, the Python code that produces line 8 in Fig. 21.8 is

```
outfile.write('            ldr r3, =' + symbol[rightindex] + '\n')
```

where rightindex is the the parameter in cg_mul() that receives the index of the right operand (y in this example).

cg_mul() calls cg_gettemp() to get the index of the next temporary variable (the code for cg_gettemp() is in Fig. 13.8). It uses this index to access the name of a temporary variable. It needs this name for the instruction on line 17 in Fig. 21.8. Thus, line 17 is dependent on what cg_gettemp() returns when it is called. Each time cg_mul() is called it produces *exactly the same assembler code* except for lines 17 (which is dependent on cg_gettemp()) and lines 1 and 8 (which are dependent on the arguments passed to cg_mul()).

```
1         ldr r0, =x          @ get address of x                    (Depends on what is passed to cg_mul)
2         ldr r0, [r0]        @ get pointer to object
3         ldr r1, [r0]        @ get type of object
4         cmp r1, #0          @ test if x is an integer
5         bne .error          @ branch to .error if not integer
6         ldr r2, [r0, #4]    @ get integer value
7
8         ldr r3, =y          @ get address of y                    (Depends on what is passed to cg_mul)
9         ldr r3, [r3]        @ get pointer to object
10        ldr r4, [r3]        @ get type of object
11        cmp r4, #0          @ test if y is an integer
12        bne .error          @ branch to .error if not integer
13        ldr r5, [r3, #4]    @ get integer value
14
15        mul r0, r2, r5      @ multiply values of x and y
16                                                                  (Depends on what cg_gettemp returns)
17        ldr r1, =.t0        @ get address of temporary variable
18        ldr r1, [r1]        @ get pointer to object
19        str r4, [r1]        @ store type in object of temp variable
20        str r0, [r1, #4]    @ store product in value field
```

Figure 21.8

The cmp instruction (compare) on line 4 in Fig. 21.8 is used to determine if the type code in r1 (obtained from the type field of the object for x) is zero:

```
4          cmp r1, #0           @ test if x is an integer
```

A zero indicates x is an integer. The cmp instruction sets flag bits in the computer that reflect the result of the compare. These flag bits are then tested on line 5 by the conditional branch instruction bne (branch on not equal):

```
5          bne .error           @ branch to .error if not integer
```

The bne instruction tests the flag bits set by the preceding cmp instruction. If the flag bits indicate the result of the compare is "not equal" (which means the type code of x is not zero, and therefore x is not an integer), then the bne instruction causes a branch to the label .error. At the label .error (not shown in Fig. 21.8), a mov instruction moves the return code 1 (which indicates an error has occurred) into r0. A pop instruction then causes a return to the caller (start-up code):

```
.error:
          mov r0, #1      @ return error code
          pop {pc}        @ pop return address into pc reg
```

These three lines are generated by the cg_epilog() function. Lines 8 to 13 perform the same operation on y as lines 1 to 6 perform on x.

After the multiplication instruction (line 15), cg_mul() stores the type code for integer (line 19) and the result of the multiplication (line 20) in the object to which the temporary variable points. cg_mul() then returns the index (which it received from the call of cg_gettemp()) of the temporary variable to its caller (which is term()).

Translating Addition/Concatenation

The function that generates the addition/concatenation code is cg_add(). It is more complicated than cg_mul() for two reasons. First, the plus sign is overloaded. It denotes addition if its operands are integers, and concatenation if its operands are strings. Thus, the assembler code has to perform both addition and concatenation. Second, the code for concatenation is itself complicated. It must allocate enough memory to hold the concatenated string and copy the concatenated string to this memory. Fig. 21.9 shows the code for cg_add().

```
1  def cg_add(leftindex, rightindex):
2      labelstr = cg_getlabel()
3      labeltemp = cg_getlabel()
4      tempindex = cg_gettemp()
5      outfile.write('          ldr r0, =' + symbol[leftindex] + '\n')
6      outfile.write('          ldr r0, [r0]\n')          # get ptr to obj
7      outfile.write('          ldr r2, [r0]\n')          # r2 has type
8      outfile.write('          ldr r1, [r0, #4]\n\n')    # r1 has ptr/val
9      outfile.write('          ldr r3, =' + symbol[rightindex] + '\n')
```

```
10      outfile.write('        ldr r3, [r3]\n')       # get ptr to obj
11      outfile.write('        ldr r4, [r3]\n')       # r4 has type
12      outfile.write('        ldr r5, [r3, #4]\n\n') # r5 has ptr/val
13      outfile.write('        cmp r2, r4\n')
14      outfile.write('        bne .error\n')
15      outfile.write('        cmp r2, #0\n')
16      outfile.write('        bne ' + labelstr + '\n')
17      outfile.write('        add r0, r1, r5\n') # integer operands
18      outfile.write('        bal ' + labeltemp + '\n')
19      outfile.write(labelstr + ':\n')              # concatenate strings
20      outfile.write('        ldr r0, =.buf\n')
21      outfile.write('        bl strcpy\n')
22      outfile.write('        mov r1, r5\n')
23      outfile.write('        bl strcat\n')
24      outfile.write('        bl strdup\n')
25      outfile.write(labeltemp + ':\n')
26      outfile.write('        ldr r1, =' + symbol[tempindex] + '\n')
27      outfile.write('        ldr r1, [r1]\n') # get ptr to obj
28      outfile.write('        str r4, [r1]\n')       # store type
29      outfile.write('        str r0, [r1, #4]\n\n') # store value
30      return tempindex
```

Figure 21.9

The `cmp` instruction on line 13 in Fig. 21.9 is used to determine if the operands have the same type by comparing the contents of `r0` with the contents of `r4`:

```
13      outfile.write('        cmp r2, r4\n')
```

Then the `cmp` instruction on line 15 is used to check if the type of x is integer:

```
15      outfile.write('        cmp r2, #0\n')
```

If the type of the left operand is not 0, then it must be a string. In that case, the `bne` instruction on line 16 branches to the code that handles strings (starting at line 19). The code starting at line 17 is executed if the operands are integers. The `bal` instruction (branch always) on line 18 branches unconditionally over the concatenation code to the code that handles the assignment to a temporary variable (at line 25).

The code starting at line 19 handles string operands. `.buf` is a 180-byte memory area created by the following directive generated by `cg_epilog()`:

```
.buf:      .space 180
```

Line 20 loads the address of `.buf` into `r0`. Then on line 21, the C library function, `strcpy`, is called. `strcpy` is passed two pointers (i.e., addresses), the first in `r0`, and the second in `r1`. It copies the string pointed to by `r1` to the location pointed to by `r0`. When line 21 is executed, `r0` has the address of `.buf`; `r1` has the address of the left operand (from the `ldr` instruction on line 8). Thus, `strcpy` copies the left operand string to `.buf`. This call does not affect the value in `r0`. Thus, `r0` retains the address of `.buf`.

The `mov` instruction on line 22 moves the address of the right operand string into `r1`. Then on line 23, the C library function `strcat` is called. It concatenates the string pointed to by `r1` (which is the right operand) to the end of the string pointed to by r0 (which is the copy of the left operand string in .buf).

If there are concatenations of strings later on in the source program, .buf will also be used for those concatenations. Thus, the concatenated string cannot be left in the .buf area for it would then get overlaid. Storage has to be dynamically allocated for the concatenated string, and the concatenated string copied to it. The C library function strdup does both the allocation and the copy. When strdup is called on line 24, r0 has the address of .buf. strdup allocates just enough storage to hold the concatenated string in .buf, and then copies the concatenated string to the allocated storage. On return from strdup, r0 has the address of the allocated storage. Note that the 180 bytes of space allocated for .buf unfortunately places an upper limit on the sizes of the strings to be concatenated. Their combined length must be less than 180. Otherwise the concatenated string cannot fit in the space allocated for .buf (see problem 2).

Starting at line 25 is the code that handles the assignment of the result (of the addition or the concatenation) to a temporary variable. At line 25, r0 holds the result of the addition or a pointer to the concatenated string. The str instruction on line 28 stores the type of the result (0 for integer, 1 for string) in the type field of the temporary variable. The str instruction on line 29 stores in the value field of the temporary variable the result of the addition or the pointer to the concatenated string in its allocated storage. cg_add() obtains the temporary variable by calling cg_gettemp() on line 4, which returns the index of the next available temporary variable. cg_add() uses this index to access the name of the temporary variable. cg_add() needs this name for the instruction on line 26. When cg_add() returns to its caller (which is expr()) on line 30, it returns the index of the temporary variable.

The cg_add() function requires two unique labels each time it is called. The function cg_getlabel() provides these labels (see Fig. 21.10). Each time cg_getlabel is called, it returns the next label in the sequence .L0, .L1, .L2, and so on. The variable labelcount holds the label sequence number.

```
1  def cg_getlabel():
2      global labelcount
3      label = '.L' + str(labelcount)
4      labelcount += 1
5      return label
```

Figure 21.10

The code generated by cg_print() is in Fig. 21.11. Here is cg_neg():

```
1  def cg_neg(index):
2      outfile.write('        ldr r0, =' + symbol[index] + '\n')
3      outfile.write('        ldr r0, [r0]\n')          # get ptr to obj
4      outfile.write('        ldr r1, [r0]\n')          # r1 has type
5      outfile.write('        cmp r1, #0\n')            # type int?
6      outfile.write('        bne .error\n')            # branch if not
7      outfile.write('        ldr r2, [r0, #4]\n')      # get value
8      outfile.write('        neg r2, r2\n')            # negate value
9      tempindex = cg_gettemp()
10     outfile.write('        ldr r0, =' + symbol[tempindex] + '\n')
11     outfile.write('        ldr r0, [r0]\n')          # get ptr to obj
12     outfile.write('        str r1, [r0]\n')          # store type
13     outfile.write('        str r2, [r0, #4]\n')      # store value
14     return tempindex
```

Handling Strings in a Compiler

When an interpreter reads in a line of source code that has escape sequences, it replaces the escape sequences with the specified codes. For example, in the following statement, the interpreter replaces the two-character backslash-n sequence with the code for the newline character:

```
print('hello\nbye')
```

Then when the string is displayed, the embedded newline character causes `'hello'` and `'bye'` to appear on separate lines:

```
hello
bye
```

If the escape sequence were not replaced, then the execution of the `print` statement would display

```
hello\nbye
```

However, compilers, as opposed to interpreters, do not replace escape sequences. For example, for the `print` statement above, our compiler generates the assembly language program in Fig. 21.11. Note that at the bottom of the assembly language program, an `.asciz` directive creates the `"hello\nbye"` string with the original escape sequence intact. If the compiler replaced the escape sequence with the newline character, as does an interpreter, then the compiler would output

```
        .asciz "hello
bye"
```

which would trigger an assembly-time error.

So how then do we handle strings in a compiler? We simply pass through all the characters in a string until we reach the quote that terminates the string. However, there is one tricky case we have to consider having to do with the terminating quote. If a quote within the string is preceded immediately by an even number of backslashes (including no backslashes), then it is the terminating quote. However, if it is preceded with an odd number of backslashes, then the quote is an embedded quote—not the terminating quote. For example, consider

```
print('A\\')     ← This quote is not the terminating quote because it is backslashed.
print('A\\\'')
```

In the first statement, the first backslash operates on the second backslash, leaving no backslash to operate on the quote at the end. Thus, the second quote is the terminating quote. In the second statement, the first backslash operates on the second backslash, leaving the third backslash to operate on the quote that follows it. Thus, this quote is an embedded quote—not the terminating quote.

```
@ Thu Feb 22 10:20:43 2018                              YOUR NAME HERE
@ Compiler     = c3.py
@ Input file   = escape.in
@ Output file  = escape.s
@---------------------------------------------- Assembler code
            .global main
            .text
main:
            push {lr}
@ print('hello\nbye')
            ldr r0, =.s0            @ get address of arg
            ldr r0, [r0]            @ get pointer to arg's object
            ldr r2, [r0]            @ get type field
            ldr r1, [r0, #4]        @ get value field into r1 for printf
            cmp r2, #0              @ int or string to be displayed?
            bne .L0                 @ branch if string
            ldr r0, =.fmt0          @ get address of format string for int
            bal .L1
.L0:
            ldr r0, =.fmt1          @ get address of format string for string
.L1:
            bl printf               @ display print statement's arg
            mov r0, #0              @ start of epilog()-generated code
            pop {pc}
            .data
.fmt0:      .asciz "%d\n"           @ format string for ints
.fmt1:      .asciz "%s\n"           @ format string for strings
.buf:       .space 180              @ buffer for concatenation
.s0:        .word .s0 + 4           @ string constant pointer
            .word 1                 @ type (1 indicates string)
            .word .s0 + 12          @ pointer to string
            .asciz "hello\nbye"
```

Depends on what is passed to cg_print() (annotation pointing to `ldr r0, =.s0`)

\n not replaced (annotation pointing to `.asciz "hello\nbye"`)

Figure 21.11

In the tokenizer for our compiler, we use the variable count to keep track of sequences of consecutive backslashes within a string (see Fig. 21.12). Initially, count is 0. On a backslash, it is incremented (see line 12 in Fig. 21.12). If the next character is also a backslash, count reverts back to 0 (see line 14). If the current character is not a backslash, count to set to 0 (see line 16). Thus, whenever, count is 0, the number of immediately preceding backslashes is even, in which case no backslash is operating on the current character. But if count is 1, then the number of immediately preceding backslashes is odd, in which case the last backslash is operating on the current character. In this case, if the current character is a quote, it is not the terminating quote because of the preceding backslash.

```
1  elif curchar == "'":    # code in tokenizer for strings
2      count = 0
3      while True:
4          curchar = getchar()
5          if curchar == '\n' or curchar == '':
6              raise RuntimeError('Unterminated string')
7          if curchar == "'" and count == 0: # terminating quote?
8              curchar = getchar()      # advance past end of string
9              token.category = STRING
10             break                    # finished processing string
11         if (curchar == '\\'):
12             count += 1
13             if count == 2:
14                 count = 0 # reset to 0 on even count
15         else:
16             count = 0    # reset to 0 if curchar not a backslash
17         token.lexeme += curchar
```

Figure 21.12

Capstone Project

Now that you know all about interpreters and compilers, a great capstone project for you is to implement the i2 and h2 interpreters using C instead of Python 3. Much of the code in the C versions will be similar to the code in the Python 3 versions—for example, the code in the tokenizer. But in the C versions, you will have to include code to handle dynamic typing. Once you have completed the C version of h2, you will have the background to study and understand the code for the actual Python 3 interpreter (it is written in C). You might ultimately become one of the programmers of a future release of Python.

Problems

1. Copy your c1.py compiler from problem 1 in chapter 13 to c3.py. Then modify c3.py as described in this chapter. Test your compiler by entering

    python c3.py c3.in c3.s

   Then run the program in c3.s by entering

    rpi c3.s   (or ./rpi c3.s)

   Alternatively, if you are on a Raspberry Pi, compile, link, and run the program in c3.s by entering

    gcc c3.s -o c3
    c3   (or ./c3)

2. Modify your `c3.py` compiler from problem 1 so that it handles string concatenation in the following way: Using the `strlen` function from the C standard library, determine the length of the strings to be concatenated. Then call `malloc`, passing it the combined length of the two strings plus 1 (for the null character at the end). Finally, using the `strcpy` function, copy the first string to the allocated storage, and then concatenate the second string to it. What is the advantage of this approach?

3. Lines 3, 4, and 5 in Fig. 21.8 are not always necessary. Why? What should the code be if the left operand in a multiplication is a constant? If the right operand is a constant? Modify your `c3.py` compiler so that `cg_mul()` and `cg_add()` do not produce unnecessary code for constant operands.

4. Why is the type code loaded into `r4` rather than `r0` on line 11 in Fig. 21.9?

5. What is the disadvantage of dynamic typing?

6. What happens if a string is missing its terminating quote?

7. Can lines 15 and 16 in Fig. 21.12 be omitted without affecting the processing of strings?

8. Modify your `c3.py` compiler from problem 1 so that repeated multiplications do not produce repeated identical sequences of assembler code. Do the same for the other code generator functions.

9. Another possible implementation of dynamic typing is for a variable or constant name to denote the type/value object rather than point to the type/value object. Then an assignment to a variable would require a type/value object copy rather than a pointer copy. For example, x would be assigned to y by copying the x object into the y object. Modify your `c3.py` compiler from problem 1 to use this alternate approach. What are the drawbacks with this approach? *Hint*: Consider user-defined types.

10. With dynamic typing, if y is assigned x, is it possible that incrementing the variable x might also increment the variable y? For example, try the following code with the Python 3 interpreter and your `c3.py` compiler.

```
x = 3
y = x
x = x + 1
print(y)      # does it output 3 or 4?
```

If there are any differences in output, then modifiy your `c3.py` compiler so that it outputs assembler code that produces the same output that the Python 3 interpreter produces. If, on the other hand, there are no differences, explain why.

11. In our implementation of `c3.py`, variables have the initial value 0 (see Fig. 21.6). However, in Python variables have no initial value. Modify `c3.py` from problem 1 so that variables have no initial value, in which case the following statement at the beginning of a program will trigger an error:

```
y = x   # x has no value
```

Appendix A: Introduction to Python

In this appendix, we present the subset of Python that you need to know to implement the interpreters and compilers we describe in this book. Don't let a lack of exposure to Python discourage you from reading this book. Python is very easy to learn. In fact, implementing an interpreter or a compiler using Python is a great way to learn the language.

If you do not already have Python 3 installed on your computer, go to `python.org` to download the latest version of Python. Be sure to get Python 3 and not Python 2. To invoke the Python interpreter via the command line, enter

```
python <filename>
```

See chapter 1 for more details on installing Python and using the command line.

Dynamic Typing

Python is a dynamically typed language. That means a variable assumes the type of the item you assign to it. For example, after the following assignment statement is executed,

```
x = 123
```

x has the type integer because 123 has the type integer. If subsequently the following assignment statement is executed, the type of x changes to string:

```
x = 'hello'
```

Because Python is a dynamically typed language, it does not have type declarations. For example, you will never see this in a Python program:

```
int x, y;
```

Multi-line Statements

Unlike C and Java, statements in Python are not terminated with a semicolon, but by a newline character (the invisible character at the end of each text line). However, a newline character does *not* end a statement if a bracketed expression—an expression bracketed with ( ), [ ], or { }—is open (i.e., the bracket matching the opening bracket has not yet been reached). For example, the following two lines of code is one statement:

```
x = (1 + 2      # parenthesized expression still open at newline
     3)         # so stmt continues to this line
```

Code Blocks

Blocks of codes in most programming language have explicit delimiters such as `begin` and `end`, or "{" and "}". Python is different. It uses indentation to delimit a block of code. For example, in the following `if` statement,

```
if x == 5:         # test if x is equal to 5
   print(1)        # first stmt in block
   print(2)
   print(3)        # last stmt in block
print(4)
```

the indented `print` statements constitute the block of code that is under control of the `if` statement. Thus, if x is not equal to 5, only 4 is displayed. If x is equal to 5, then 1, 2, and 3 are displayed followed by 4. Because indentation is syntactically significant, correct indentation is essential when writing Python code.

The number of columns to indent is a matter of taste. We like three-column indentations although four-column indentation is the Python standard. Three-column indentation is still easy for the eye to spot, and it makes it less likely that your program will run past the right margin of an 80-column page.

An easy way to indent is to hit the tab key. On some text editors (like `notepad`), hitting the tab key injects the tab character rather than some fixed number of spaces into the text file you are creating or editing. If you use such an editor, you must use the space bar exclusively or the tab key exclusively to indent the statements within any one code block. An even easier way to indent is to use a text editor that will automatically indent for you.

A Python program must start in the leftmost column. For example, the following single line, left justified, is a complete program:

```
print('hello')
```

But if the `print` statement is indented, then it becomes a code block. A code block is legal only as part of some of other statement (for example, an `if` statement). Thus, the `print` statement above is not a legal program if it is indented.

Arithmetic Operations

The arithmetic operations in Python are addition, subtraction, multiplication, exponentiation, floating-point division, integer division, and remainder. For example, the following `print` statements display 7, 3, 10, 25, 2.5, 2 and 1, respectively:

```
print(5 + 2)    # addition: displays 7
print(5 - 2)    # subtraction: displays 3
print(5 * 2)    # multiplication: displays 10
print(5 ** 2)   # exponentiation: displays 25
print(5 / 2)    # floating-point division: displays 2.5
print(5 // 2)   # integer division: displays 2
print(5 % 2)    # remainder: displays 1
```

Note that "/" specifies floating-point division. Thus, it produces a floating-point result (i.e., a number with a fractional part) even if both of its operands have the type integer. In contrast, "//" specifies integer division. It produces an integer result (the fractional part of the result is discarded).

Strings

Strings in Python can be delimited with either a pair of single quotes or a pair of double quotes. For example,

```
print('hello')      # displays hello
print("hello")      # displays hello
```

To embed in a string a quote different from the delimiting quotes, simply insert the quote in the string. For example,

```
print("it's")       # displays it's
```

To embed a quote that is of the same type as the delimiting quotes, precede the quote with a backslash. For example,

```
print('it\'s')      # displays it's
```

To embed a backslash in a string, precede it with another backslash. For example, the following print statement displays A\B:

```
print('A\\B')       # displays A\B
```

To determine if a string is a prefix of another string, use the startswith() method. For example, the following if statement tests if the string in s starts with '.t':

```
if s.startswith('.t'):
    print('it does')
```

The replace() method creates the string that results when the first string argument is replaced by the second string argument in a copy of the given string. For example, suppose s is assigned 'but'. Then the following statement replaces the 'u' substring in a copy of the s string with 'oa', and then assigns the modified copy to t. The s string is unaffected, but t is assigned 'boat'.

```
t = s.replace('u','oa')    # replaces 'u' with 'oa'
```

A shorthand way of specifying a string with a repeated sequence is by using the repetition operator "*". For example, the following statement assigns the string 'xxxxx' to s:

```
s = 'x'*5
```

"*5" means "repeat 5 times." Thus, 'x'*5 is the string containing five x's. In the following sequence, t is assigned a string consisting of 30 spaces.

```
i = 30
t = ' '*i        # t is assigned string consisting of 30 spaces
print(t + '^')   # position of caret determined by value in i at run time
```

Thus, the `print` statement displays a caret (`'^'`) in column 31.

The individual characters in a string can be accessed via an index. For example, if `s` is a string variable that holds the string `'dog'`, then `s[0]` is `'d'`, `s[1]` is `'o'`, and `s[2]` is `'g'`. The individual characters are themselves strings.

The *null string* is the string that contains no characters. It has zero length. It is represented with two quotes of the same type with no intervening characters. For example, `""`.

Concatenation

Concatenation is the operation which joins two strings to make a new string. The plus operator is overloaded. That is, it has more than one meaning. It specifies either addition or concatenation, depending on the types of its operands. If the operands are numbers, "+" means addition; if the operands are strings, "+" means concatenation. For example, the following two `print` statements display 5 and 32:

```
print(3 + 2)      # addition: displays 5
print('3' + '2')  # concatenation: displays 32
```

Assignment Operator

A single equal sign is the assignment operator. For example, the following statement assigns 1 to `x`:

```
x = 1
```

A commonly used shorthand for

```
x = x + 1
```

is

```
x += 1
```

The combination operator "+=" means add the left and right sides, then assign the result to the left side. Thus, `x += 1` means add `x` and 1, and assign the result to `x`.

Functions

The first line of a function consists of the keyword word `def`, followed by the function name, followed by parentheses, followed by a colon. For example, here is a program that has a function named `sample` (the line numbers are not part of the program):

```
1 def sample():          # this is the start of the function definition
2     print('morning')
3     print('bye')        # end of function definition
4 print('good')
5 sample()               # this stmt "calls" sample()
```

A function is executed only if it is called. Thus, the first statement executed in the program above in on line 4. Line 5 then calls the `sample()` function (calling a function causes it to be executed). The program displays

good
morning
bye

The body of a function is a code block (i.e., a sequence of one or more statements that are indented). Functions can appear in any order. However, a function can be called only after the interpreter has "seen" the definition of that function. For example, here is a Python program that displays "hello" and "bye". It starts with the call of `f()` at the bottom end of the program.

```
1 def f():
2     print('hello')
3     g()                # forward reference ok here
4
5 def g():
6     print('bye')
7 f()                    # this call must follow the definition of f()
```

At the time of the call of `f()` on line 7, the interpreter has already seen the definitions of the `f()` and `g()` functions (because the interpreter scans the program from top to bottom). Thus, the call of `f()` on line 8 and the call of `g()` on line 3 are legal. If, however, the call of `f()` is moved to line 4, the call of `g()` on line 3 would then be illegal because the interpreter at that point has not yet seen the definition of `g()`.

We use the following terminology regarding function calls. The items within parentheses in a function call are called *arguments*. The variables within parentheses on the first line of a function definition are called *parameters*. When a function is called, the values of the arguments are automatically assigned to the corresponding parameters. For example, in the following program, z + 5 and 50 are arguments; x and y are parameters. The values of z + 5 and 50 and assigned to x, respectively, when `f()` calls `g()`:

```
1 def g(x, y):           # x and y are parameters
2     print(x + y)       # displays 75
3 z = 20
4 def f():
5     g(z + 5, 50)       # z + 5 and 50 are arguments
6 f()
```

`f()` calls `g()` on line 5. Thus, we refer to `f()` as the *calling function*, and `g()` as the *called function*.

Functions can return values. For example, the following function adds or concatenates its parameters, depending of the type of the parameters and returns the result to the calling function:

```
1 def addorconcat(x, y):
2     result = x + y
3     return result
```

Consider the following two assignment statements:

```
4 y = addorconcat(3, 2)        # y is assigned 5
5 y = addorconcat('3', '2')    # y is assigned '32'
```

When the first statement above is executed, the arguments 3 and 2 are assigned to their corresponding parameters, x and y, in the function. The function then executes, adding x and y, and assigning the sum 5 to result. The return statement then returns the value in result to the caller, in effect replacing the call with the value returned. Thus, the assignment statement on line 4 in effect becomes

```
y = 5
```

When assignment statement on line 5 is executed, the strings '3' and '2' are assigned to the parameters x and y, respectively. For this call, x and y are strings. Thus, the plus sign on line 2 means concatenation, and therefore the assignment statement on line 5 in effect becomes

```
y = '32'
```

The parameters of a function are local variables in that function. Thus, in the preceding example, the parameter y is distinct from the variable y on lines 4 and 5.

A recursive function is a function that calls itself. For example, r() is a recursive function:

```
1 def r():
2     print('hello')
3     r()              # r() calls itself
4 r()
```

Each time r() is called, it calls itself. Thus, the calling of r() theoretically never stops. Actually, it will ultimately stop. The interpreter will terminate the program when the recursion depth reaches some upper limit. To avoid this, recursive calls are always within an if statement. At some point during recursion, some condition should occur that causes the if statement to not execute the recursive call, causing the repeated recursions to stop. For example, in the following program, on each call of countdown(), the value of the parameter n is one less than on the preceding calls. When n reaches zero, the recursion stops.

```
1 def countdown(n)
2     if n > 0:              # recurse only if n is positive
3         print(n)
4         countdown(n - 1)   # next n is one less the current n
5 countdown(10)
```

This program displays the integers from 10 down to 1.

Global and Local Variables

A local variable in a function can be used only inside that function. A global variable can be accessed from any function that does not have an identically named local variable, and it can be assigned a new value in any function that declares it global.

Consider the following program in which we have local and global variables:

```
1  x = 1             # x is global here
2  y = 2             # y is global here
3  z = 3             # z is global here
4  def f():
5      global x      # makes x global in this function
6      x = y         # x and y are global variables here
7      z = 20        # z is a local variable here
8  f()
9  print(x)          # displays 2
10 print(y)          # displays 2
11 print(z)          # displays 3
```

On lines 1, 2, and 3, x, y, and z are outside functions. Thus, they are automatically global variables. Inside f(), x is declared global on line 5. Thus, x on line 6 is the global variable x (i.e., it is the same variable as the x on line 1). The global variable y on line 2 is not declared global inside f(). Nevertheless, the y inside f() (on line 6) is the global variable y (it is the same variable as the y on line 2).

Now here is the confusing characteristic of globals: z outside f(), like y, is a global variable. But z inside f() (on line 7), is a local variable. Why is y global inside f(), but z is local inside f()? Neither is declared global by f(). The reason why z is local inside f() is because it is assigned a value (on line 7). In Python, it is illegal to assign a global variable a value within a function unless it is declared global. Thus, z on line 7 cannot be global, and therefore must be local. The variable y, on the other hand, is not assigned a value. So it is the global variable y.

Two or more functions can have identically named local variables. For example, in the following program, f() and g() both have a local variable x:

```
1  def f():
2      x = 1         # this is the local variable x in f()
3      g()
4      print(x)      # displays 1
5  def g():
6      x = 7         # does not change local variable x in f()
7  f()
```

Although the local variable in f() and g() are identically named, they are not the same variable. Thus, the assignment of 7 to x in g() does not affect the value of the local variable x in f().

Each time a function is called, its local variables are created. On exit from a function, its local variables are destroyed. Thus, *local variables do not retain their values between function calls*. A variable must be global to retain its value between function calls. For example, suppose you want a function cg_gettemp() to have access to a variable named tempcount whose value is initially 0, and is increased by 1 on every call of cg_gettemp(). Suppose tempcount is used only by cg_gettemp(). It, nevertheless, has to be a global to retain its value between calls of cg_gettemp(). Thus, cg_gettemp() should be structured as follows:

```
def gettemp():
    global tempcount
    ...
    tempcount += 1   # increment tempcount for next call of cg_gettemp()
```

To give it its initial value, tempcount should be initialized outside of any function (so it is global) before the first call of cg_gettemp():

```
tempcount = 0
```

print Statement

The print statement can have zero or more arguments. Multiple arguments should be separated by commas. Here are some examples:

```
print()            # nothing displayed, goes to next line
print(1)           # displays 1, goes to next line
print(1, 2)        # displays 1 2 then goes to the next line
print(1, 2,)       # displays 1 2 then goes to the next line
```

If multiple arguments are specified, they are displayed with a single space between them. After displaying the values of its arguments, the print statement moves the cursor to the beginning of the next line, unless end = '' is the last argument. For example, the following display 1, 2, and 3 on the same line:

```
print(1, 2, end = '')   # does not move cursor to next line
print(3)
```

A format specification can be specified in a print statement (similar to the format specification in the printf() function in C). For example, the print statement,

```
print('x = %5d y = %d' % (x, y))
```

displays its first argument. But before displaying it, print() replaces the conversion codes, %5d and %d, with the values of x and y, respectively, converted to decimal. %5d specifies conversion to decimal and a field width of 5. %d specifies conversion to decimal and a field width just sufficient to hold the corresponding value. Suppose x is 2 and y is 3. The values of x and y inside the computer are in binary. The print statement above converts the binary values in x and y to decimal (because of the "d" in the conversion codes), and replaces the conversion codes with the decimal representation of the values of x and y, using the specified field widths. Thus, the print statement above displays

```
x =     2 y = 3
```

The value of x occupies five columns (four spaces plus the "2") because of the "5" in the conversion code %5d. The value of y occupies just enough columns to hold the value 3 (i.e., just one column).

The conversion code for a string is %s. For example, the following statement displays the string 'hello' right justified in a field of width 50.

```
print('%50s' % 'hello')
```

input() Function

The input() function prompts the user and reads data from the keyboard, returning it *in string form*. For example, the following statement

```
x = input('enter integer')
```

displays the prompt

```
enter integer
```

When an integer is then entered via the keyboard, it (*in string form*) is assigned to x.

if Statement

An if statement has as optional else part. Here are examples of the two variations of the if statement:

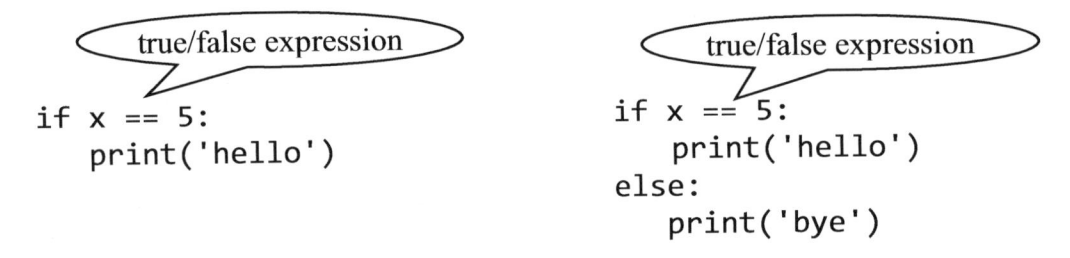

```
                  true/false expression                        true/false expression
if x == 5:                                  if x == 5:
    print('hello')                              print('hello')
                                            else:
                                                print('bye')
```

In an if statement, following the keyword if is anything that evaluates to true or false. If the keyword else is used in an if statement, it should start in the same column as if and be followed by a colon.
 Python has the true/false constants True and False (spelled with a leading capital letter). Every Python object evaluates to either True or False. Specifically, None, 0, 0.0 and any empty data structure evaluate to False. Examples of empty data structures are [ ] (an empty list), { } (an empty dictionary), ' ' (string of zero length delimited with single quotes), and "" (string of zero length delimited with double quotes). Any nonzero number and any non-empty data structure evaluate to True. Thus, when the following if statement is executed, "hello" is displayed.

```
x = 1
if x:                  # 1 is treated as True
    print('hello')     # hello is displayed
```

A true/false expression can be constructed using any of the following relational operators:

Relational operator	Meaning
<	less than
<=	less than or equal
==	equal
!=	not equal
>	greater than
>=	greater than or equal

For example, x <= y is true if x is less than y. Otherwise, it is false.

if statements can be nested. In a nested if statement, an else followed by an if can be written as elif. For example, the following statement displays "A", "B", "C", "D", or "F", depending of the value of grade:

```
if grade >= 90:
    print('A')
elif grade >= 80:    # elif means else if
    print('B')
elif grade >= 70:
    print('C')
elif grade >= 65:
    print('D')
else:
    print('F')
```

Expressions can be combined with the Boolean operators or, and, and not. The "or" operator gives a true result if either or both of its operands are true. Otherwise, it gives a false result. The "and" operator gives a true result only if both operands are true. The "not" operator gives the flipped truth value of its operand. For example, in the following if statement,

```
if x == 1 or y == 2:
    print('got 1 or 2 or both')
```

the expression "x == 1 or y == 2" evaluates to true if x is 1 *or* y is 2. Otherwise, it is false. If we replace "or" with "and", then the expression is true only if both x is 1 *and* y is 2. Now let's add the "not" operator. We get

```
if not(x == 1 or y == 2):
    print('x not 1 and y not 2')
```

The "not" operator here flips the truth value of (x == 1 or y == 2). The expression "x == 1 or y == 2" is true if either x is 1 or y is 2. Thus, "not(x == 1 or y == 2)" is true if x is not 1 *and* y is not 2. The "not" operator has high precedence. Thus, to apply it to the expression "x == 1 or y == 2", the expression has to be surrounded with parentheses.

while Statement

The `while` statement is a looping statement with a leading exit test. For example, the following program displays the numbers from 1 to 10:

```
1  i = 1
2  while i <= 10:     # loop body executed while i <= 10 is True
3      print(i)
4      i += 1
```

(exit-test expression points to `i <= 10` on line 2)

The body of a `while` statement is a code block. It is executed repeatedly as long as the exit-test expression ("`i <= 10`" in the example above) is true. When it goes false, the loop is exited. Execution then proceeds with the statement that follows the `while` loop. It is essential that the body of a `while` statement do something that eventually makes the exit-test expression go false. Otherwise, an *infinite loop* (i.e., a loop that never stops) results. For example, if we delete the statement on line 4 that increments `i` in the example above, we would then have an infinite loop.

A `while` loop ends when the exit-test expression goes false. It also ends if a `break` statement within the loop body is executed. For example, the following program displays numbers up to 5 only. After 5 is displayed, the `break` statement on line 5 causes a break out of the loop.

```
1  i = 1
2  while i <= 10:
3      print(i)
4      if i == 5:
5          break      # causes a break out of the loop
6      i += 1
```

Because the `while` statement has a leading exit test, its standard setup is awkward for a loop that naturally does not have a leading exit test. To handle such a loop, use a `while` statement with an `if/break` structure configured as follows:

```
while True:
    ⋮                           # stmts before the exit test
    if exit-test_expression:    # this is the exit test
        break
    ⋮                           # stmts after the exit test
```

When the exit-test expression in the `if` statement goes true, the `break` statement is executed, causing a break out of the loop. With this structure, the exit test is wherever you put the `if/break` statement. For example, the following is a program that reads in integers, and accumulates their sum until a negative number is entered. A negative number signals the end of the data. It causes an exit from the loop. The negative number is not data to be accumulated. Its function is simply to signal the end of the data. Thus, it should not be added to the sum. That is the reason why the loop is set up so that the exit occurs immediately after a negative number is entered.

```
1 sum = 0
2 while True:
3     x = int(input('enter integer: '))  # prompt user
4     if x < 0:                          # check for a neg number
5         break                          # exit loop
6     sum += x                           # add x to sum
7 print('sum = ' + str(sum))             # display final sum
```

The `input()` function returns the integer in string form. So before line 4 can be executed, the string returned by `input()` has to be converted to integer form. The `int()` function on line 3 performs the required conversion. It converts the number returned by `input()` to integer form. To perform the concatenation on line 7, both operands have to be strings. The `str()` function converts the number in `sum` to string form. It is passed the number in `sum`; it returns that number in string form. The converted number is then concatenated to `'sum = '`, and the result is displayed. Here is a sample run of the program:

```
enter integer: 5
enter integer: 3
enter integer: -1
sum = 8
```

Files

To read a text file, it first must be opened. The following statement opens the file `t.in` for reading:

    infile = open('t.in', 'r')

The `'r'` argument indicates that the file is to be read. `infile` here is an arbitrary name (use any name you like) that represents the file in the program code. Once opened, the entire file can be read in as one long string. The following statement reads the entire `infile` file into `source`:

    source = infile.read()

To create and write to a file named `c1.s`, open the file with

    outfile = open('c1.s', 'w')

`outfile` here is an arbitrary name (use any name you like) that represents the file in the program. The `'w'` argument indicates that the file is to be written. To write a line to the file, use the `write()` method. For example, the following call of `write()` writes one line containing "hello" to the `c1.s` file:

    outfile.write('hello\n')

The `write()` method writes out precisely the string it is passed. It does not append a newline character to the string it is passed. Thus, if you want a newline character, you should include it in the argument passed to `write()`, as in the example above.

To close a file, use the `close()` method. For example, the following statement closes `outfile`:

```
outfile.close()
```

It is essential to close output files. Otherwise, when your program ends, the file may not contain all the items written to it.

Classes

A class is essentially a blueprint for an object. When an object is created from a class, the object is created according to the specifications in the class. Objects contain functions and variables. We call a function that is defined in a class a *method*.

The following class specifies four variables, `self.line`, `self.column`, `self.category`, `self.lexeme`, and one method, `__init__()`:

```
1 class Token:
2     def __init__(self, line, column, category, lexeme):
3         self.line = line         # line number of the token
4         self.column = column     # column in which token starts
5         self.category = category # category of the token
6         self.lexeme = lexeme     # token in string form
```

The items in the `__init__` method with the prefix "self." are the variables (`self.line`, `self.column`, `self.category`, `self.lexeme`). The items without the prefix "self." are the parameters. The parameters receive values when the `__init__` method is called. The values in the parameters are then assigned to the variables (lines 3 to 6).

The following statement creates and initializes an object from the `Token` class:

```
t = Token(1, 20, None, 'x')
```

This statement

1. creates an object from the `Token` class. Specifically, it allocates a block of memory big enough to hold the variables specified in the class.

2. it calls the `__init__` method defined in the `Token` class, passing it the address of the block of memory that holds the object's variables, and the arguments `1, 20, None`, and `'x'`. These arguments are received, respectively, by the `self, line, column, category`, and `lexeme` parameters of the `__init__` method (see line 2 in the `Token` class). The `__init__` method then assigns to the variables of the object the corresponding parameters (see lines 3, 4, 5, and 6).

3. it assigns the address of the block of memory that holds the object's variables to `t`.

The result is the following structure:

```
t ──→  ┌──────┐
       │  1   │ line
       ├──────┤
       │  20  │ column
       ├──────┤
       │ None │ category
       ├──────┤
       │ 'x'  │ lexeme
       └──────┘
```

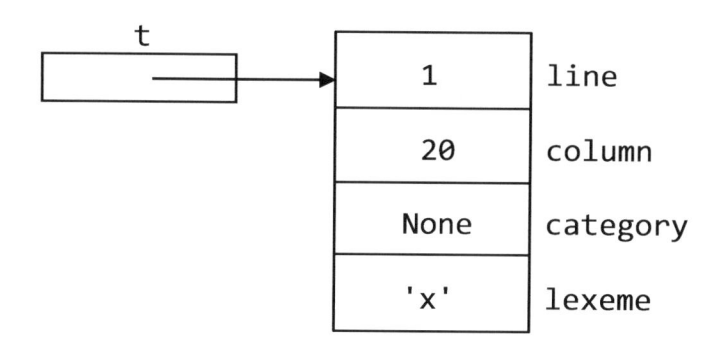

We can now access the variables in our object via t. For example, to assign NAME to the category variable in the t object, use

    t.category = NAME

Think of t.category as meaning the category variable in the object pointed to by t. Be sure to remember that the variables of an object are always accessed via a pointer—specifically, via the pointer that is pointing to the block of memory that holds the object's variables.

When the __init__ method is called as a result of the execution of

    t = Token(1, 20, None, 'x')

five arguments are passed: the address of the memory block that holds the object's variables, and the four arguments explicitly specified (i.e., 1, 20, None, 'x'). Thus, on entry to __init__, we have the following structure:

```
                Token object
    self        ┌──────┐
    ──────→     │      │ line
                ├──────┤
                │      │ column
                ├──────┤
                │      │ category
                ├──────┤
                │      │ lexeme
                └──────┘
    (parameter)

       ┌──────┐
       │  1   │ line
       ├──────┤
       │  20  │ column
       ├──────┤
       │ None │ category
       ├──────┤
       │ 'x'  │ lexeme
       └──────┘
       (parameters)
```

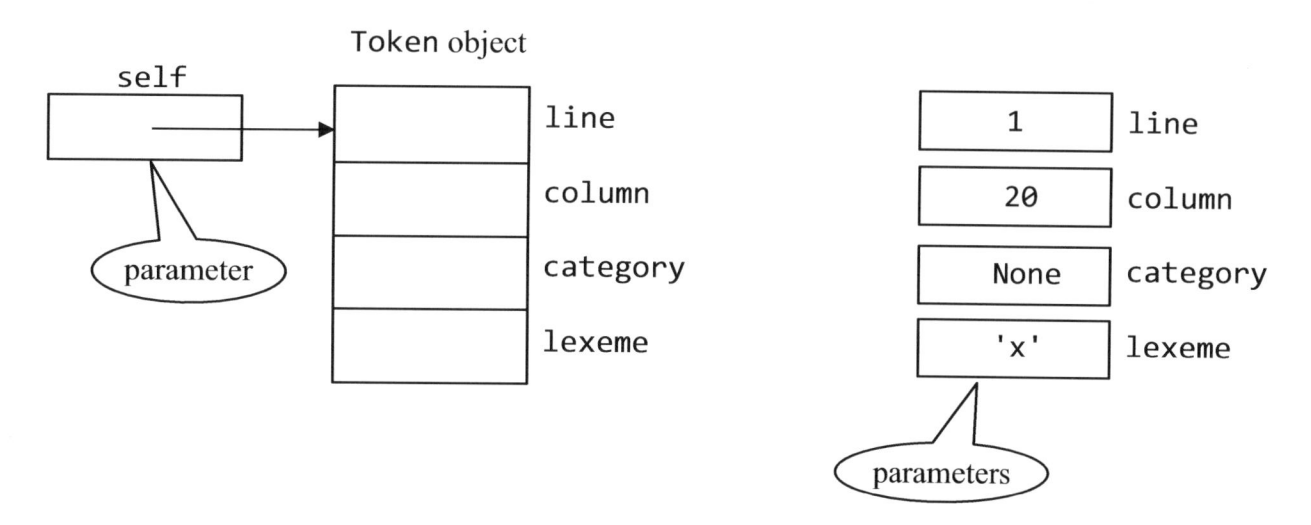

Within __init__, to access a parameter, we specify its name. To access a variable in the object, we specify its name prefixed with the name of the pointer that is pointing to the block of memory that holds the object's variables. Thus, *within* the __init__ method, we access the object's variables by prefixing their names with "self.". For example, to assign the parameter lexeme to the variable in the object named lexeme, we use

```
self.lexeme = lexeme
```

The name of the initializer method in a class is always "`__init__`". It starts with two underscore characters and ends with two underscore characters. Beware that when printed or displayed, each two-character underscore sequence in the name of the initializer usually appears as one long underscore character. When you enter the initializer's name, be sure to enter two underscores, then "`init`", and then two more underscores.

Exceptions

An exception is an unusual event that occurs during the execution of a program. When an exception occurs, an object is created that represents the event. This object then propagates up the call chain. If it is not caught, it causes the termination of the program. When caught, what happens depends on the code in the `except` block that catches it.

Errors detected by the Python interpreter during execution automatically cause exceptions. The execution of a `raise` statement also causes an exception. In the following example, the call of the `parser()` function is in a `try` block. The `try` block is followed by an `except` block. The `except` block catches any `RuntimeError` exception that occurs during the execution of the code in the `try` block.

```
1 try
2     parser()
3 except RuntimeError as emsg      # catches RuntimeError exceptions
4     print(emsg)                  # displays error message
5     sys.exit(1)                  # terminates program
```

The `except` block above specifies `RuntimeError` on line 3 as the type of exception it should catch. Suppose during the execution of the `parser()` function, the following statement is executed:

```
raise RuntimeError('Illegal operation')
```

It creates a `RuntimeError` exception. The exception propagates up to the `try` block where it is caught by the `except` block shown above. The error message in the `raise` statement is automatically assigned to the variable specified in the `except` block that follows the keyword `as`. Thus, in the example above, `emsg` is assigned the error message `'Illegal operation'`. The `except` block is then executed. In this example, it displays the error message from the `raise` statement and then terminates the program by executing

```
sys.exit(1)
```

To check if an input/output error has occurred, use a `try` and a `except` block. Set up the `except` block to catch `IOError` exceptions. For example, the following code opens and reads the file `i1.in`. If an I/O error occurs, the `except` block is executed:

```
1  try:
2      infile = open('i1.in', 'r')  # opens file for reading
3      source = infile.read()       # reads the entire file
4  except IOError:                  # catches IOError exceptions
5      print('Cannot read input file i1.in')
6      sys.exit(1)                  # terminates the program
```

`RuntimeError` is an exception type that is built into Python. We can also create our own exception types using a class. For example, the following class definition creates a new exception type named `Returnsignal`:

```
class Returnsignal(Exception)
    pass
```

To raise this type of exception in a program, use

```
raise Returnsignal()
```

The body of the `Returnsignal class` is executed when it is raised. But in this example, we do not want the body to do anything. So we use the `pass` statement as the body of the exception class. The `pass` statement is the Python statement that does nothing when executed.

Lists

A *list* is an indexed data structure. The elements in a list do not have to be all of the same type. In fact, an element in a list can be another list. The following statement creates an empty list named `zlist`:

```
zlist = []
```

To append an item to the end of a list, use the `append()` method. For example, after the following statements are executed, `zlist` contains the elements `'hello'` and 234:

```
zlist.append('hello')
zlist.append(234)
```

If we then execute

```
print(zlist)
```

the following is displayed:

```
['hello', 234]
```

An element of a list can be accessed via its index. Indices start from 0. Thus, in `zlist` we created above, `'hello'` is at index 0, and 234 is at index 1. The following two statements display "hello" and "234":

```
print(zlist[0])   # displays element at index 0
print(zlist[1])   # displays element at index 1
```

Negative indices are relative to the end of the list. For example, `zlist[-1]` is the last element in the list. `zlist[-2]` is the second from the last element in the list, and so on.

To remove the last element appended to a list, use the `pop()` method. For example, the statement

```
x = zlist.pop()
```

pops 234 off `zlist` and assigns it to `x`, after which the list no longer contains the element 234. To determine if an item is in a list, use the `in` operator. For example, the following `if` statement tests if 234 is in `zlist`:

```
if 234 in zlist:
    print('it is there')
```

To determine the index of an element in a list, use the `index()` method. For example, the following statement determines the index of `'hello'` in `zlist`:

```
index = zlist.index('hello')
```

The simplest way to process each element in a list in order is to use a `for` loop along with the `in` operator. For example, the following `for` loop displays each element in `zlist`:

```
for i in zlist:
    print(i)
```

splitlines() Method

The following statement opens the text file `i1.in` for reading:

```
infile = open('i1.in', 'r')
```

If we then execute

```
source = infile.read()
```

the `i1.in` file is read into `source` as one long string. If we then execute

```
lines = source.splitlines()
```

`lines` is assigned the list consisting of the text lines in `source`. Each text line is a separate element of the `lines` list.

Dictionaries

A *dictionary* is an unordered collection of key-value pairs. An element of a dictionary is accessed via its key. The following statement creates an empty dictionary named `d`:

```
d = {}
```

The following statements add the key/value pairs `'x'`/`'up'` and `'y'`/77 to the dictionary d:

```
d['x'] = 'up'
d['y'] = 77
```

Use the key that is paired with a value to access that value in a dictionary. For example, the following statement displays the value paired with the key `'y'`:

```
print(d['y'])      # displays 77
```

To determine if a key is in a dictionary, use the `in` operator. For example, the following `if` statement tests if the key `'y'` is in the dictionary d:

```
if 'y' in d:
    print('it is there')
```

The keys in a list do not have to be all of the same type. Similarly, the values in a list do not have to be all of the same type.

Accessing Command Line Arguments

Suppose you run the Python program in `t.py` by entering on the command line

```
python cla.py 12 5
```

We call `cla.py`, `hello`, and `123` *command line arguments*. Command line arguments are provided to the `cla.py` program via a list named `sys.argv`. Thus, for the command line above, `sys.argv[0]` is `'cla.py'`, `sys.argv[1]` is `'12'`, and `sys.argv[2]` is `'5'`. All the elements in the `sys.argv` list are in string form. Thus, in the preceding example, arithmetic computations *cannot* be performed on `sys.argv[1]` and `sys.argv[2]` (because their type is string). They have to be converted to integers or a floating-point numbers before they can be used in arithmetic computations. Use the functions `int()` and `float()` to do these conversions. For example, the following Python program adds the second are third command line arguments (after converting them to integer with the `int()` function) and then displays the result:

```
import sys
result = int(sys.argv[1]) + int(sys.argv[2])
print(result)
```

To use `sys.argv`, you should have the following statement at the beginning of your program:

```
import sys
```

len() Function

The `len()` function returns the length of multiple-component structures like strings, lists, and dictionaries. For example, the following statement displays the number of elements in the `zlist` list:

```
print(len(zlist))
```

Use the `len()` function to determine the number of command line arguments. For example, the following program displays the number of command line arguments:

```
print(len(sys.argv))
```

isalpha(), isdigit(), isalnum(), and isspace() Methods

`isalpha()` returns `True` if its string consists exclusively of letters, and `False` otherwise. `isdigit()` returns `True` if its string consists exclusively of digits, and `False` otherwise. `isalnum()` returns `True` if its string contains exclusively letters and/or digits, and `False` otherwise. `isspace()` returns `True` if its string consists exclusively of *whitespace* (i.e., space, tab, newline, return, form feed, or vertical tab characters), and `False` otherwise. For example, the following program displays `True, False, True, False`:

```
1 a = 'hello'
2 print(a.isalpha())   # displays True
3 print(a.isdigit())   # displays False
4 print(a.isalnum())   # displays True
5 print(a.isspace())   # displays False
```

Time and Date

`time.strftime('%c')` returns in string form the current time and date. For example, the following statement displays the current time and date:

```
print(time.strftime('%c'))
```

To use `time.strftime('%c')`, insert the following statement at the beginning of your program:

```
import time
```

Problems

1. Write a program that displays your name 10 times. Use a loop.

2. Write a program that reads a text file and outputs an exact copy to another file. Access the input and output file names from the command line.

3. Same as problem 2, but each line in the output file should be prefixed with its line number. The line number for each should occupy four spaces, right justified.

4. Write a program that executes a loop that prompts the user for a number, squares the entered number, and displays the square. Your loop should continue until the user enters 0.

5. Write a program that reads in 10 integers, appending each onto a list. It then displays the list from beginning to end using a loop, accessing each element via its index. Next, it displays the list from end to beginning using a loop, accessing each element via a negative index. Finally, it displays the list from end to beginning, accessing the elements of the list without using indices. *Hint*: Use the `pop()` method.

6. Write a function that is passed two lists. Your function should concatenate the elements of the second list onto the first list, and then return the modified first list. Write a program that tests your function.

7. Write a program which calls the function `getgrade()` repeatedly until `getgrade()` returns a valid grade. `getgrade()` should prompt for and read in from the keyboard an integer in the range 0 to 100 and return it to the caller. If, however, the grade entered is outside the range 0 to 100 inclusive, `getgrade()` should raise a `RuntimeError` exception, indicating an invalid grade was entered. When your program receives a valid grade from `getgrade()`, it should display in which quartile the grade is in: first (75-100), second (50-74), third (25-49), or fourth (0-24).

8. Write a program that creates a dictionary whose key/value pairs are `'a'`/1, `'b'`/2, ..., `'z'`/26. Then prompt for and read in a letter and display its corresponding number value obtained from your dictionary.

9. Write a program that reads in 10 strings from the keyboard. Count the number of strings that start with `'pr'`. Display this count. Use a loop.

10. Write a program that reads in a positive integer into n. Your program should then display `True` if n is a perfect number, and `False` otherwise A *perfect number* is a number whose positive divisors excluding itself sum up to the given number. For example, the positive divisors of 6 excluding 6 are 1, 2, and 3. Because $1 + 2 + 3 = 6$, 6 is a perfect number.

11. Write a program that reads in a text file that consists of some standard English text. Your program should count the number of occurrences of each letter of the alphabet and display each letter with its count. What are the six most frequently used letters?

12. Write a program that reads in a string and determines if it is a palindrome (i.e., a string that reads the same backwards as forwards).

13. Write a program that computes the following sum: $2 + 1/2! + 1/3! + \cdots + 1/100!$ Is the sum equal to an important constant in mathematics? "!" denotes the factorial function. n! is the product of the integers from 1 to n. For example, $5! = 1 \times 2 \times 3 \times 4 \times 5 = 120$.

14. Write a program that reads in a positive integer into n. Your program should then sum up the first n positive odd numbers and display the sum. What is the relation between the value of n and the computed sum?

15. Read in a positive number into x. Then execute the following statement 100 times:

    ```
    x = math.sqrt(x)
    ```

    Does the value of x converge on a particular number, regardless of its initial value? Try values both less than and greater than 1. To use `sqrt()`, import the `math` module.

16. Write a program that reads in a positive integer into n. Your program should then display n rows. Each row should have consecutive integers starting from 1 and have one more integer than the preceding row. The first row should contain only 1. For example, if 3 is entered, then your program should display

    1
    1 2
    1 2 3

Appendix B: Decimal, Binary, and Hexadecimal

Decimal is a positional numbering system. That is, associated with each position in a decimal number is a weight. For example, in the decimal number 573, the digits 3, 7, and 5 have the weights 1, 10, and 100, respectively. Because the 5 digit is in the position whose weight is 100, the 5 contributes 5×100 to the value of the number. Thus, the value of 573 is 5×100 + 7×10 + 3×1. Weights in a decimal number increase by a factor of 10 from each position to the next, from right to left.

Binary, like decimal, is a positional numbering system. In binary, the weights increase by a factor of 2. For example, in the binary number 01011, the weights from right to left are 1, 2, 4, 8, and 16:

$$\frac{0 \quad 1 \quad 0 \quad 1 \quad 1}{16 \quad 8 \quad 4 \quad 2 \quad 1} \text{ weights in decimal}$$

Thus, the value of the binary number 01011 is 0×16 + 1×8 + 0×4 + 1×2 + 1×1 = 11 in decimal.

In hexadecimal, the weights increase by a factor of 16. For example, in the hexadecimal number 573, the weights from right to left are 1, 16, and 256:

$$\frac{5 \quad 7 \quad 3}{256 \quad 16 \quad 1} \text{ weights in decimal}$$

Thus, the value of the hexadecimal number 573 is 5×256 + 7×16 + 3×1 = 1395 in decimal. Hexadecimal uses 16 symbols corresponding to the value 0 to 15: 0, 1, 2, ..., 9, A, B, C, D, E, and F. The values of the hexadecimal digits A, B, C, D, E, and F are 10, 11, 12, 13, 14, and 15 decimal, respectively. For example, here is the hexadecimal number 1F5 with the weight of each digit:

$$\frac{1 \quad F \quad 5}{256 \quad 16 \quad 1} \text{ weights in decimal} \qquad \text{F equal to 15 decimal}$$

The value of the hexadecimal number 1F5 is 1×256 + F×16 + 5×1 = 501 in decimal.

Conversion from hexadecimal to binary is simple: Simply replace each hexadecimal digit with the 4-bit binary number with the same value. For example, the values of the hexadecimal digits 1, F, and 5 in binary are 0001, 1111, and 0101, respectively. Thus, the binary number with the same value as the hexadecimal number 1F5 is 000111110101. Conversion from binary to hexadecimal is also simple: Break up the binary number into 4-bit groups. Then replace each group with the hexadecimal digit with the same value. For example, to convert the binary number 111110101 to hexadecimal, break into 4-bit groups (add 0 bits to the left to extend the leftmost group to 4-bits). We get 0001 1111 0101. Then replace each group with its hexadecimal equivalent. We get 1F5.

Because the conversions between binary and hexadecimal are so easy, and it is difficult for us humans to read, write, and remember binary numbers, hexadecimal is often used to represent the binary numbers inside a computer. For example, the contents of the registers and memory shown in Fig. 11.5 are shown in hexadecimal, but the actual contents are binary

Appendix C: Answers to Selected Problems

Chapter 1

1) `gcc` is not in your work directory but in a directory that the OS searches.

5) The Java interpreter in your web browser prevents a Java program embedded in a web page from doing any harm to your computer system. But for compiled code, there is no protective mechanism.

Chapter 2

1) $\{a^i b^j \mid i, j \geq 0\}$

2) No. ab is in (a|b)* but not in a*|b*.

4) This is the set of strings that have at least one b: a*b(a|b)*

7) [a]b+ = (a|λ)bb* = abb*|bb*

Chapter 3

1) <S> → <A> | <B>
   <A> → 'a'<A> | λ
   <B> → 'b'<B> | λ

4) <S> → 'a'<S> | 'b'<A>   or   <S> → <A>'b'<A>
   <A> → 'a'<A> | λ   <A> → 'a'<A> | λ

8) <S> → 'a'<S>'a' | 'b'<S>'b' | 'a' | 'b' | λ

Chapter 4

5) The parser cannot determine from the current token alone which production to apply—both <S> productions generate a leading 'a'.

    <S> → 'a'<A>
    <A> → 'a'<B>
    <B> → 'a'<C>
    <C> → 'a'<C> | 'd'

8) On line 46, we need to test if the current token is 'a'. On line 52, we do not need to test the current token. If control reaches line 52, the current token has to be 'c' by virtue of the `if` statement on line 50.

10) <S> → 'a'(<B>|<C>)

```
def S():
    consume('a')
    if token = 'b':
        B()
    elif token = 'c':
        C()
    else:
        raise RuntimeError('Expecting b or c')
```

Chapter 5

3) <S> → <A><B>'d'   {'a', 'b', 'd'}
    <A> → 'a'<A>'c'   {'a'}
    <A> → λ   {'b', 'c', 'd', 'e'}
    <B> → 'b'<A>'e'   {'b'}
    <B> → λ   {'d'}

5) <S> → <S>'a'   {'a'}
    <S> → 'a'   {'a'}

This grammar is not suitable for recursive-descent parsing because the predict sets for the <S> productions are not disjoint. If the S() function applies the right side of the first production, it calls itself without advancing. Then on re-entering S(), S() would call itself again. The recursive calls would never end. The first production is called a *left recursive production* because its left side appears leftmost on its right side. Left recursive productions are not suitable for recursive-descent parsers.

7) Factor out <A> from the two productions to get <S> → <A>(<C>|'d'). This technique is called *left factoring*.

```
def S():
    A()
    if token = 'c':
        C()
    elif token = 'd':
        advance()
    else:
        raise RuntimeError('Expecting start of <C> or \'d\'')
```

12) The parser has to examine not only the current token but the token after that to determine which <S>production to apply. If the current token and the one following it are both 'a', it should apply the production <S> → 'a'<S>. If the current token is 'a' and the token following it is the end-of-input marker, then the production <S> → 'a' should be applied. For other cases of the current token and the token following it, the parser should raise an exception. This grammar is called an LL(2) grammar because it requires a lookahead of *two* symbols (the current token and the token following it) to determine which production to use. The first "L" in "LL(2)" indicates that the parser scans the input string starting from the left side. The second "L" indicates that the parser determines the leftmost derivation of the input string. A *leftmost derivation* is a derivation of a string in which the leftmost nonterminal at every step is replaced (this is what a recursive-descent parser does in effect). For example, the following derivation is a leftmost derivation:

<S> ⇒ <A><B> ⇒ a<A><B> ⇒ aa<A><B> ⇒ aaa<B> ⇒ aaab

— leftmost nonterminal is replaced

The best type of grammar for recursive-descent parsing is an LL(1) grammar. The "1" indicates that the parser has to examine only one token—the current token—to determine which production to apply when there is a choice.

Chapter 6

3) `prevchar` is declared global so that it retains its value between calls of `getchar()`.

4) `curchar` is initialized to a space because otherwise line 86 would access `curchar` before it is assigned a value. The space is discarded by line 87 so it has no effect on the tokenizing of the first token. Similarly, `prevchar` is initialized to the newline character because otherwise line 137 would access `prevchar` before it is assigned a value. The newline character signals a new line to `getchar()`, which makes sense because the first line is a new line.

Chapter 7

6) No. When `simplestmt()` is called, the current token is necessarily the start of a statement.

8) Yes if implementation corresponds to the grammar in Fig. 7.3.

Chapter 8

4) C does not support dynamic typing so the interpreter would have to include type analysis code. But Python supports dynamic typing so we do not have to include type analysis code in our interpreter. If, however, the source language was like C, then C would essentially be as easy to use as Python.

5) Pure interpreters parse a loop on each iteration of the loop. A hybrid interpreter parses it only once.

7) Interpreted because they are executed as soon as they are entered.

Chapter 9

2) Check your answer by entering on the command line

   python -m dis p0902.py

   Ignore the RETURN_VALUE instruction at the end of the dis listing.

3) x = 2*3 + 4

Chapter 10

2) Yes. Test the more frequently occurring opcodes first to minimize execution time.

3) co_values is used only within the interpreter.

4) No. For code with no loops, the pure interpreter should be a little faster because it does have the overhead associated with the compile step in a hybrid interpreter.

Chapter 11

1) See the file p1101model.s.

4) See the file p1104model.s.

9) The literal pool follows the 20,000 words inserted by the .space directive. Thus, it is too far away from the first ldr instruction (which accesses the address of a from the literal pool).

Chapter 12

1) See the file p1201model.s.

Chapter 13

4) If multiple users are running the same program on a computer system, they can all share the code in the .text segment. Thus, only one copy of the .text segment would need to be loaded into memory. If the computer system has two memory subunits, it can place the .text segment in one and the .data segment in the other. Then instructions could be fetched at the same time data is fetched.

8) An symbol table index uniquely identifies a variable. A name does not. For example, a program could have two variables, one local and one global, with the same name.

Chapter 14

4) The maximum absolute value of non-negative and negative numbers differ by one. For example, with eight bits (a bit is a binary 0 or 1), the values that can be represented range from −128 to +127. Note that for negative numbers, the maximum absolute value is 128 but only 127 for non-negative numbers. In the expression x-128, the minus sign indicates subtraction. The 128 is a positive number. But in the expression x+-128, the 128 is a negative number. If 8 bits are used to represent numbers, in the former case, the 128 is too big (because it is a positive number), but in the latter case, it is okay because it (with the minus sign preceding it) is a negative number. Thus, the required check depends on the type of the minus sign. The tokenizer does not know if a minus sign preceding a number indicates subtraction or a negative number. But the parser does. Thus, the check should be in the parser.

Chapter 15

2) Yes if implemented as specified.

3) The pure interpreter parses only what it executes.

4) The interpreter based on this parser performs a separate operation for each relational operator. Thus, each relational operator must be handled individually.

Chapter 16

5) If the exit-test expression is false, a pure interpreter has to skip over the body of the loop. But if the loop body is not delimited with braces, indentation, or some other kind of marker, the parser has to parse the loop body to determine where it ends. But then this extra parsing of the loop body would cause the loop body to be executed after the exit-test expression has gone false.

Chapter 17

6) pc = pc + 1 + co_code[pc]

Chapter 18

4) gcc has access to the C standard library and start-up code.

6) Yes

7) No. Some registers may be used for temporary variables.

Chapter 19

3) No. An argument in a function call can be another function call which would then use (and therefore corrupt) the `arglist` in use by the original call.

4) The Python 3 interpreter does not but the `i3.py` interpreter does.

10) Because of the assignment statement that assigns 10 to x and no global declaration of x within the function, the Python interpreter treats x as a local variable. But then the `print` statement is illegal because it is accessing a local variable before it has been assigned a value. When `i3.py` processes the `print` statement, it has not yet executed the assignment to x within the function definition. So it treats x within the function as a global, and executes the `print`, displaying 5, and then terminates normally.

Chapter 21

4) Because the contents of `r4` will not be corrupted by a call to a C library function. So we can load a value into `r4` and use it later in the program even if there is an intervening call of a C library function.

Index

`.ascii`, 109
`.asciz`, 109
.bashrc, 5
`.data`, 97, 159
`.global`, 94, 96
`.text`, 94, 97
`.word`, 94

`__init__()`, 46

abstract syntax tree, 182
add, 104
address, 89
`advance()`, 26, 59
alphabet, 12
ambiguous grammar, 20
`append()`, 65
argument, 210
arithmetic expressions, 19
arithmetic operation, 207
ASCII, 106
assemble, 75
assembler, 88
assembly language, 75, 88, 128
assignment operator, 209
AST, 182

backtracking, 37, 44
backward branch, 142, 150
`bal`, 200
BASIC, 9
bcc32c, 4, 128
`BINARY_MULTIPLY`, 76
bit, 70, 88
`bl`, 98, 103
`bne`, 199, 200
Boolean operator, 215
bottom-up parser, 25
branch, 90
byte, 70, 88
bytecode, 9, 70, 148

C standard library, 106
`c1.py`, 127
`c2.py`, 169
`c3.py`, 204
category, 46, 50

central processing unit, 88
`cg_`, 117
`cg_add()`, 118, 156, 199
`cg_assign()`, 156, 161
`cg_epilog()`, 123, 195
`cg_getlabel()`, 201
`cg_gettemp()`, 120, 198
`cg_mul()`, 120, 156, 198
`cg_print()`, 156
`cg_prolog()`, 123, 195
`co_code`, 71
`co_consts`, 71
`co_names`, 71
code block, 7, 132, 207
command line arguments, 223
command line program, 1
compile time, 157
compiler, 115, 156, 182, 192
complementation, 14
concatenation, 13, 199, 209, 211, 217
constant folding, 157, 191
consume(), 27, 59
context-free grammar, 16
conversion code, 108
`curchar`, 27, 50
current character, 26

dedentation, 7, 132
derivation, 17
dictionary, 222
dis form, 75, 76
disassembler, 75
disjoint sets, 37
dynamic typing, 206

echo, 95
end-of-line character, 6
`enter()`, 120, 160
entry point, 96
EOL, 7
epilog, 123
`except` block, 220
exception, 220
Executable and Linkable Format, 103
execution time, 157
exit-test expression, 142
extended regular expressions, 15

files, 217
FIRST set, 39
float(), 223
floating-point, 131
FOLLOW set, 39
format string, 109
forward branch, 142, 150
functiondef(), 178
functions, 209

gcc, 4, 108
generate, 17
getchar(), 49
gigabyte, 89
global declarations, 176
global symbol table, 171
global variable, 212
globalsdeclared, 171
globalsdeclaredstack, 176
grade, 68

h1.py, 87
h2.py, 146, 154
h3.py, 191
h4.py, 191
hexadecimal, 78, 91
hybrid interpreter, 8, 71, 78, 148, 182

i1.py, 68
i2.py, 146
i3.py, 180
if statement, 214
IL, 8, 182
immediate instruction, 94
implementation language, 6
indentation, 7, 132
infinite loop, 216
infunction, 171
initializer method, 46
input(), 214
instring, 132
int(), 223
intermediate language, 8
intersection, 14
IOError, 220
isalnum(), 224
isalpha(), 224
isdigit(), 224
isspace(), 224

java, 9

javac, 9

label, 94
labelcount, 201
lambda production, 17
language over an alphabet, 12
last-in-first-out, 64
ldr, 94
left recursion, 229
leftmost derivation, 230
len(), 224
lexeme, 46, 50
lexer, 55
lexical analyzer, 55
libc, 106
linker, 95
list, 221
list form, 75
literal pool, 102
little endian, 91
LL(1) grammar, 37, 230
local symbol table, 171, 175
local variable, 212
localsymtabstack, 176

machine language, 88
machine language instruction, 4, 9
main(), 48
malloc(), 106, 205
method, 218
mnemonic, 75, 88
mov, 94, 199
mul, 116

NAME, 58
nano, 3
needword, 158
nested structure, 32
newline character, 6
nonterminal symbol, 16
notepad, 3
null string, 12
nullable string, 38

object file, 95
object module, 95
offset, 99
opcode, 70, 88
operandstack, 64
or operator, 14

p1.py, 62, 141

parameter, 210
parse tree, 20, 182
parser, 25, 35, 57, 136
parsing, 8
`pc`, 84
`pc`-relative addressing, 100
peephole optimization, 128
perfect number, 225
pipeline, 91
plus operator, 13, 19
pointer, 46, 84
pop operation, 64
postfix, 87, 155
predict set, 36
predictive parsing, 30
`prevchar`, 49
`print` statement, 213
`printf()`, 106, 108
production, 16
prolog, 123
pure interpreter, 8, 64, 142, 171
push operation, 64
Python Virtual Machine, 70

`raise`, 220
Raspbian, 103
recursive function, 32, 211
recursive-descent parser, 25, 29
`reg`, 160
register, 88
register allocation, 159
regular expression, 14
regular grammar, 24
regular language, 14
relational operator, 214
repetition operator, 68, 84, 208
`replace()`, 208
returnstack, 175
`RuntimeError`, 221

`scanf()`, 106
scanner, 55
selection set, 36
semantic analysis, 141
set-builder notation, 12
sign, 66
source language, 6
source program, 5
`sourceindex`, 49
`sp.py`, 28

splitlines(), 68, 222
square bracket operator, 14, 138
stack, 64
star operator, 13, 19, 22, 31
start symbol, 16
starting quote, 132
start-up code, 108, 199
`str`, 201
`strcat()`, 106
`strcpy()`, 106, 200
`strdup()`, 201
string over an alphabet, 12
strings, 208
`strlen()`, 205
supervisor mode, 98
`svc`, 94
symbol table, 64, 119
syscall, 107

`t1.py`, 48
target language, 6
target program, 6
`tempcount`, 156
temporary variable re-use, 156
`Terminal`, 1
terminal alphabet, 16
terminal string, 17
terminal symbols, 16
terminating quote, 132
token, 6, 45, 46, 59
`Token` class, 46
token manager, 55
`tokenindex`, 59
tokenizer, 10, 25, 45, 129
`tokenlist`, 47, 59
top-down parser, 25
TOS, 76
TOS1, 76
`try` block, 220

union, 14
universe of strings, 13
`UNSIGNEDINT`, 58
user mode, 98

vertical bar operator, 14, 20, 138, 139

`while` statement, 216
whitespace, 224
word, 89